W9-CEC-759

BIX

SCOTT CHANTLER

GALLERY 13

NEW YORK   LONDON   TORONTO   SYDNEY   NEW DELHI

GALLERY 13
AN IMPRINT OF SIMON & SCHUSTER, INC.
1230 AVENUE OF THE AMERICAS
NEW YORK, NY 10020

FIRST GALLERY 13 HARDCOVER EDITION APRIL 2020

GALLERY 13 AND COLOPHON ARE TRADEMARKS OF SIMON & SCHUSTER, INC.

FOR INFORMATION ABOUT SPECIAL DISCOUNTS FOR BULK PURCHASES, PLEASE CONTACT SIMON & SCHUSTER SPECIAL SALES AT 1-866-506-1949 OR BUSINESS@SIMONANDSCHUSTER.COM.

THE SIMON & SCHUSTER SPEAKERS BUREAU CAN BRING AUTHORS TO YOUR LIVE EVENT. FOR MORE INFORMATION OR TO BOOK AN EVENT, CONTACT THE SIMON & SCHUSTER SPEAKERS BUREAU AT 1-866-248-3049 OR VISIT OUR WEBSITE AT WWW.SIMONSPEAKERS.COM.

MANUFACTURED IN THE UNITED STATES OF AMERICA

1 3 5 7 9 10 8 6 4 2

LIBRARY OF CONGRESS CATALOGING-IN-PUBLICATION DATA IS AVAILABLE.

ISBN 978-1-5011-9078-0
ISBN 978-1-5011-9079-7 (EBOOK)

WE ACKNOWLEDGE THE SUPPORT OF THE CANADA COUNCIL FOR THE ARTS.

INTRODUCTION

Leon Bix Beiderbecke was one of the unlikeliest of jazz heroes. A white kid who grew up in a prosperous, religious home in conservative Davenport, Iowa, he ended up as an outlier in what was then predominantly African-American music just beginning to spread north out of New Orleans. Nonetheless, in a span of years as short as they were creatively fertile, Bix wrote and recorded some of the landmark music in the early history of the genre. These included a lyrical and inventive reworking of "Singin' the Blues" with his musical soul mate Frank Trumbauer in 1927, and "In a Mist," an astonishing composition from the same year that blends elements of jazz and classical music. This much, at least, is beyond dispute.

But since his untimely death in 1931, Bix's life and art have also taken on more than a hint of legend, as has been the case with many other doomed musicians who have followed in his wake. There's a distinct pattern to these tragic stories, and Bix just may have provided the blueprint. Through the Beat Generation and continuing even into the twenty-first century, Bix has become a sort of patron saint for misunderstood (and often self-destructive) artist types. All of which is to say: He's a hard guy to nail down.

Someone recently said to me that Bix is like an inkblot; people see what they want to see in him. I've found that's true of many things in life, but have learned it's especially true of Bix. Nearly everything in the story you're about to read was sourced from some previous biography—but naturally, those biographies don't always agree with one another. Some Bix historians (and the Beiderbecke family itself, it should be noted) don't seem to agree with *any* of them, crying foul at the varying degrees of mythologizing that's settled in over the past nine decades. Some insist that Bix was not a rebel at all, but a choirboy whose halo has been tarnished by storytellers out to make a quick buck, and that his parents were actually nothing but fully supportive from the beginning.

Personally, I don't buy it.

People often give their past selves the benefit of their current wisdom. Memory is notoriously unreliable. And Bix himself was more than an occasional liar. So whose version of the events do you believe?

There's more to truth than cold fact, and that's never been clearer to me than in the schism between how some historians choose to interpret Bix as opposed to how artists do. There's something about Bix's story—romanticized or not—that's immediately recognizable to anyone who's ever struggled to express themselves. Whose parents might not understand or approve. Who feel trapped by the circumstances of their lives—be it geography, economics, religion, or the color of their skin. Or maybe by their own worst instincts.

So let me be clear: some of the scenes you'll see depicted in this work are apocryphal at best. I've also combined characters, compressed and reordered events, made my own (informed, but admittedly subjective) judgments on what might have been true, and all the other things you do when creating a readable story based on historical subjects.

I also freely admit that I've appropriated Bix's life to serve as a framework upon which to hang a personal experiment with visualizing musical rhythms (as well as the "rhythm" of life), and to convey my own feelings about the rewards and potential risks of a life lived creatively. In those respects, this is as much my own biography as it is his. I've now ended up in a place that *feels* right, at least to me, knowing what I know about being an artist from an unlikely place, working in an unlikely medium.

Your own mileage may vary, and that's cool with me. Let's discuss and debate it all over a cold drink on a hot summer's day at Bix Fest, which is held every year in his hometown of Davenport, not far from where he heard the music drifting across the water from the riverboats on the mighty Mississippi. We'll raise a glass to the music, the mystery, and the man himself.

Whoever he was.

Scott Chantler
November 2019

"MUTE, TO A DEGREE, HE WOULD ALWAYS BE; VERBAL COMMUNICATION WOULD NEVER BE HIS MEDIUM."

-RALPH BERTON, *REMEMBERING BIX*

"THE LISTENING MUSICIAN, WHATEVER HIS GENERATION OR HIS STYLE, RECOGNIZES BIX AS A MODERN, MODERNISM BEING NOT A STYLE BUT AN ATTITUDE."

-BENNY GREEN, *THE RELUCTANT ART*

"BIX IS A VERY CLEVER EXCUSE-MAKER, AND I THINK HE SOMETIMES FOOLS EVEN HIMSELF IN A WAY."

-HEADMASTER JOHN WAYNE RICHARDS OF LAKE FOREST ACADEMY

Part One

DAVENPORT BLUES

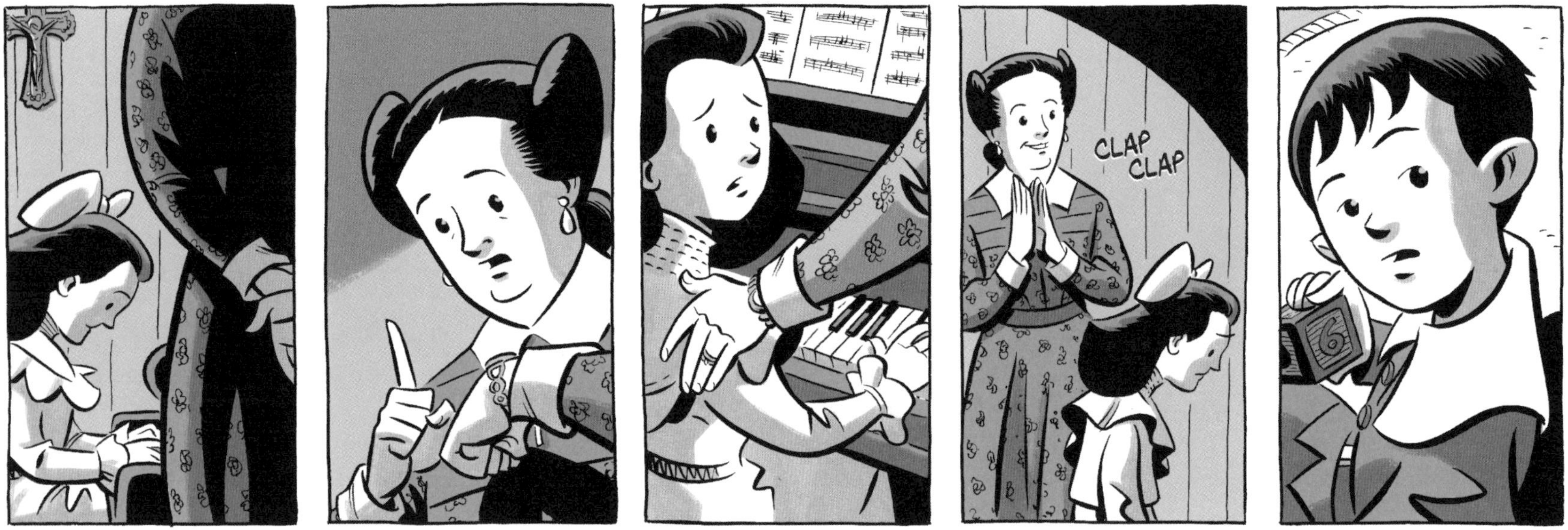
CLAP
CLAP

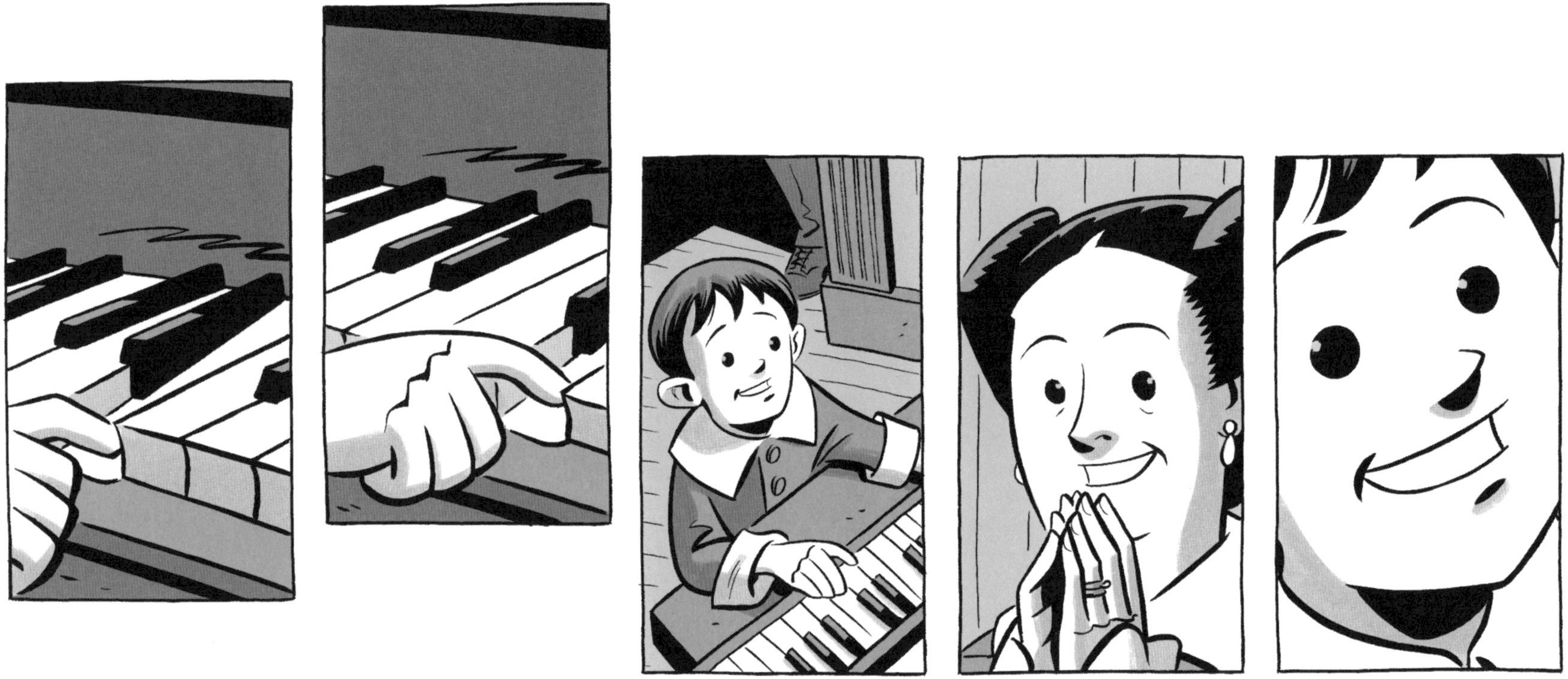

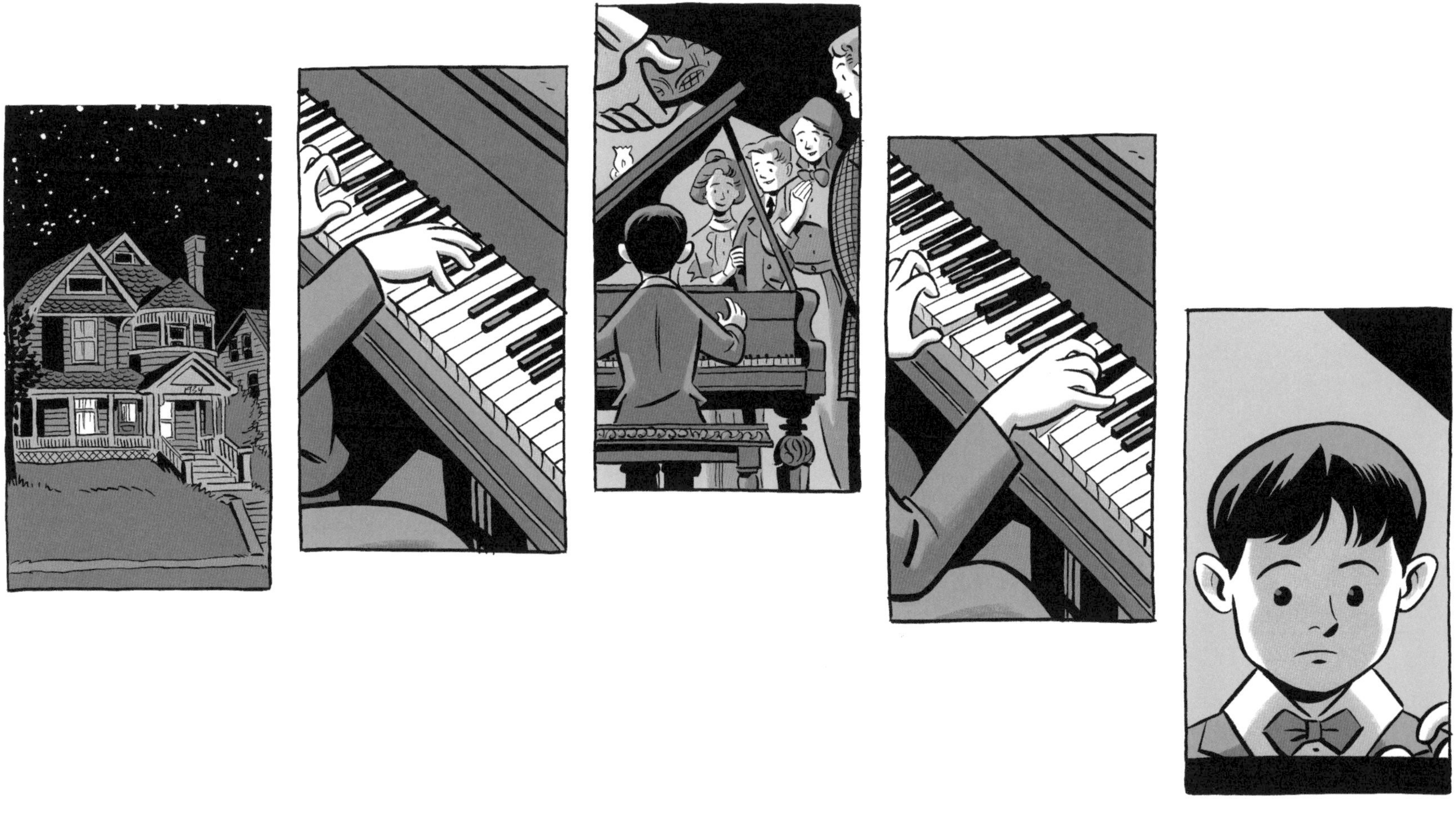

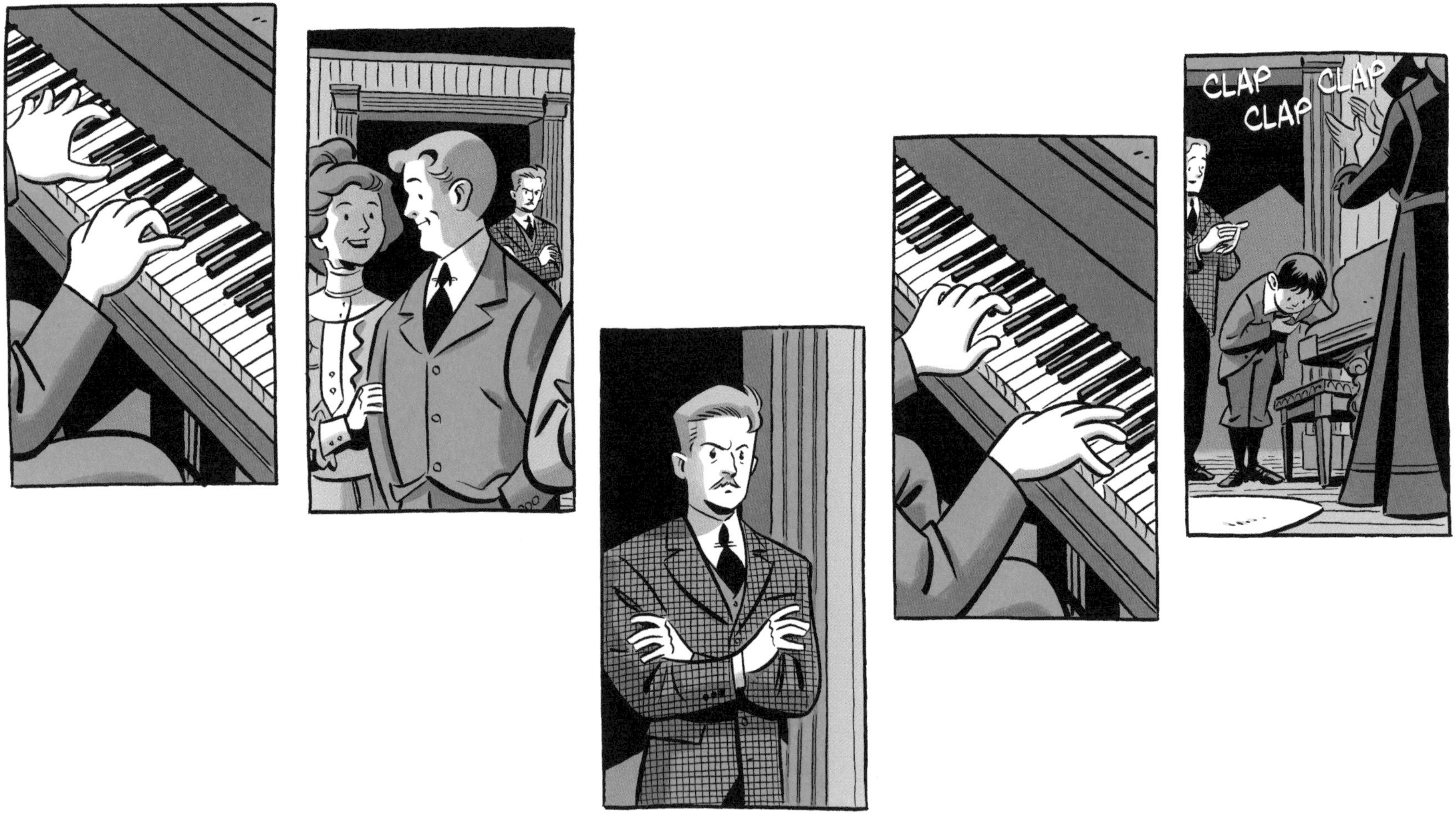
CLAP
CLAP
CLAP

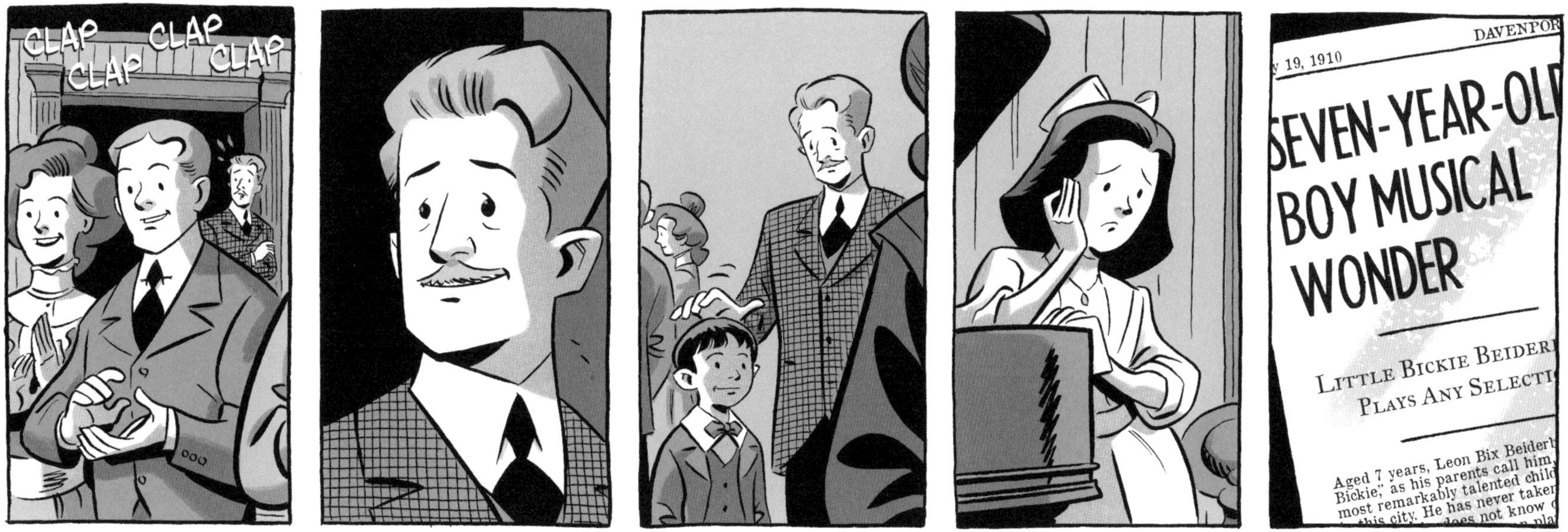
CLAP
CLAP
CLAP
CLAP
DAVENPOR
y 19, 1910
SEVEN-YEAR-OL
BOY MUSICAL
WONDER
LITTLE BICKIE BEIDER
PLAYS ANY SELECTI
Aged 7 years, Leon Bix Beiderb
Bickie," as his parents call him,
most remarkably talented child
this city. He has never taken

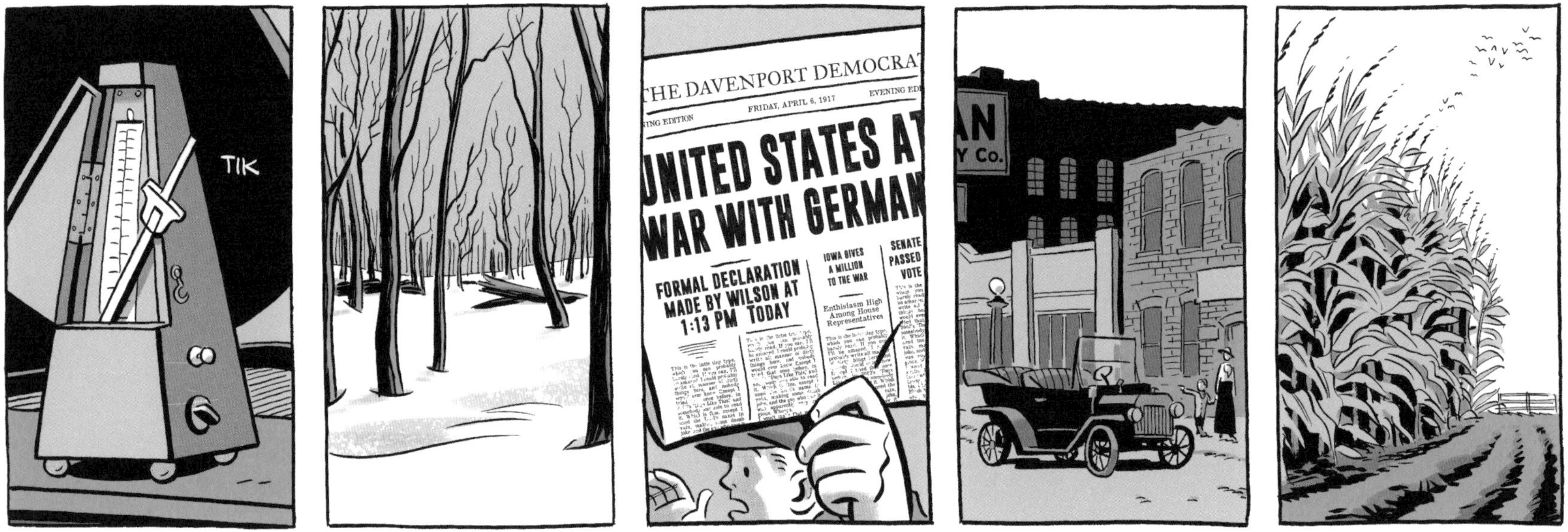
TIK
THE DAVENPORT DEMOCRAT
FRIDAY, APRIL 6, 1917
EVENING ED
ING EDITION
UNITED STATES AT
WAR WITH GERMAN
FORMAL DECLARATION MADE BY WILSON AT 1:13 PM TODAY
IOWA GIVES A MILLION TO THE WAR
Enthisiasm High Among House Representatives
SENATE PASSED VOTE
AN
Y Co.

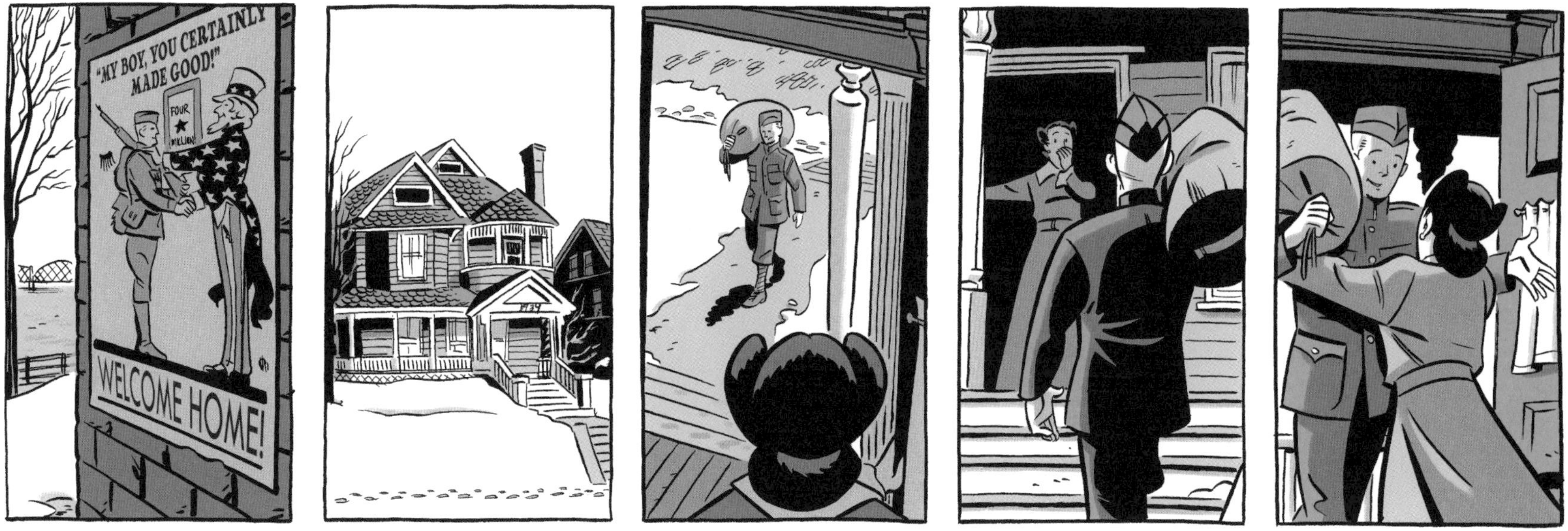
"MY BOY, YOU CERTAINLY MADE GOOD!"
FOUR
WELCOME HOME!

GRAPHOPHONE

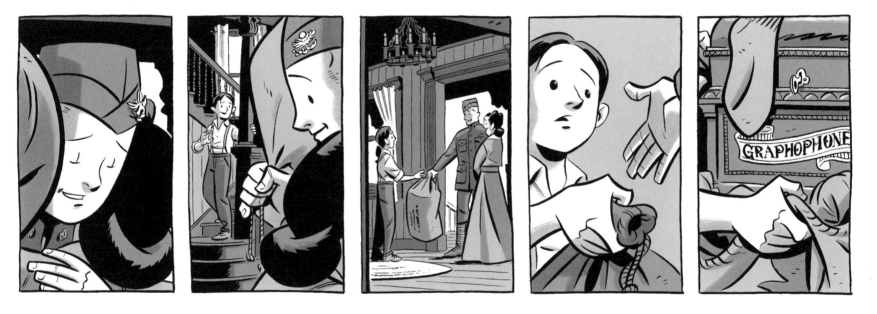

Victor
For Dancing
Tiger Rag - One Step
(D.J. La Rocca)
Original Dixieland Jazz Band
18472-B

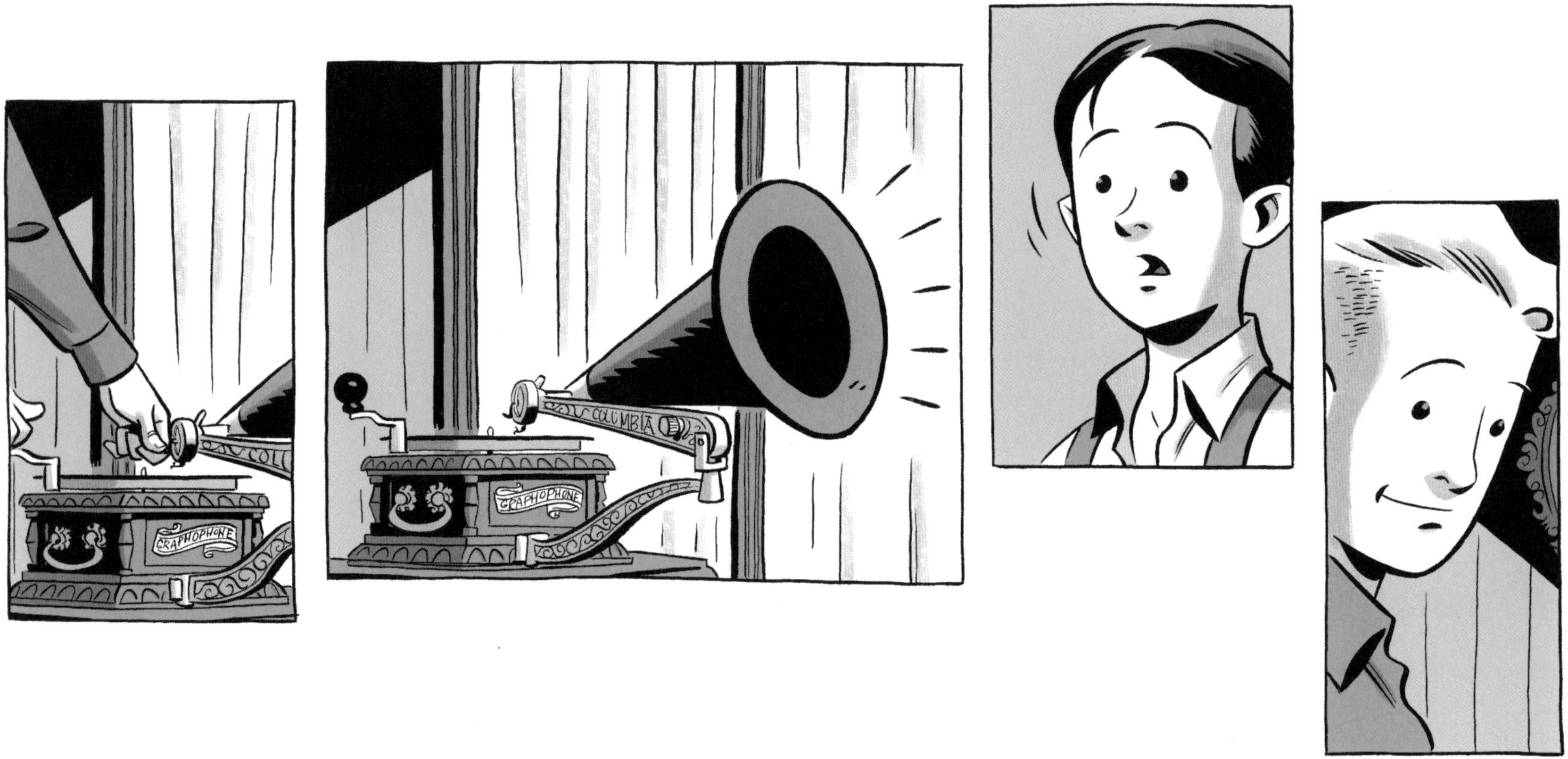
GRAPHOPHONE
COLUMBIA
GRAPHOPHONE

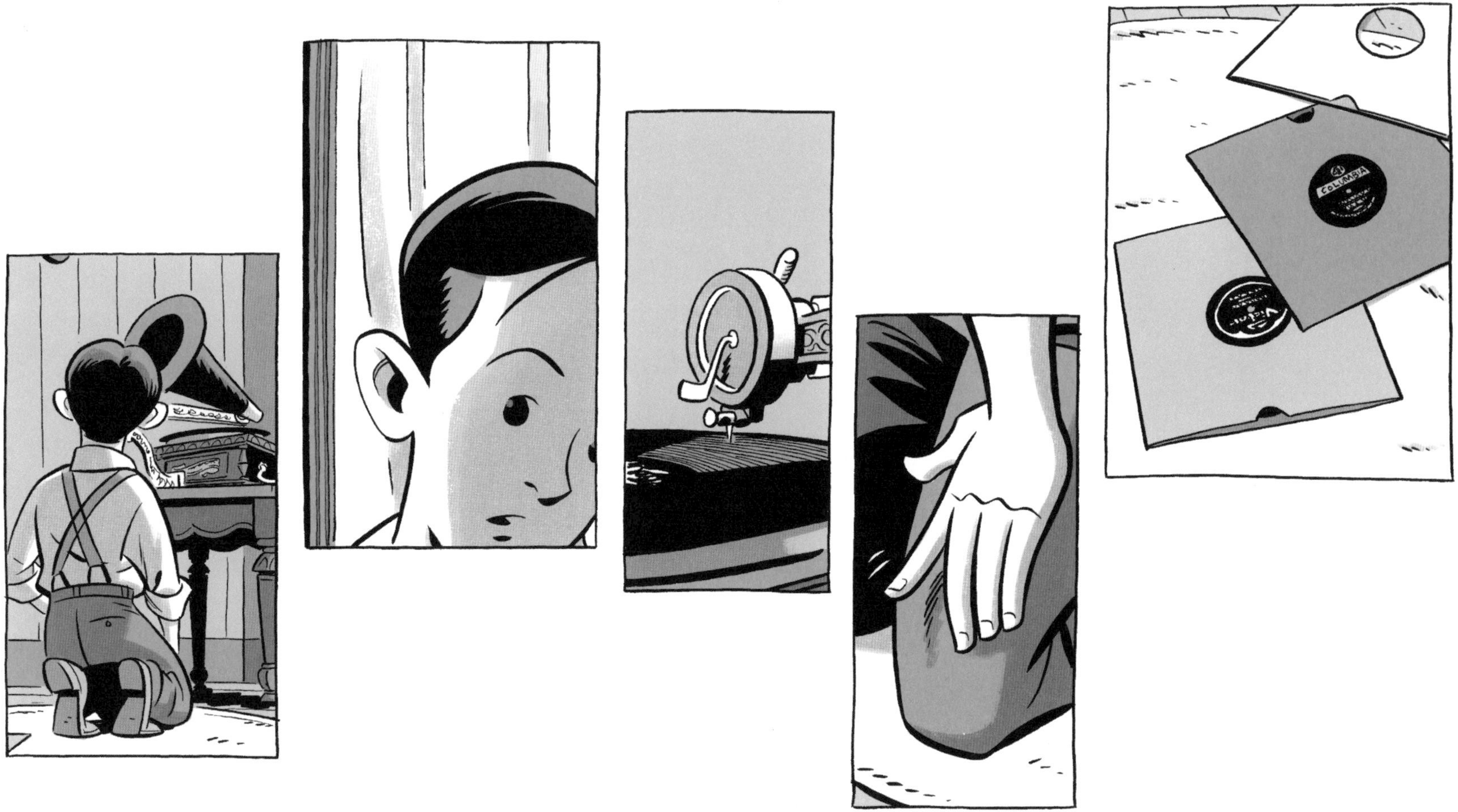
COLUMBIA

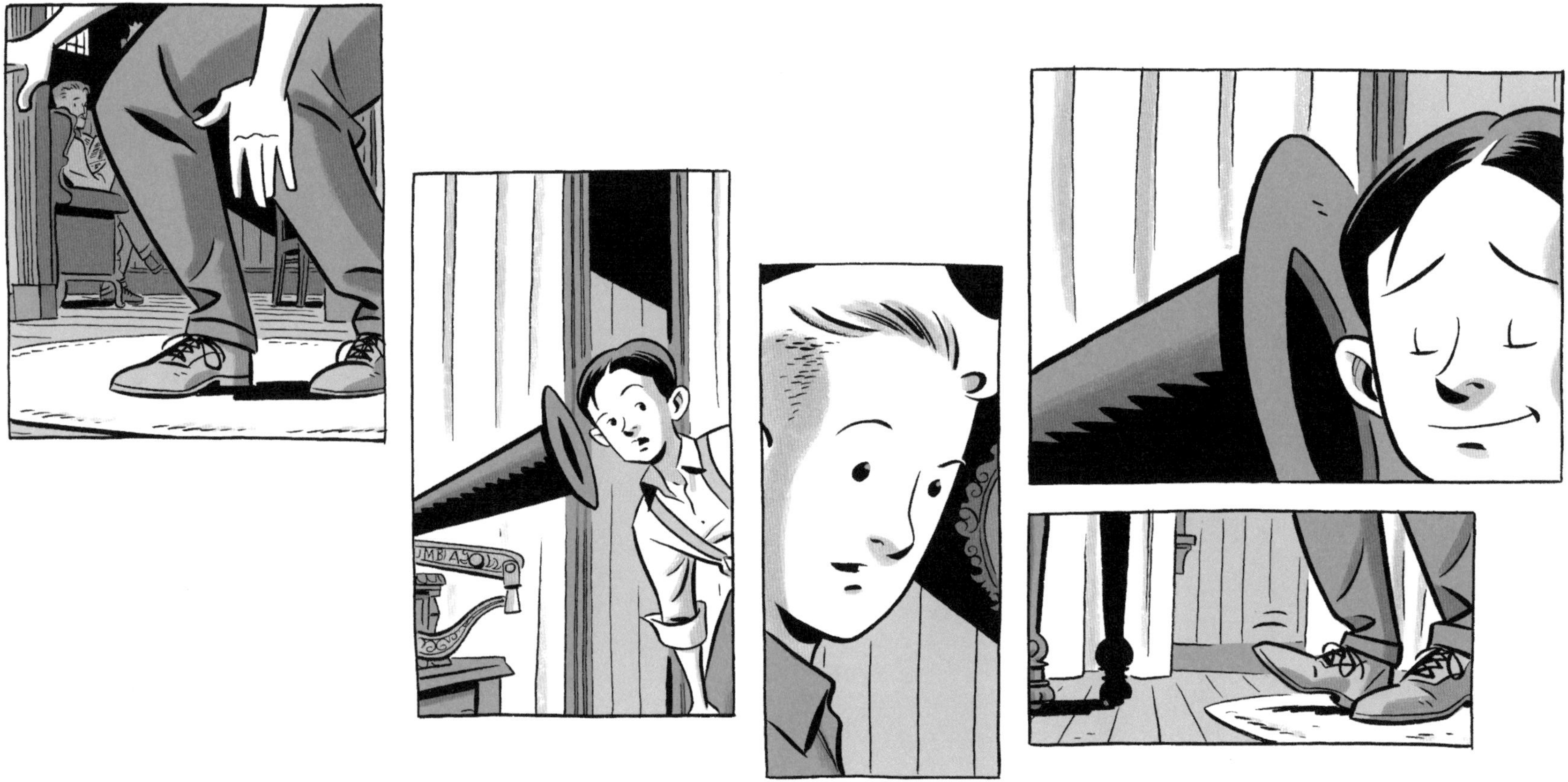

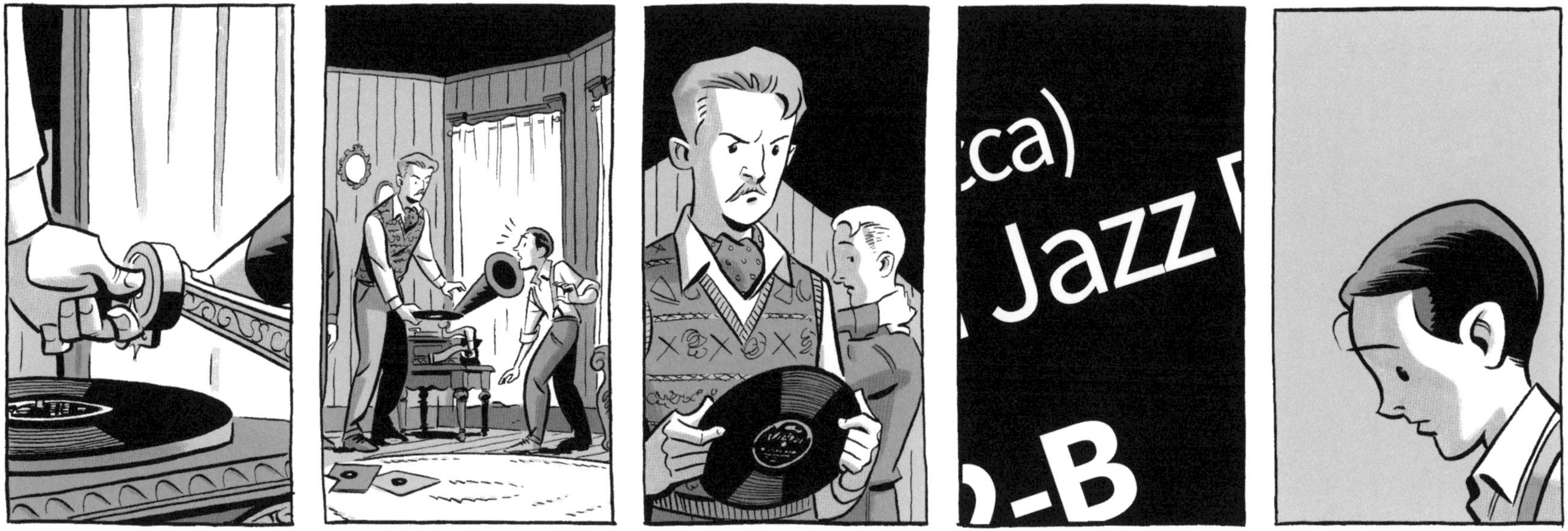
ca)
Jazz
-B

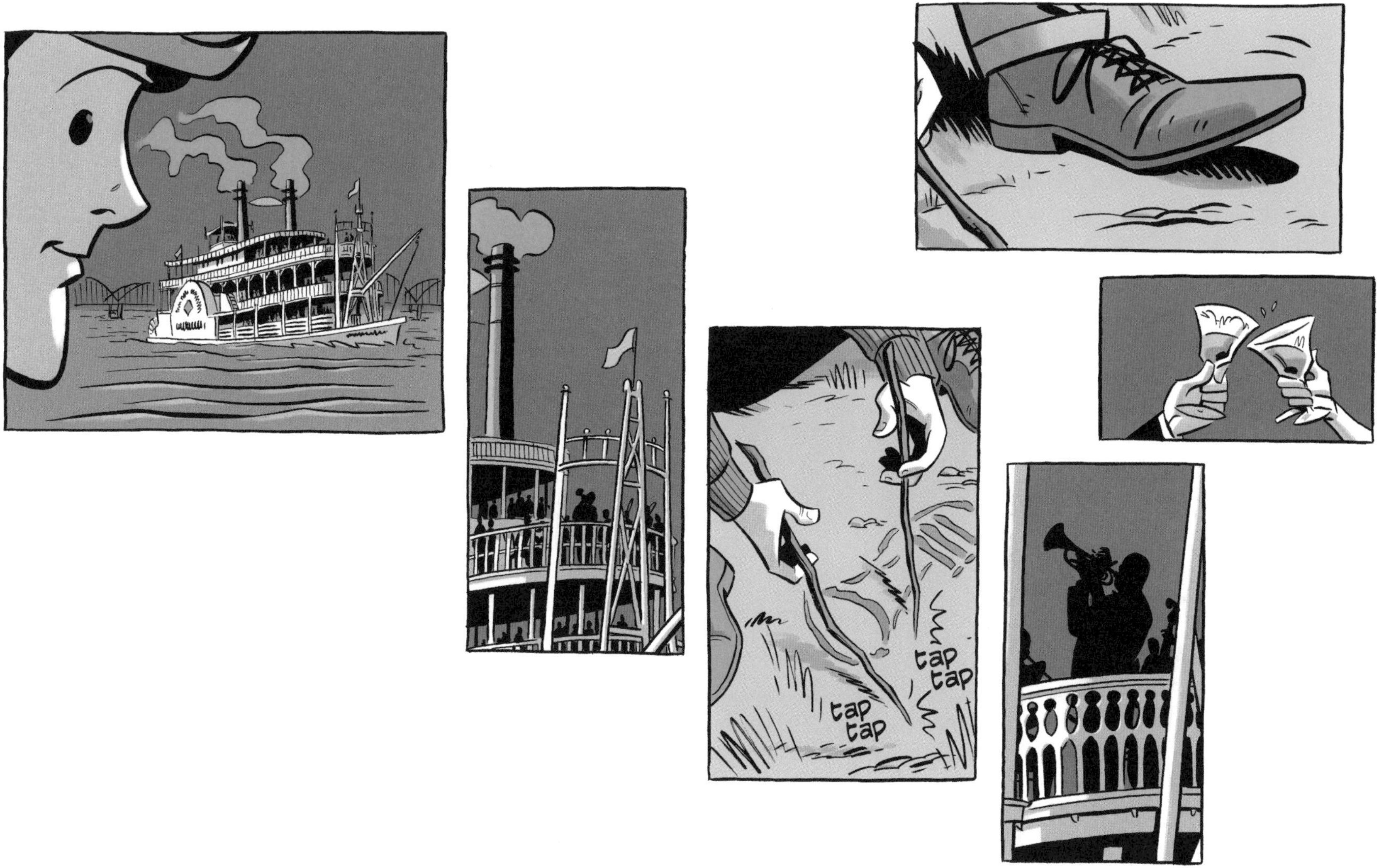
tap
tap
tap
tap

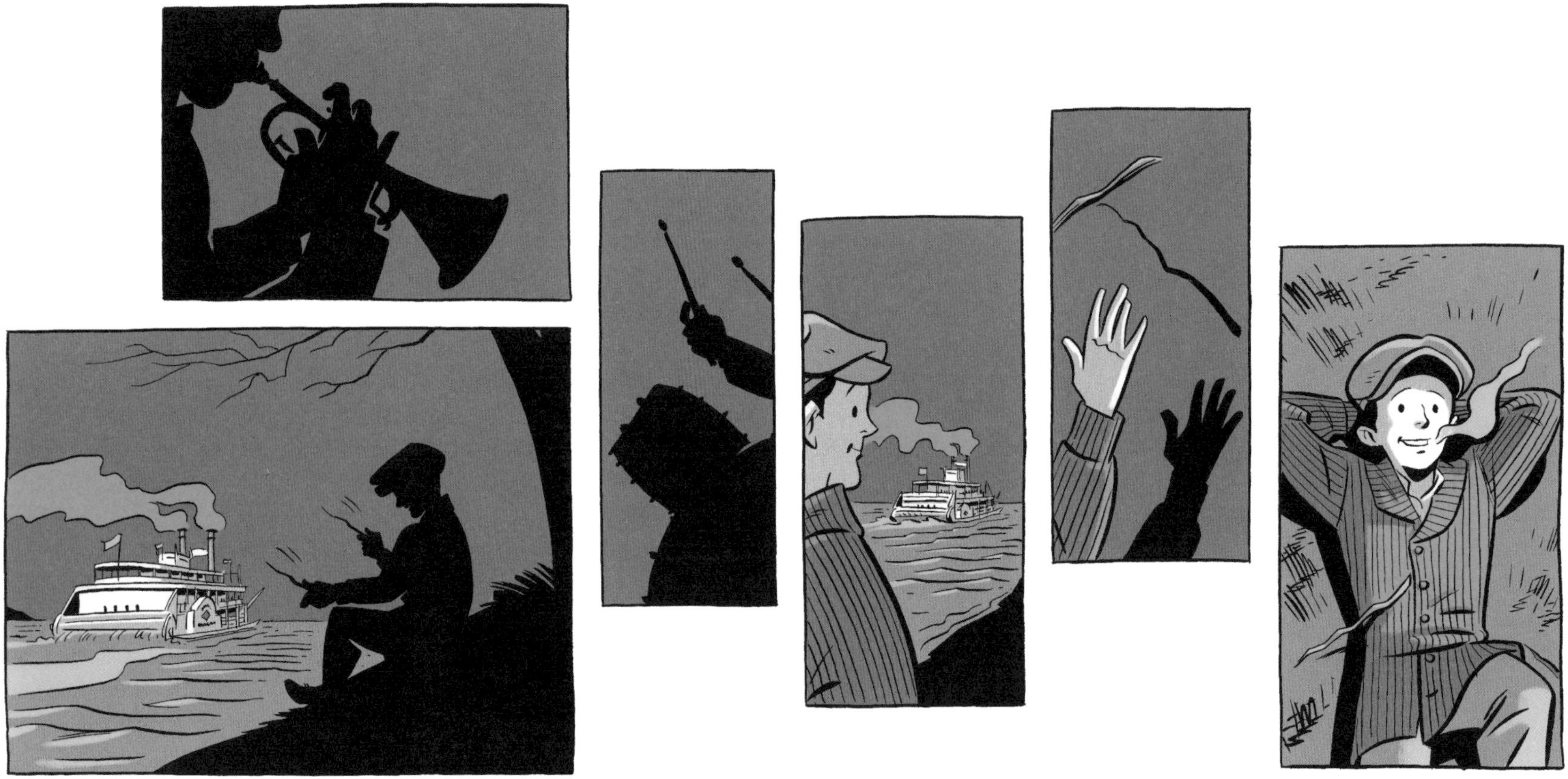

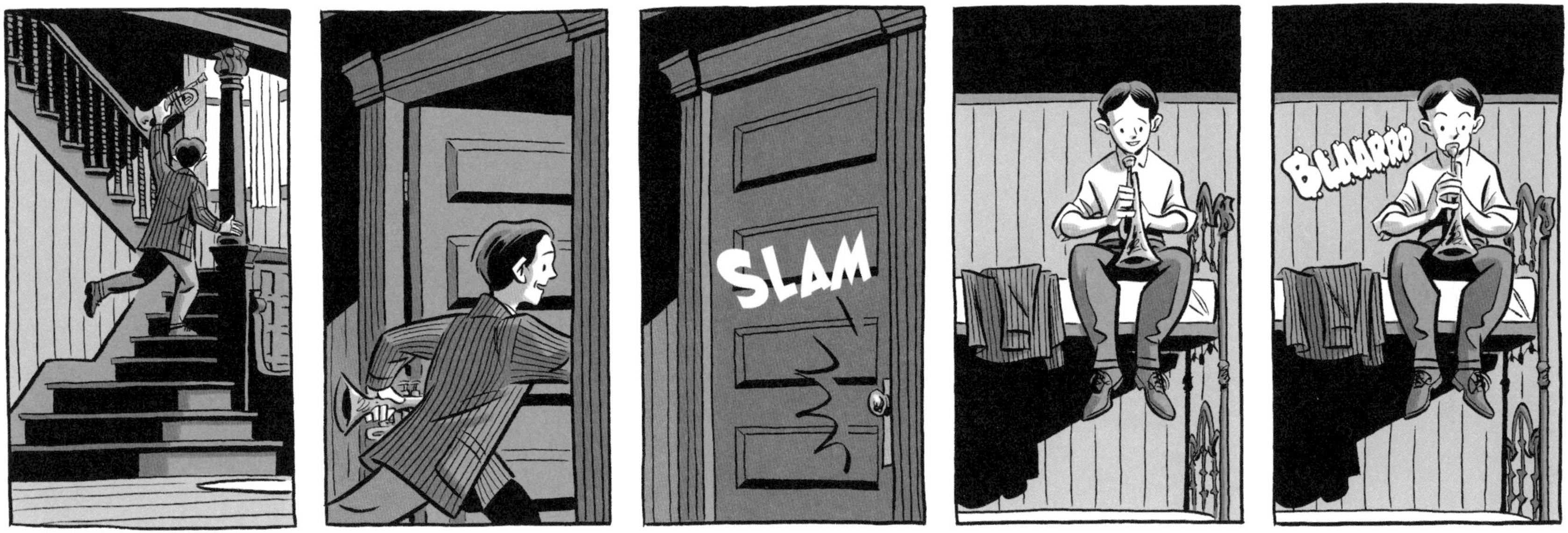
SLAM
BLAARRP

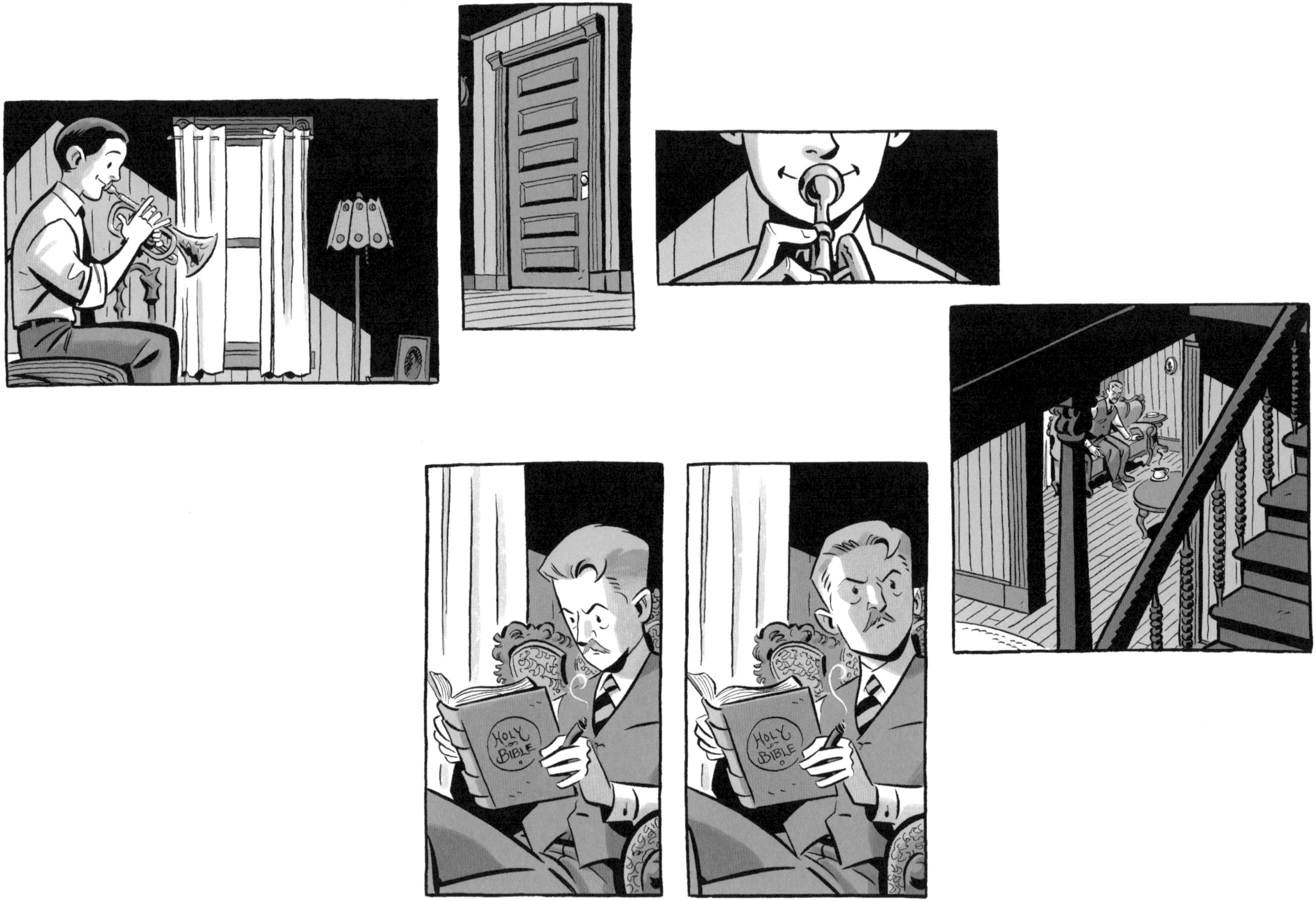
HOLY BIBLE
HOLY BIBLE

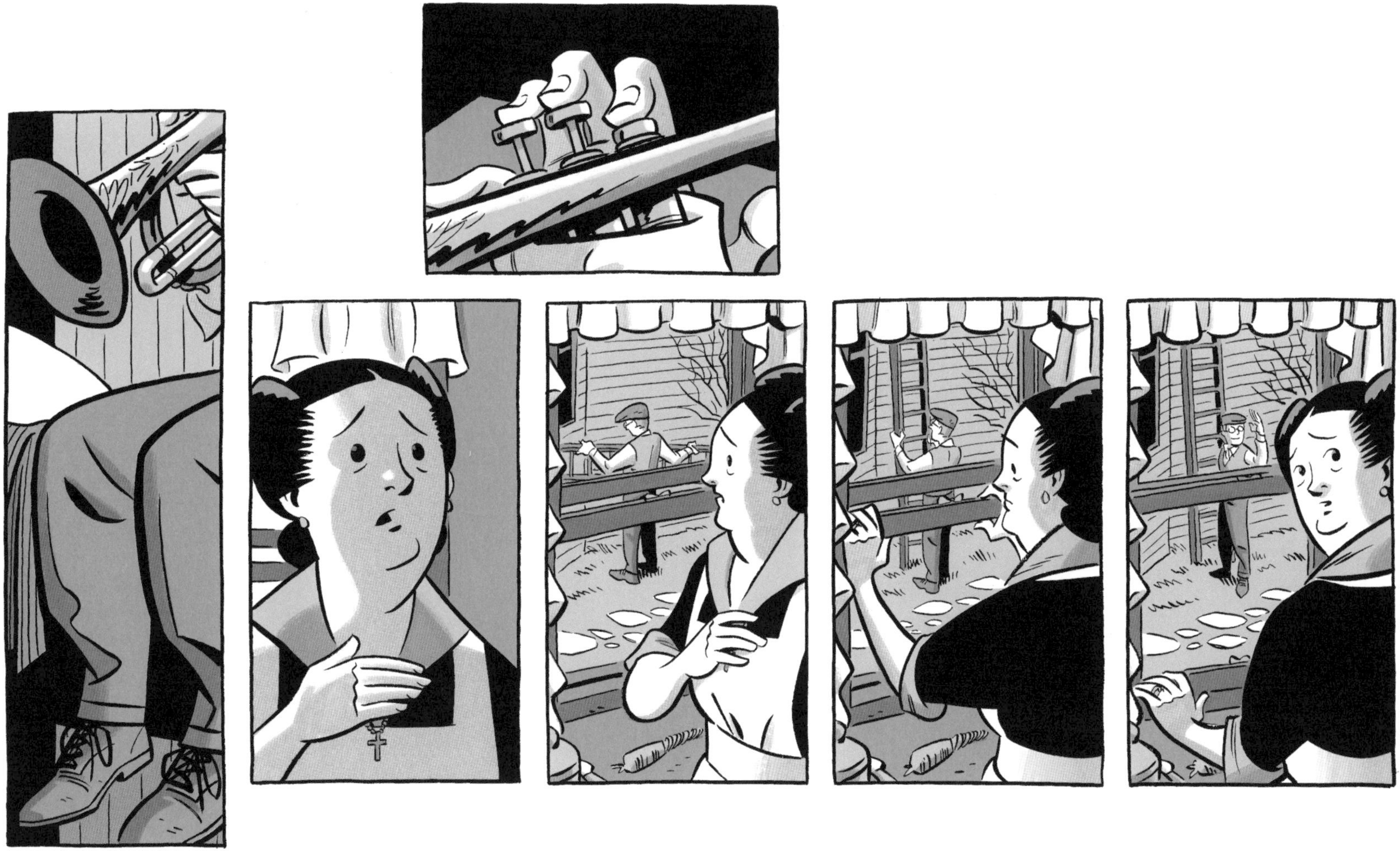

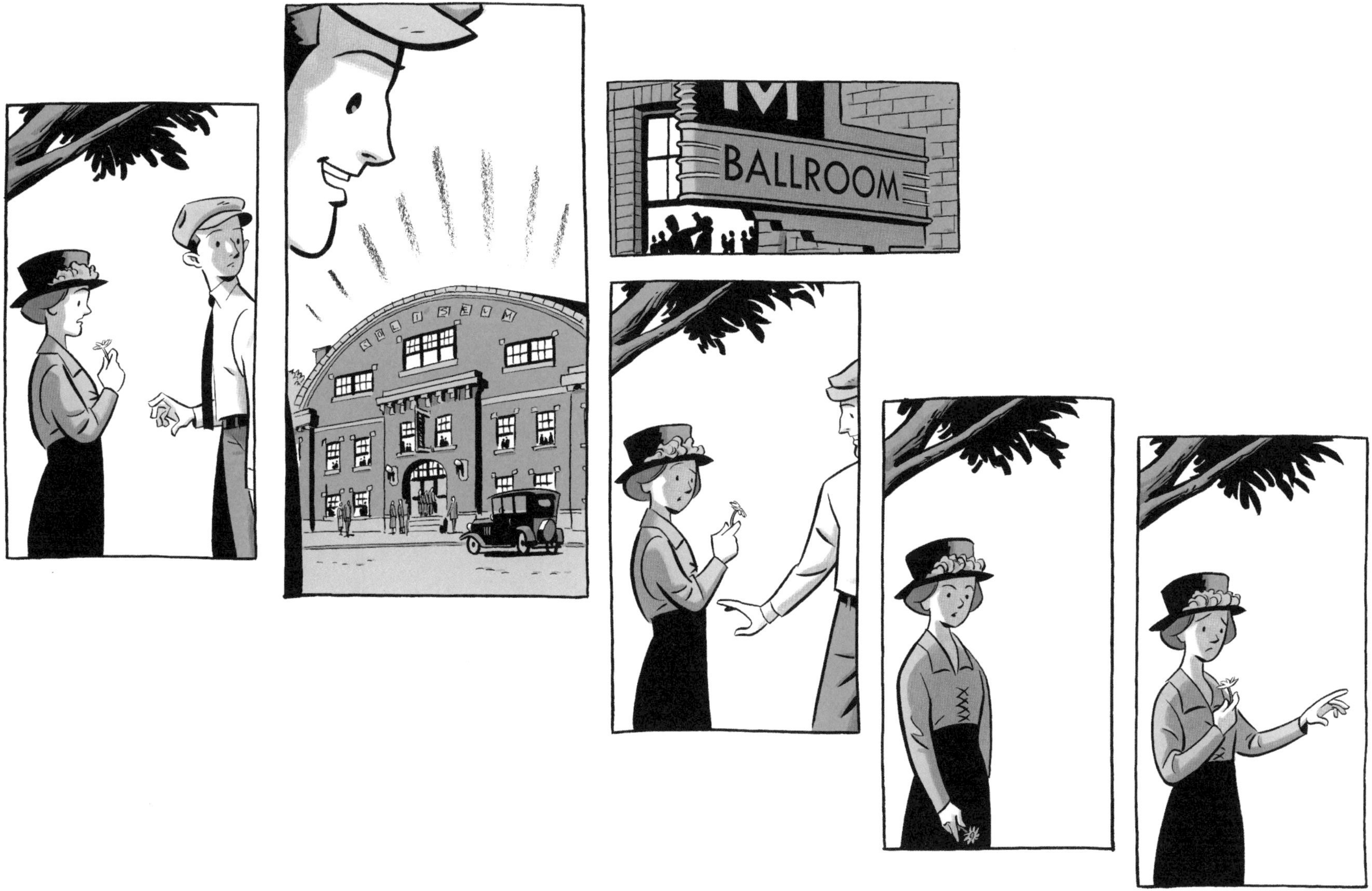
BALLROOM

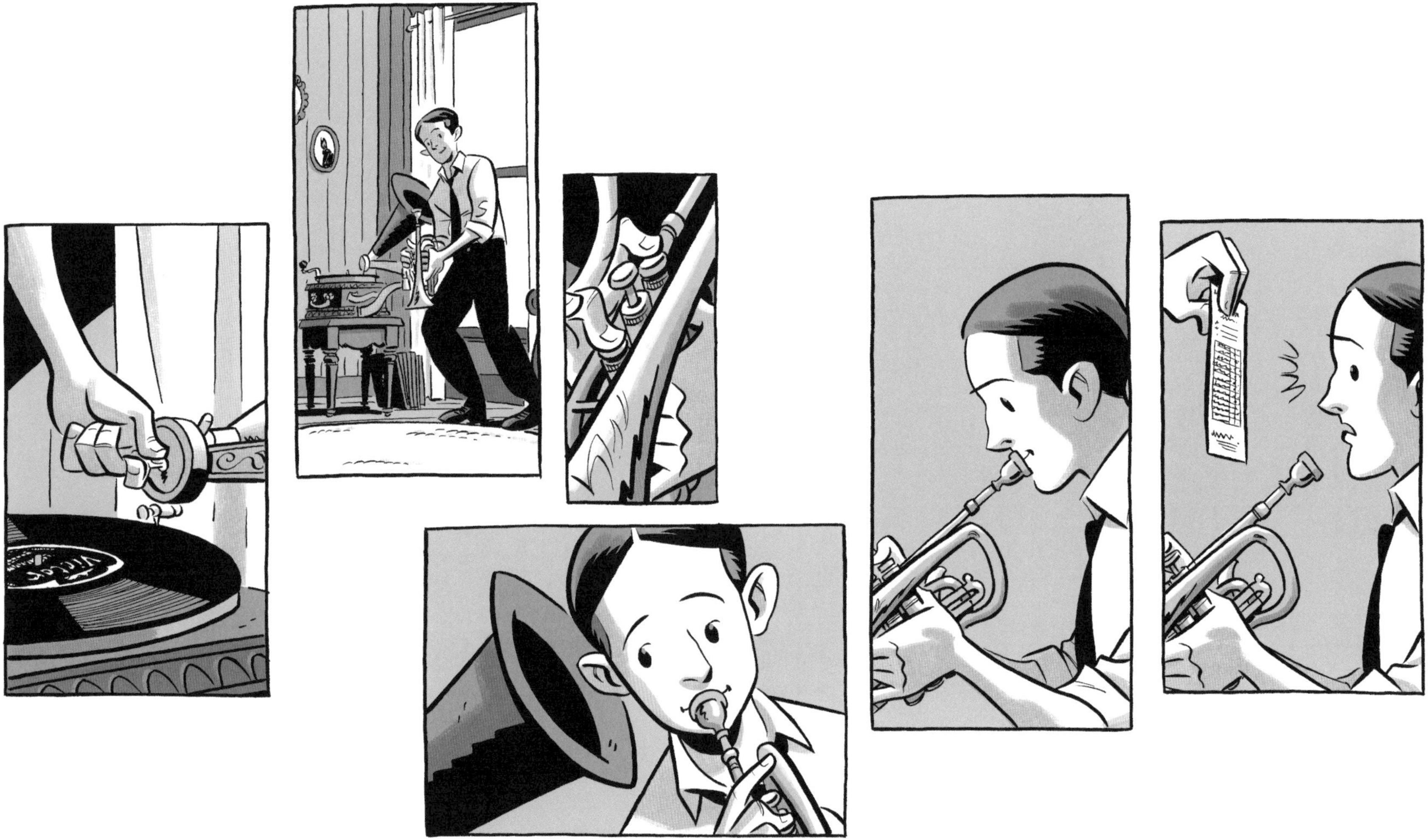

IOWA PUBLIC SCHOOL

DAVENPORT H
REPORT CAR

Report of *Bix Beiderbecke*
Grade 11
Date
Teacher

Studies	
English Literature	D+
English Usage	D
Spelling	F
Writing	D
Social Science	C-
Mathematics	F
General Science	D
Art	C
Shop	D
Physical Education	D+
Elements of Business	F
Citizenship	

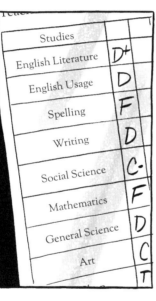

Studies	
English Literature	D+
English Usage	D
Spelling	F
Writing	D
Social Science	C-
Mathematics	F
General Science	D
Art	C

The Rock Island News
ROCK ISLAND, ILLINOIS, SATURDAY, JANUARY 17, 1920
PROHIBITIO
BEGINS TOD
Dream of Reformers
Century Goes Into

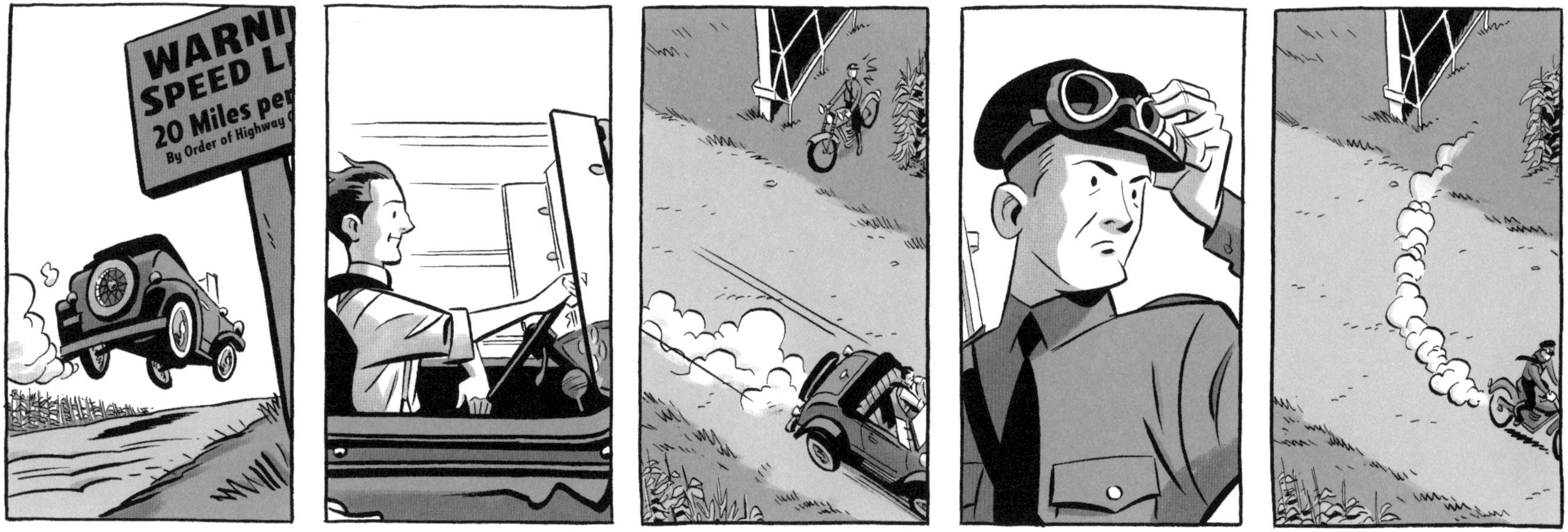
WARNI
SPEED LI
20 Miles per
By Order of Highway

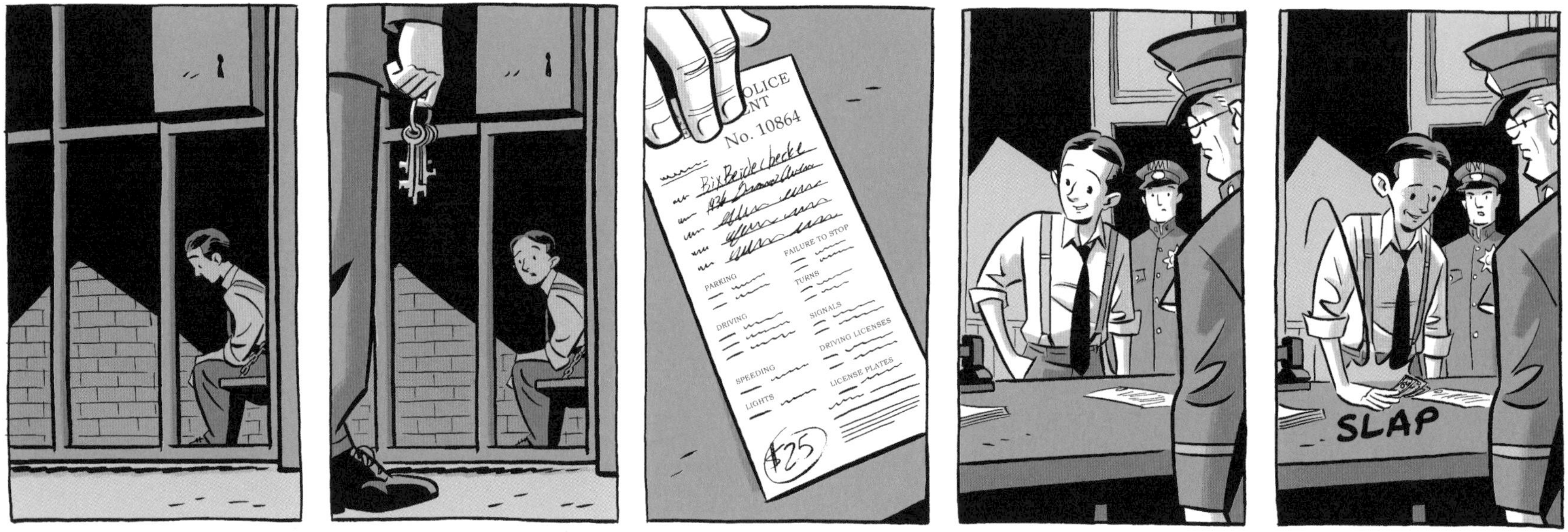
No. 10864
Bix Beiderbecke
FAILURE TO STOP
PARKING
TURNS
DRIVING
SIGNALS
DRIVING LICENSES
SPEEDING
LICENSE PLATES
LIGHTS
$25
SLAP

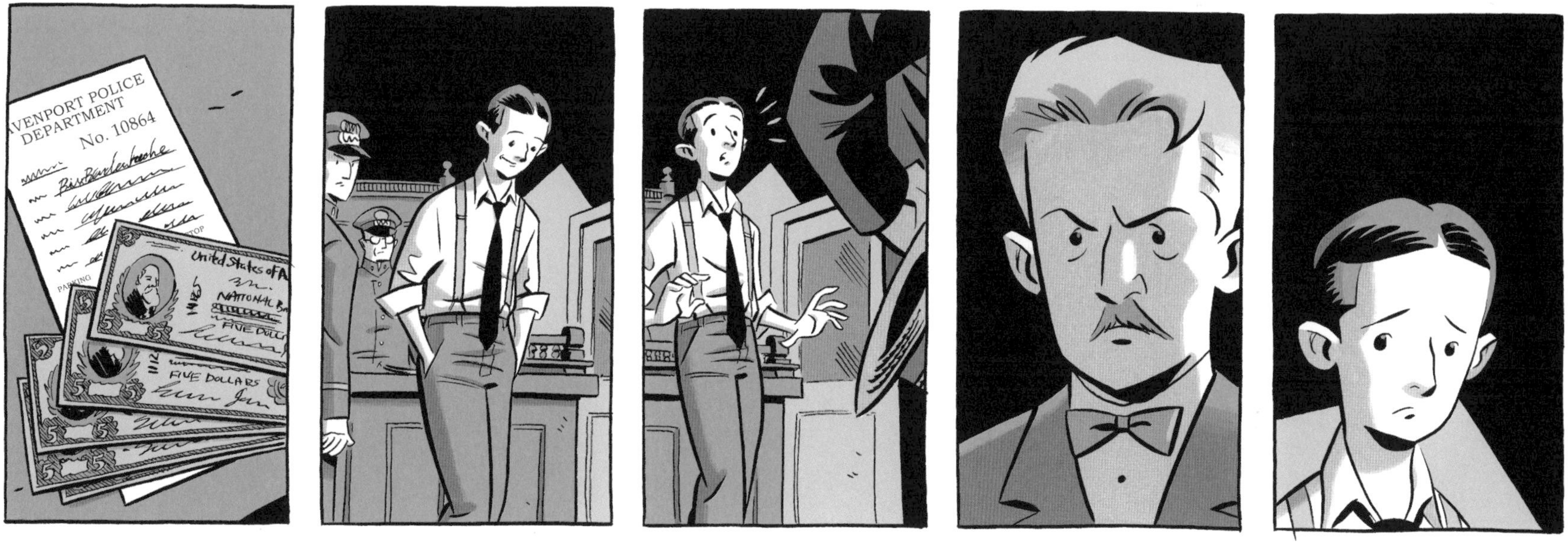
AVENPORT POLICE
DEPARTMENT
No. 10864
FIVE DOLLARS

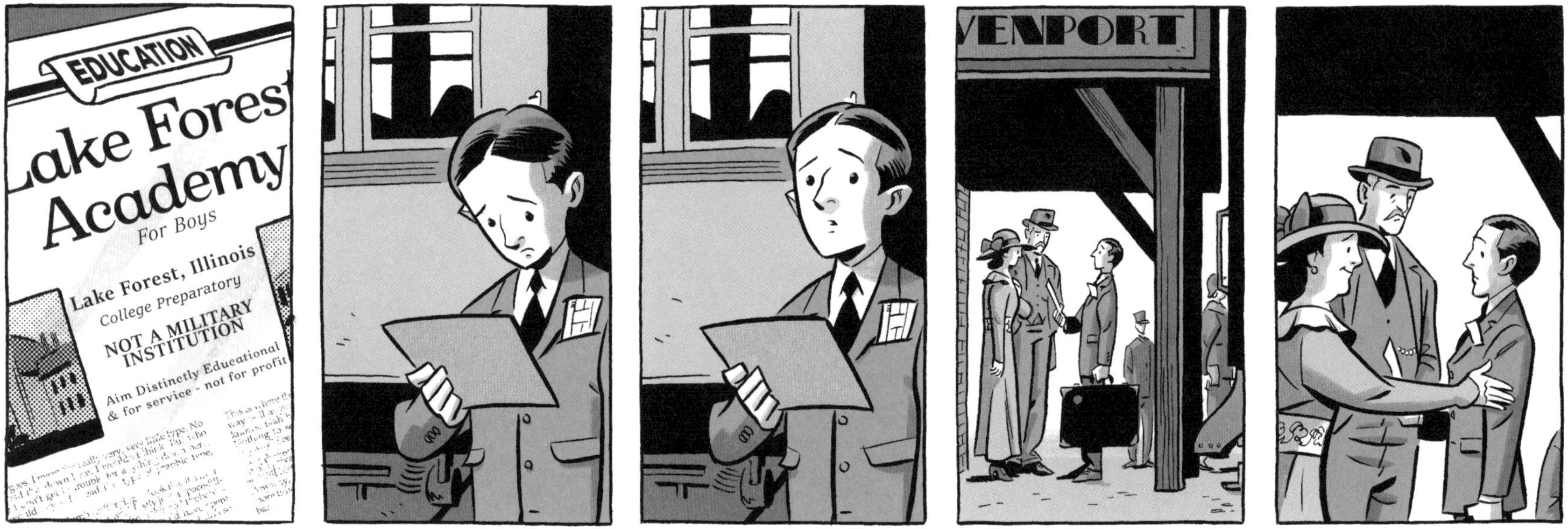
EDUCATION
ake Fores
Academy
For Boys
Lake Forest, Illinois
College Preparatory
NOT A MILITARY INSTITUTION
Aim Distinctly Educational & for service - not for profit
VENPORT

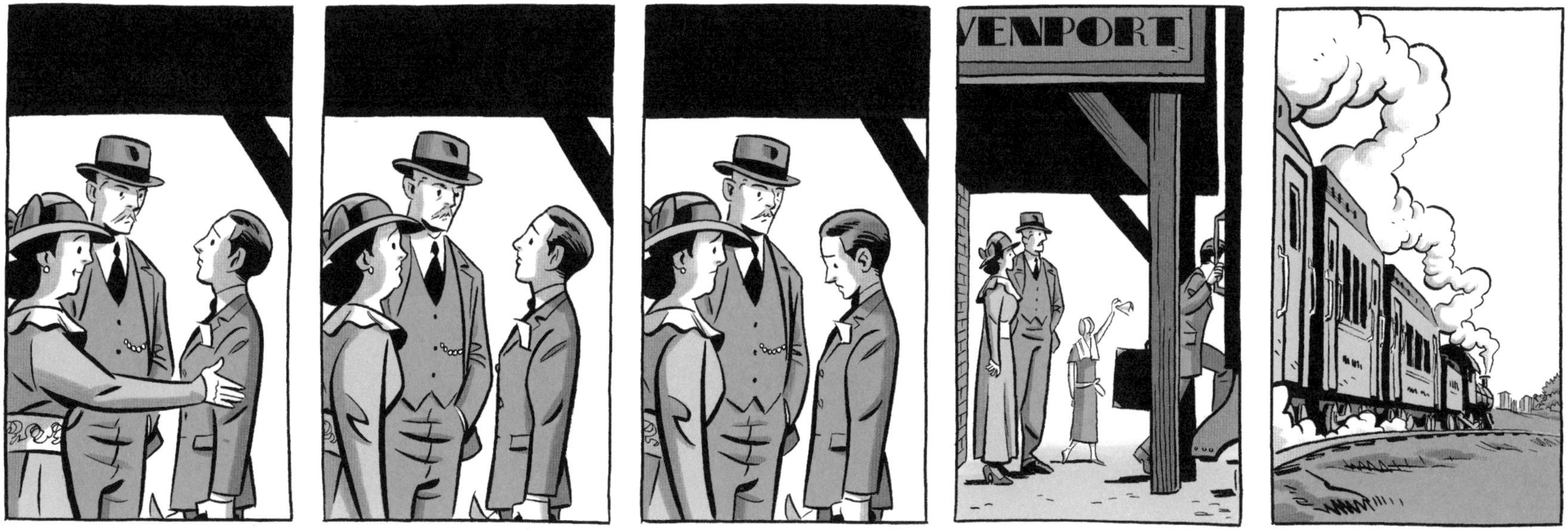
VENPORT

LAKE FOREST
TO CHICAGO
↑ 30 MILES

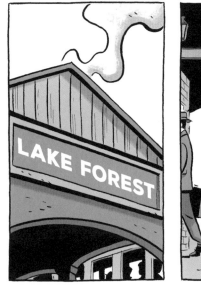

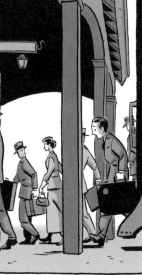

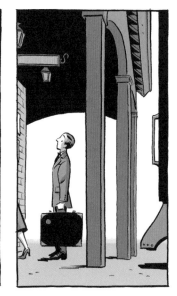

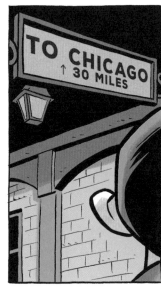

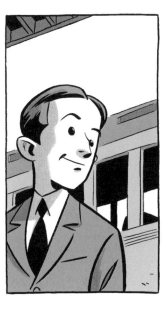

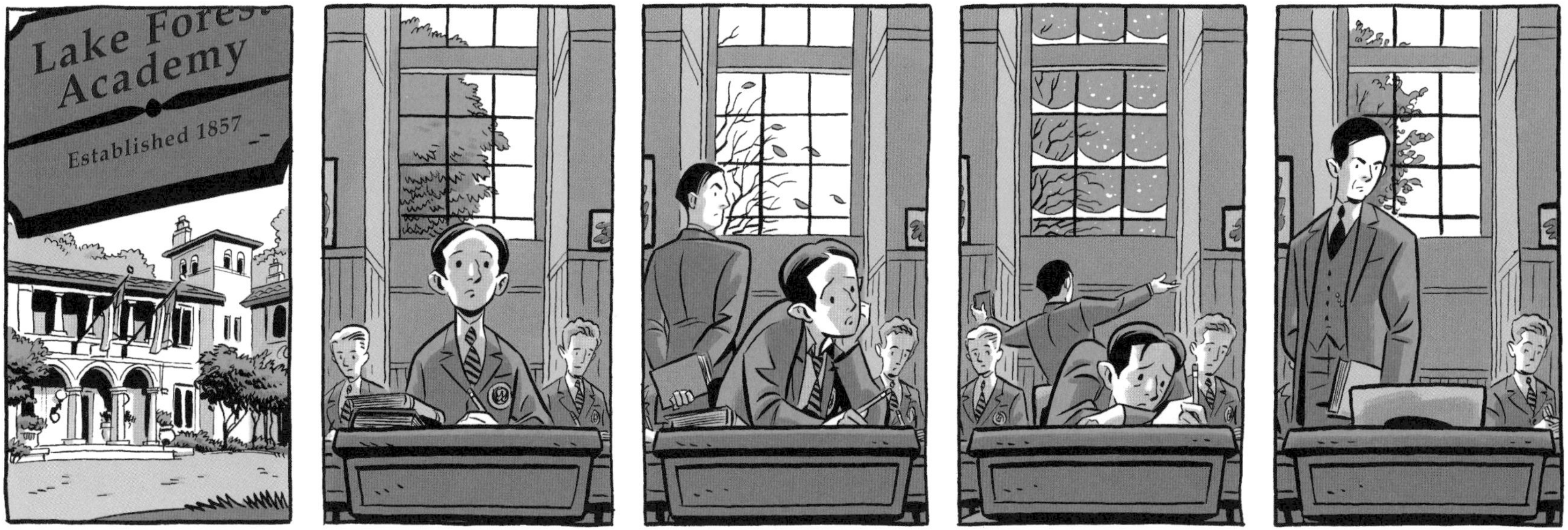
Lake Fores
Academy
Established 1857

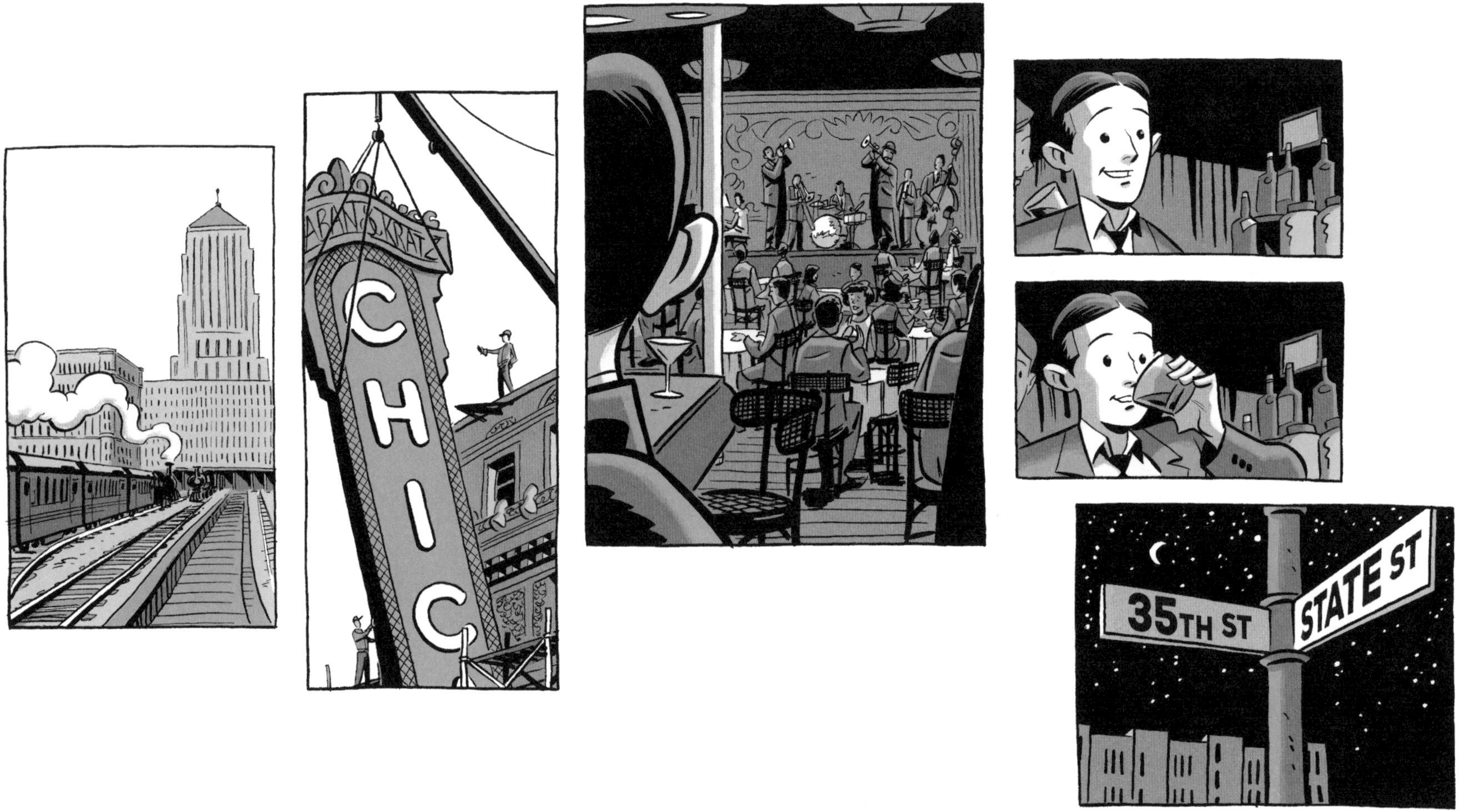
35TH ST
STATE ST

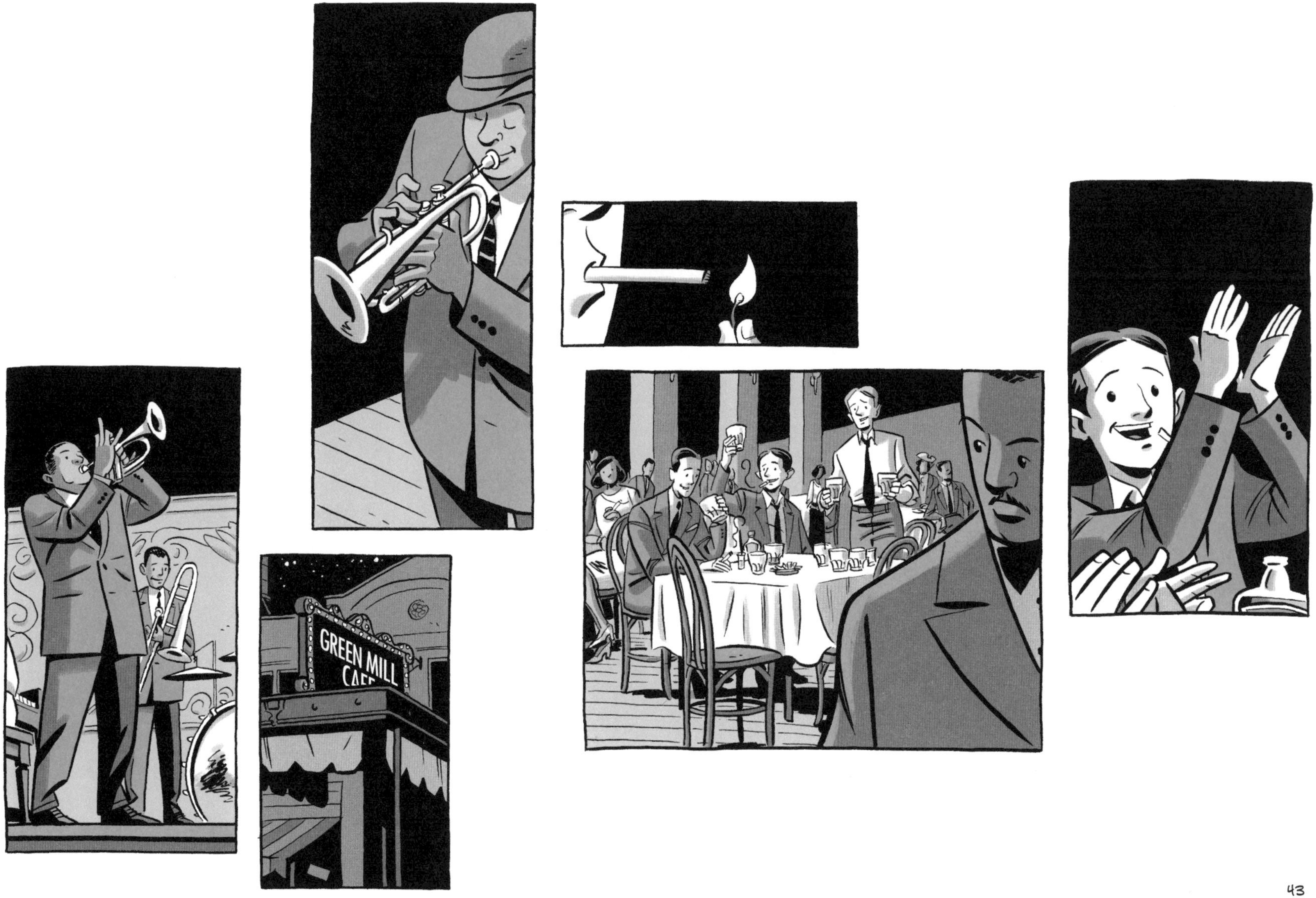
GREEN MILL

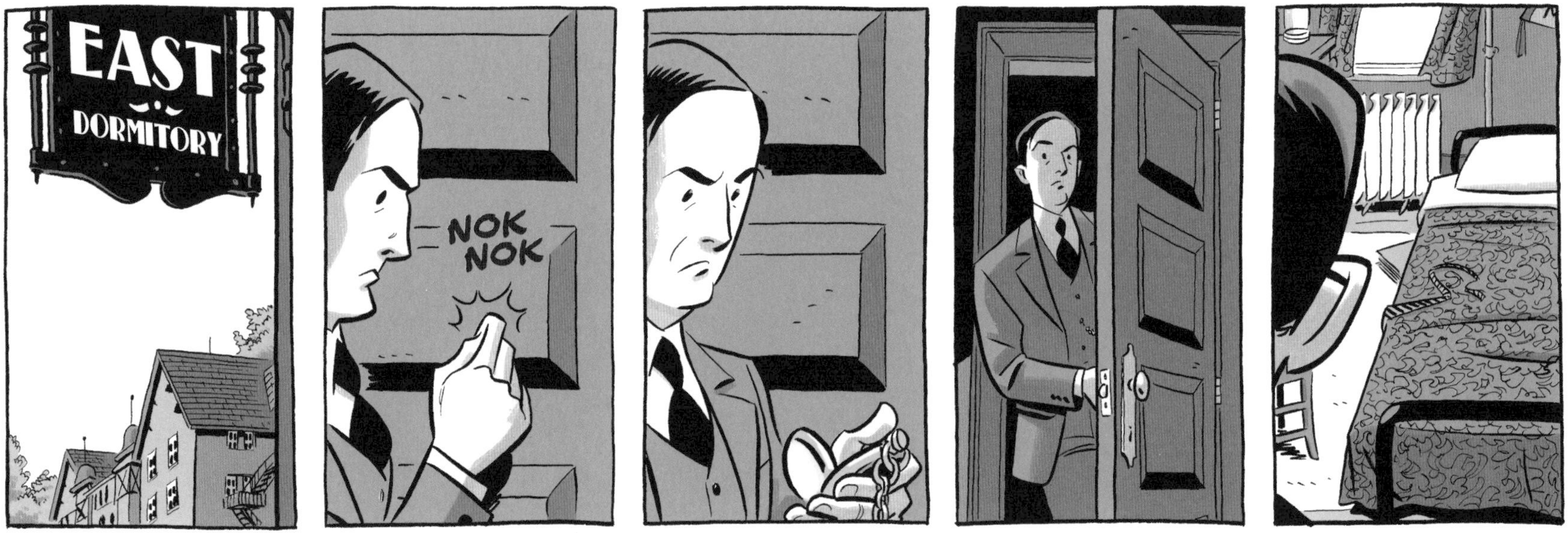
EAST
DORMITORY
NOK
NOK

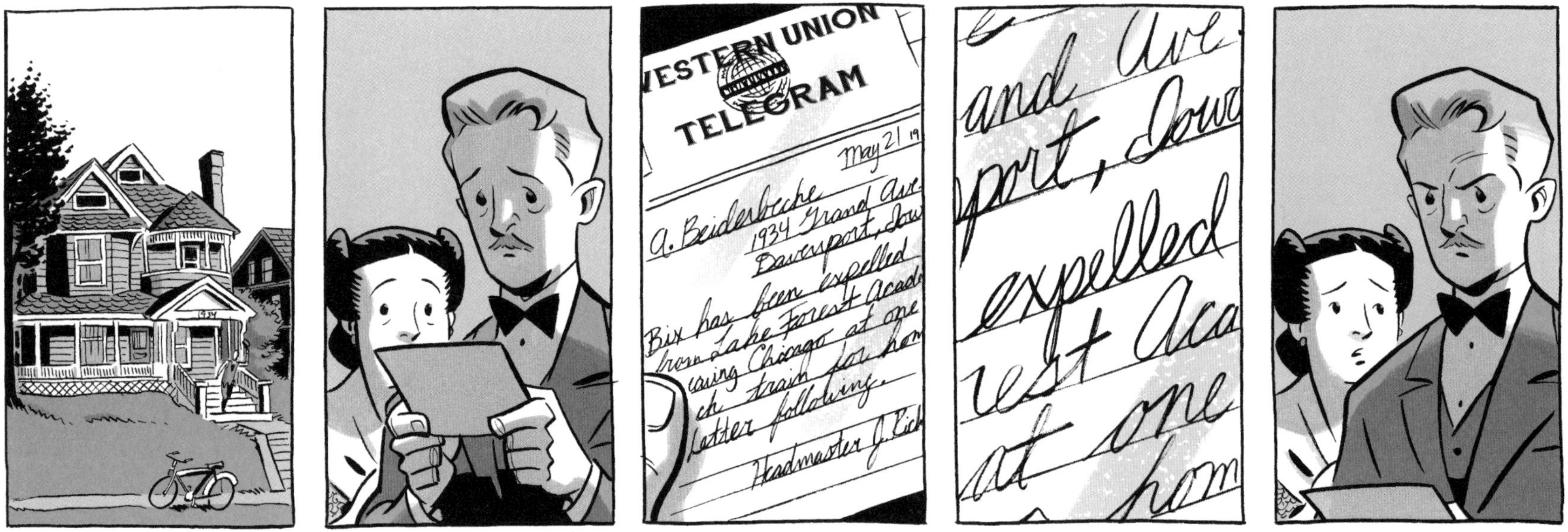
WESTERN UNION
TELEGRAM
May 21 19
A. Beiderbecke
1934 Grand Ave.
Davenport, Iow
Bix has been expelled
from Lake Forest Acad
leaving Chicago at one
ch train for hom
Letter following.
Headmaster J. Rich
and Ave.
port, Iow
expelled
est Aca
at one
hom

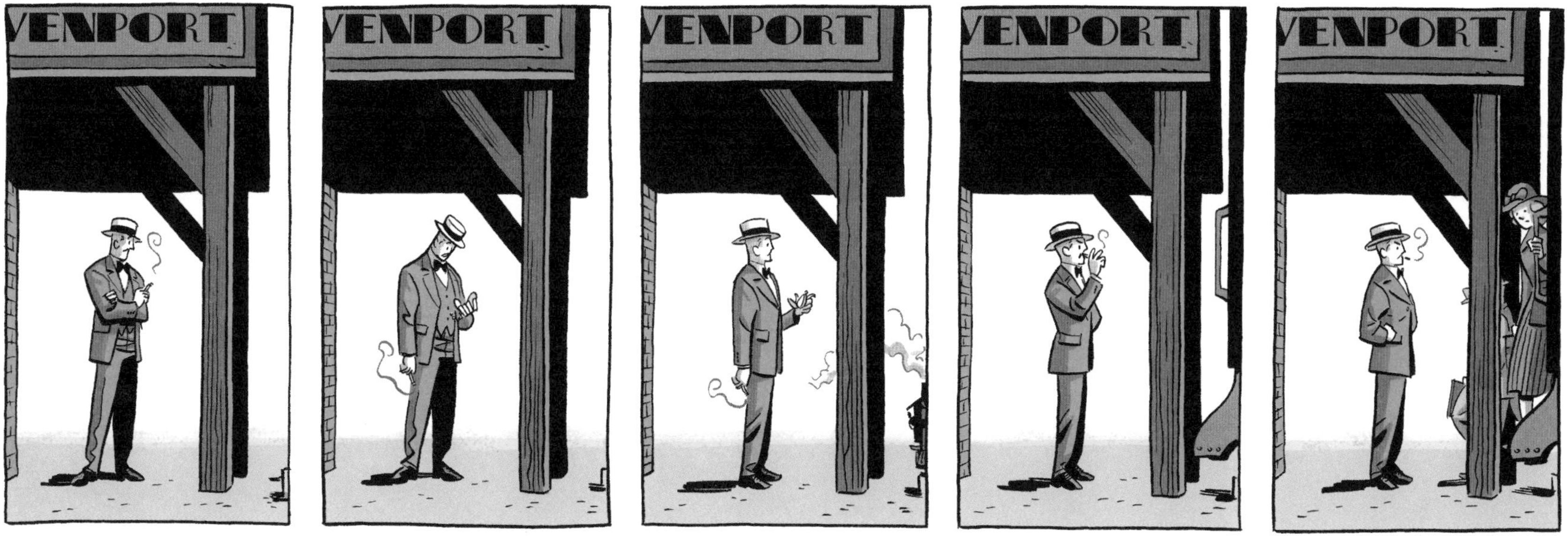
VENPORT
VENPORT
VENPORT
VENPORT
VENPORT

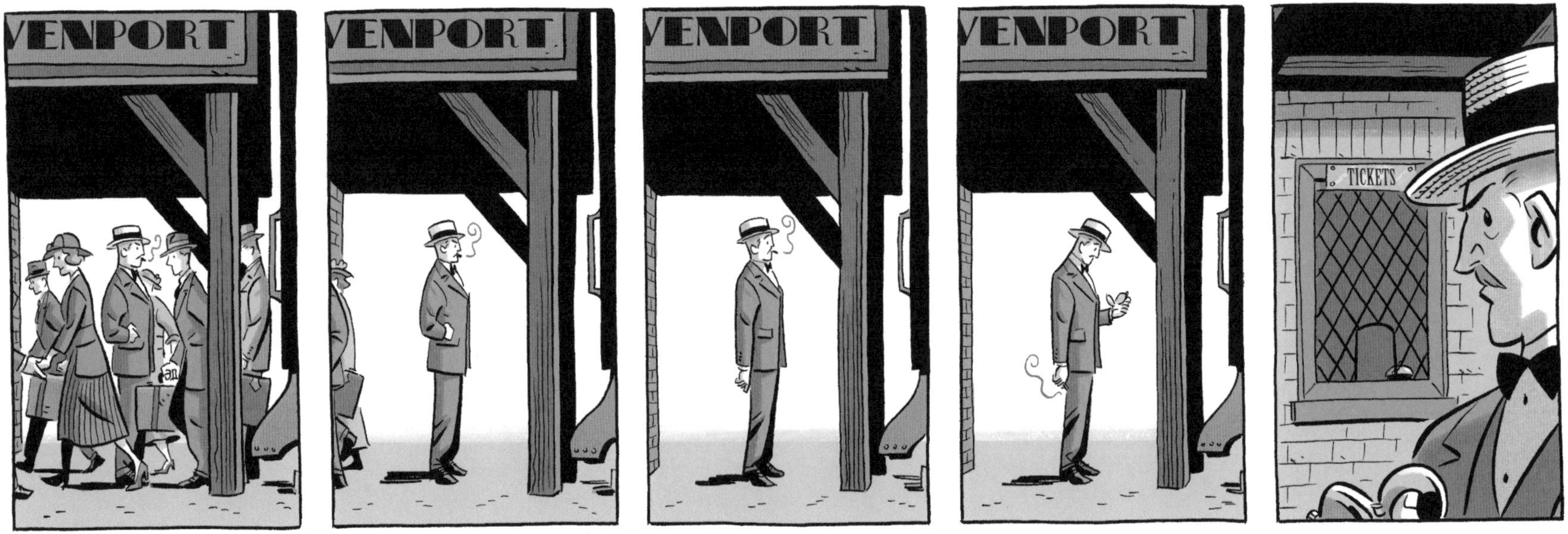
VENPORT
VENPORT
VENPORT
VENPORT
TICKETS

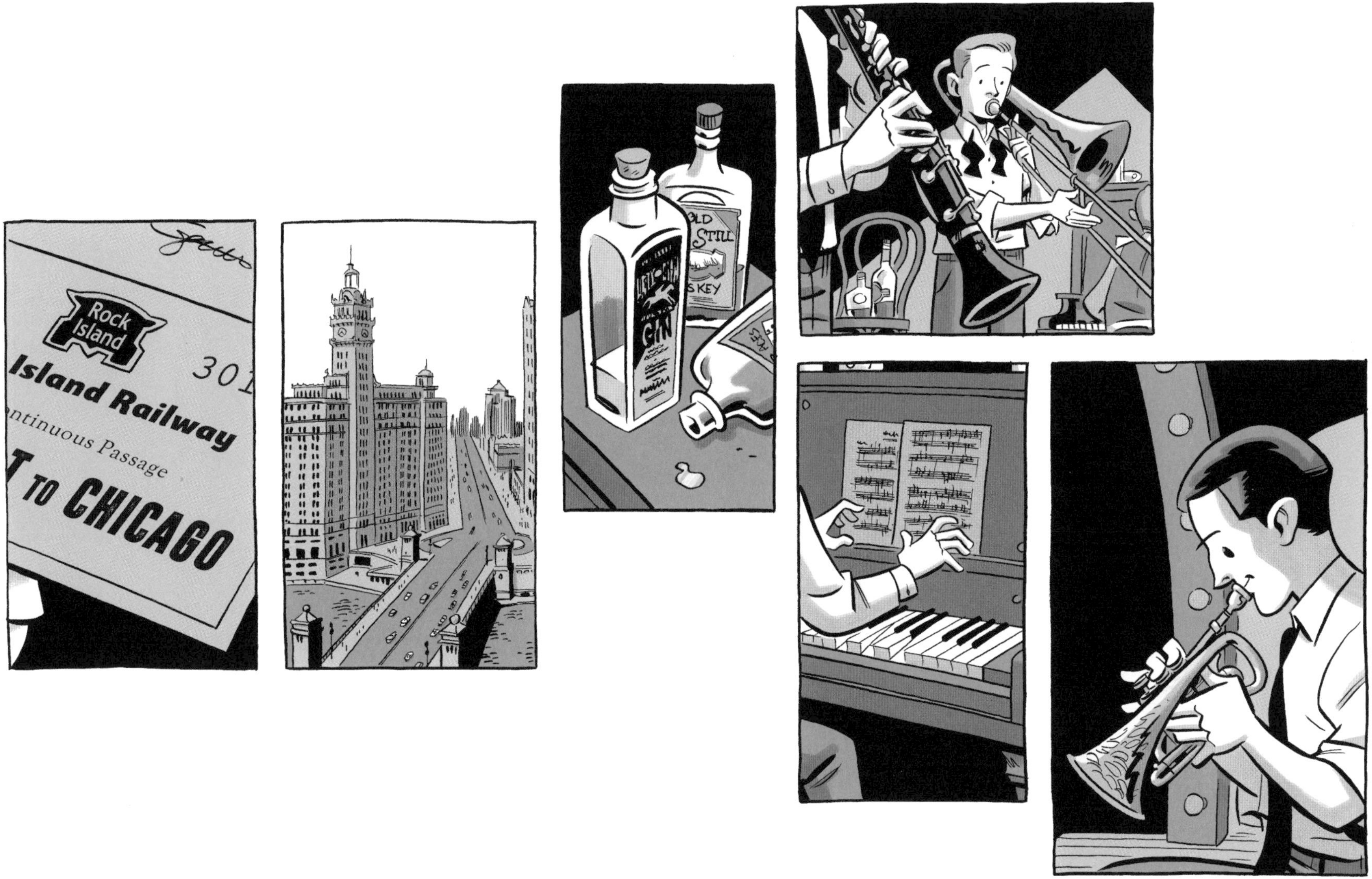
Rock Island
Island Railway
301
ntinuous Passage
T TO CHICAGO
OLD STILL
SKEY
GIN

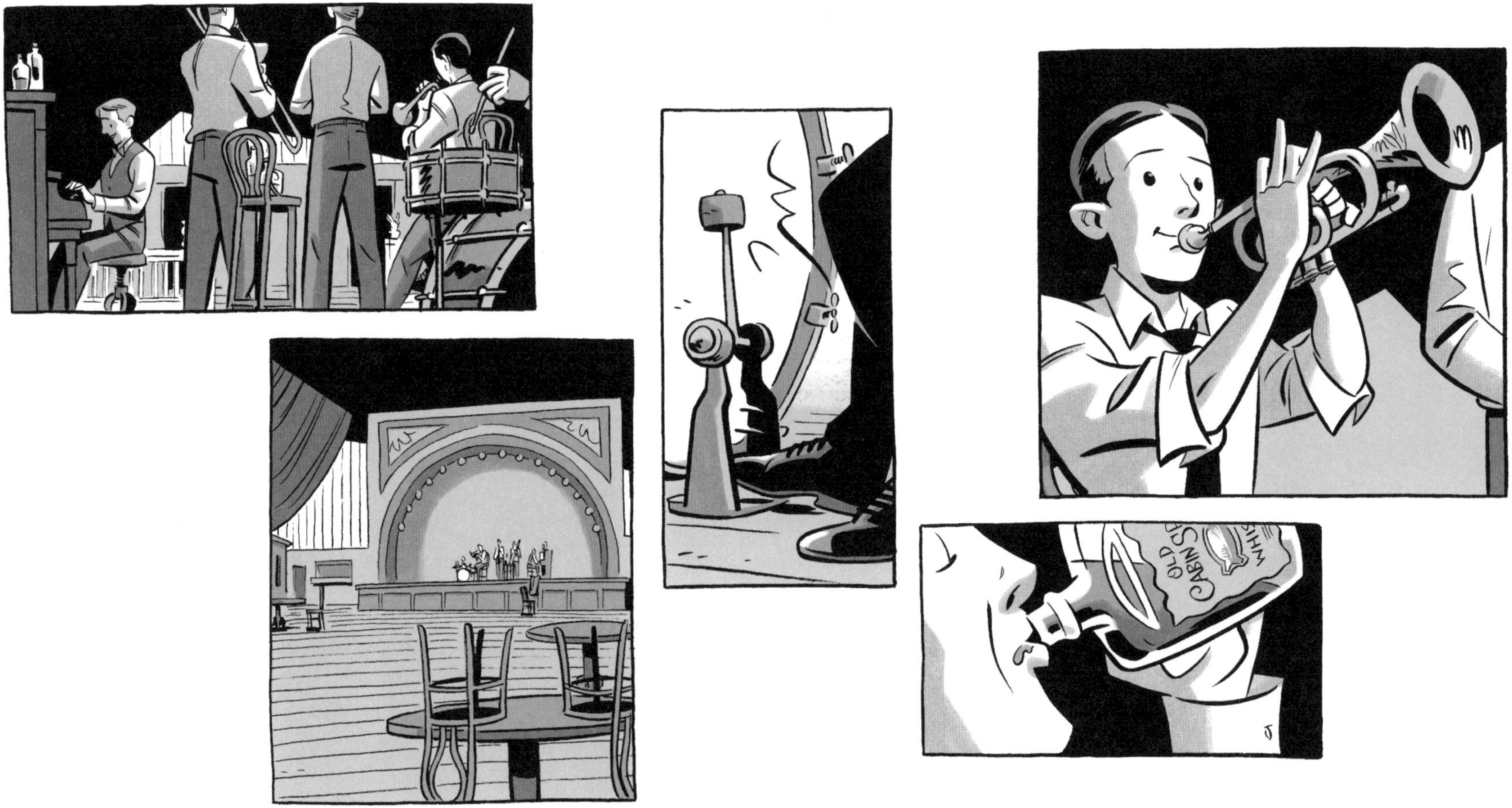
OLD CABIN

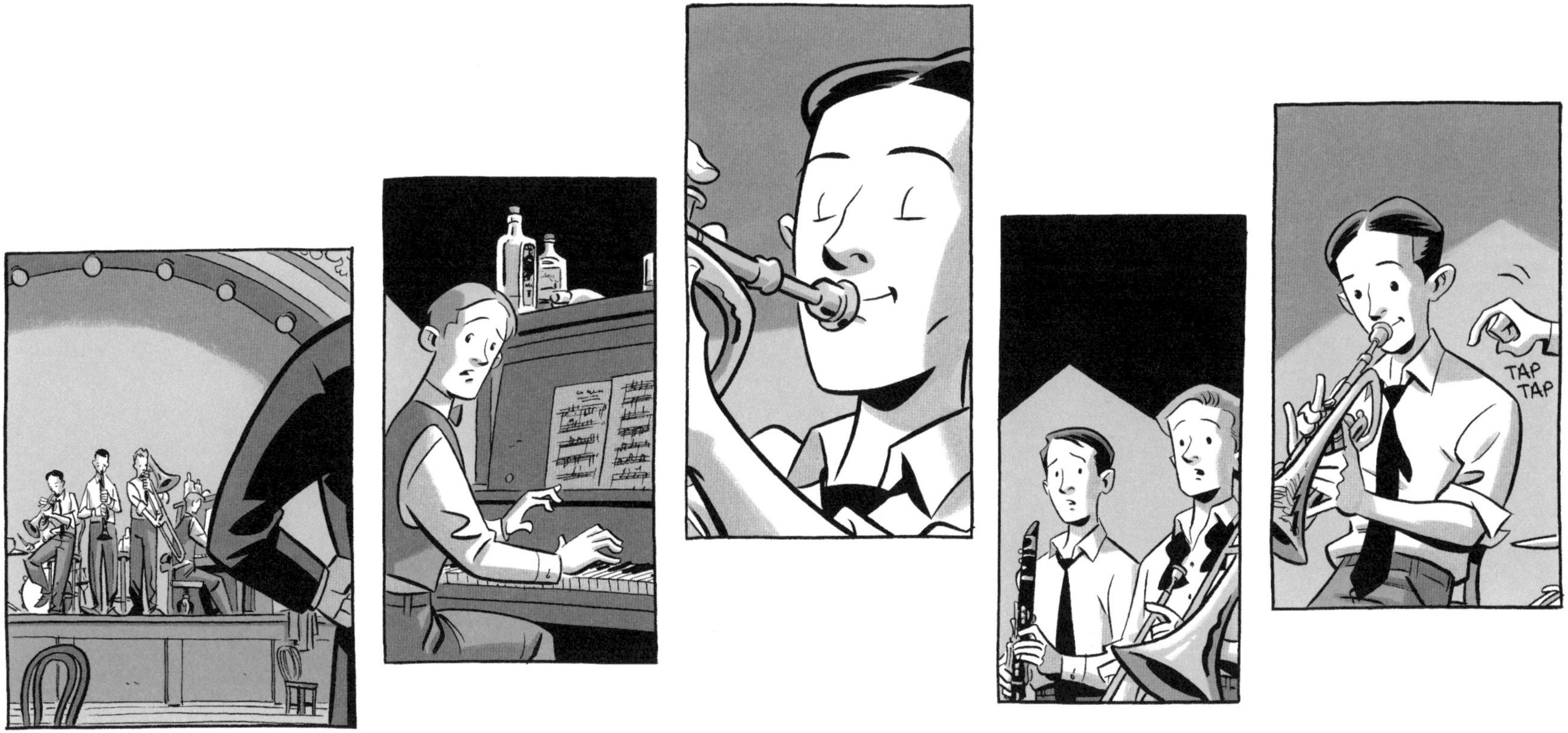
TAP
TAP

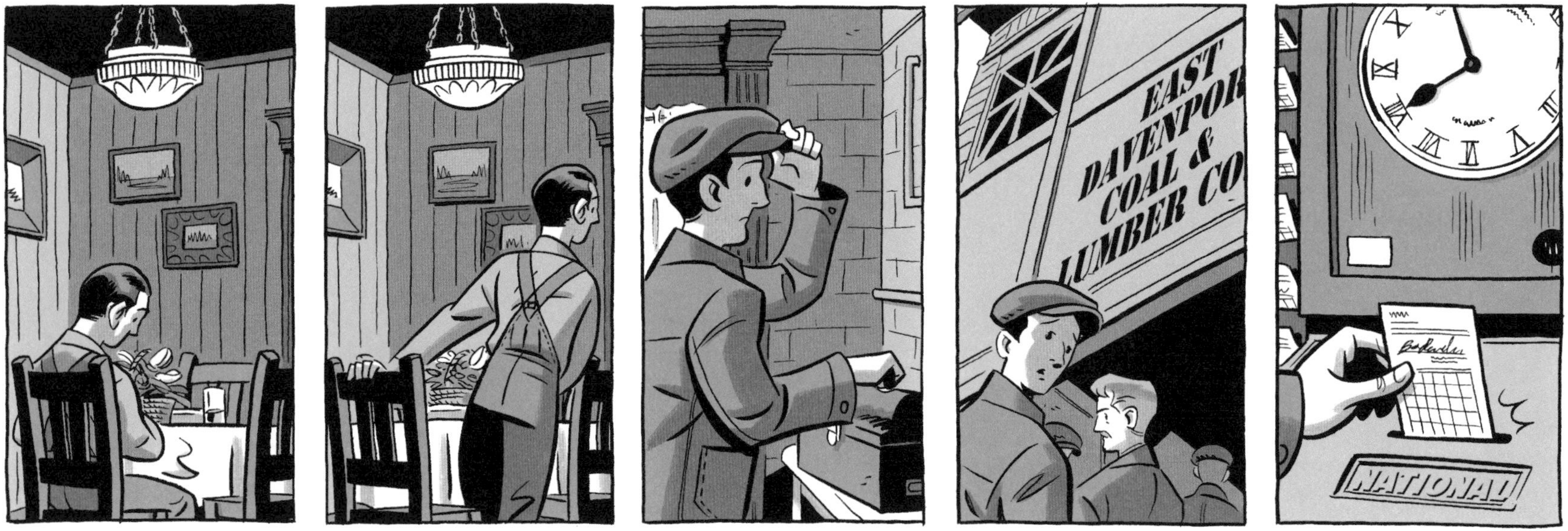
EAST
DAVENPOR
COAL &
LUMBER CO
NATIONAL

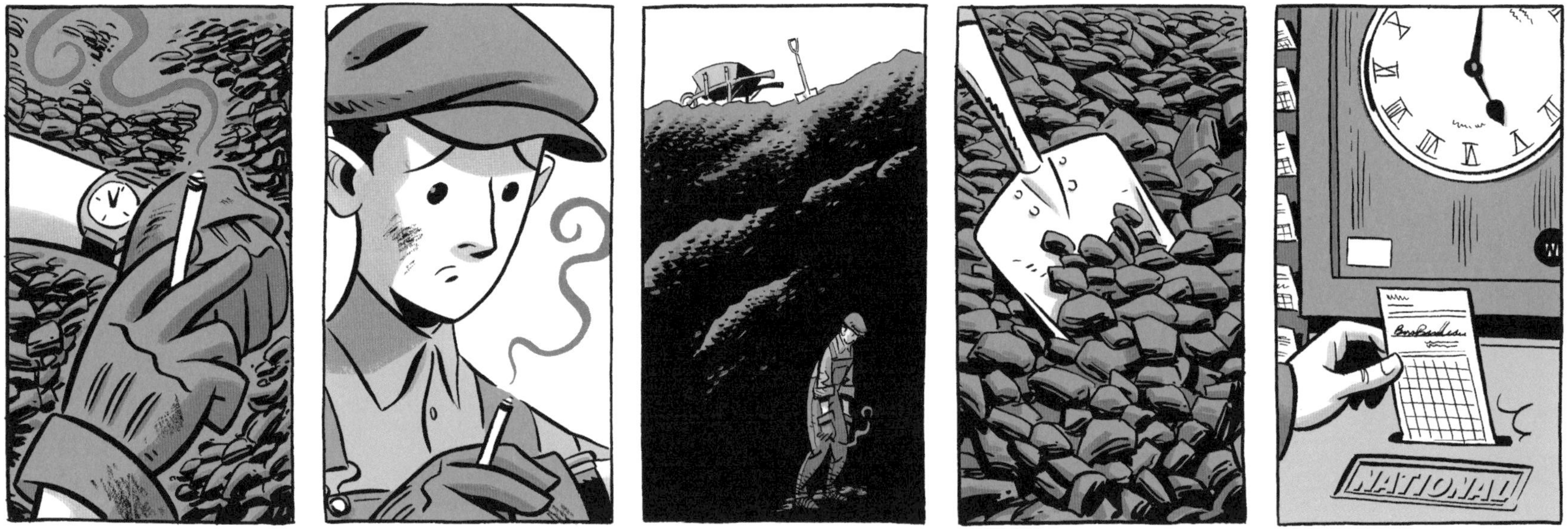
NATIONAL

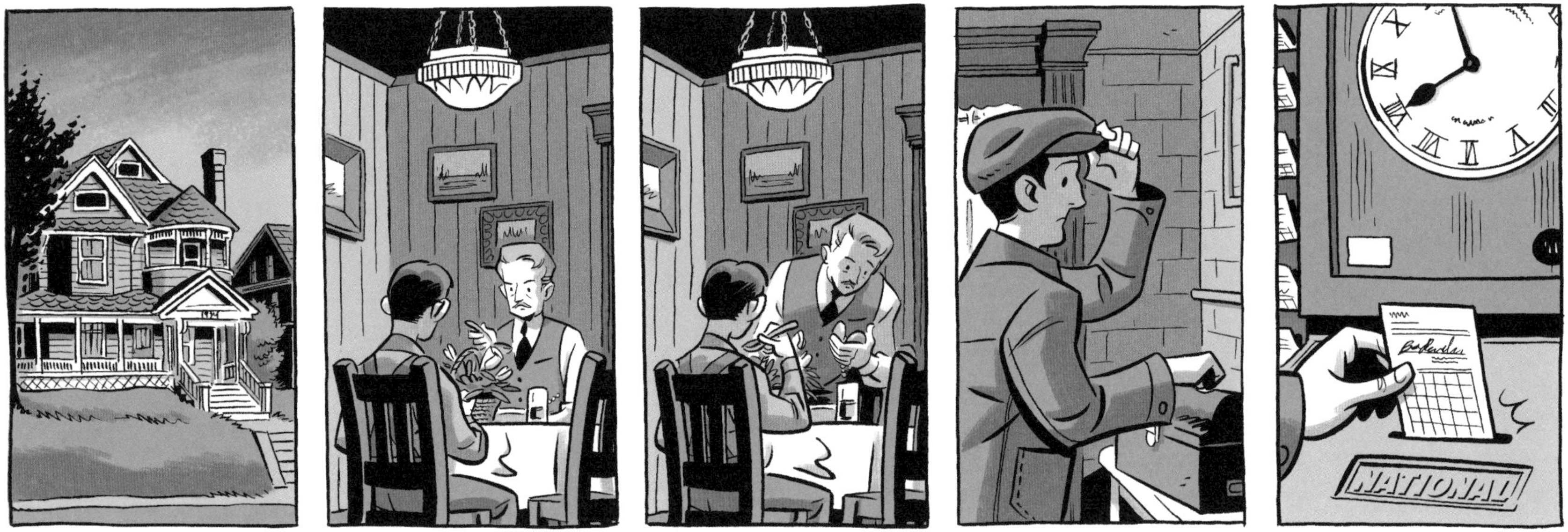
NATIONAL

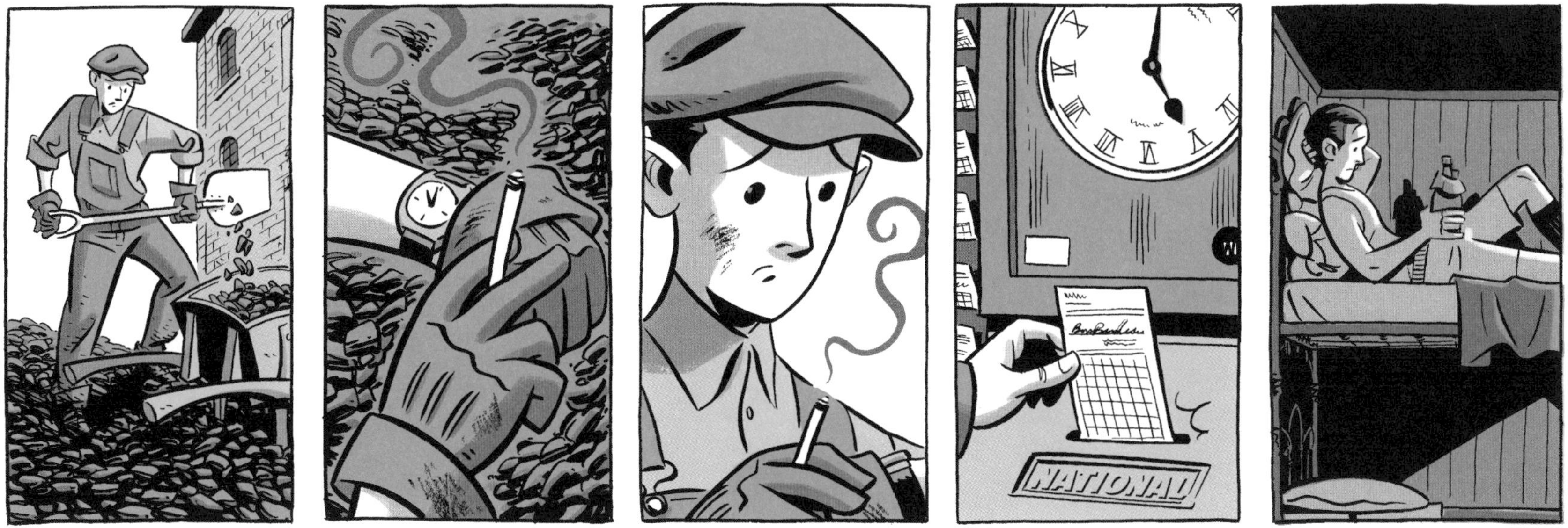
NATIONAL

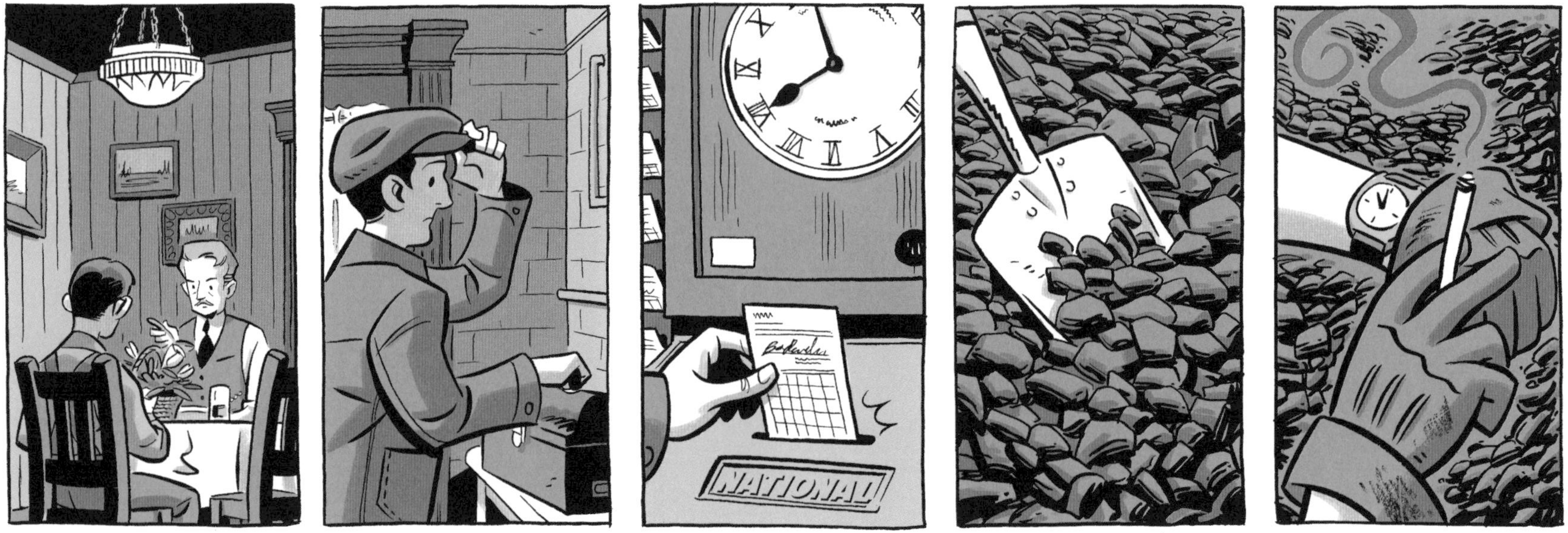
NATIONAL

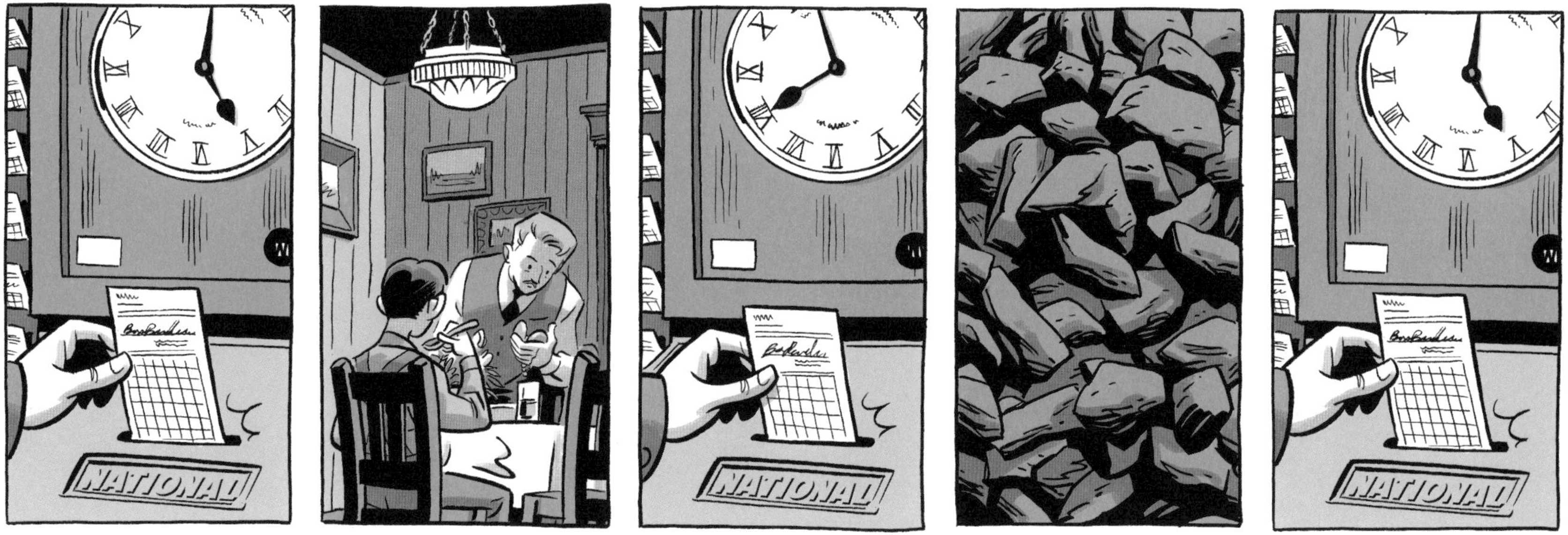
NATIONAL
NATIONAL
NATIONAL

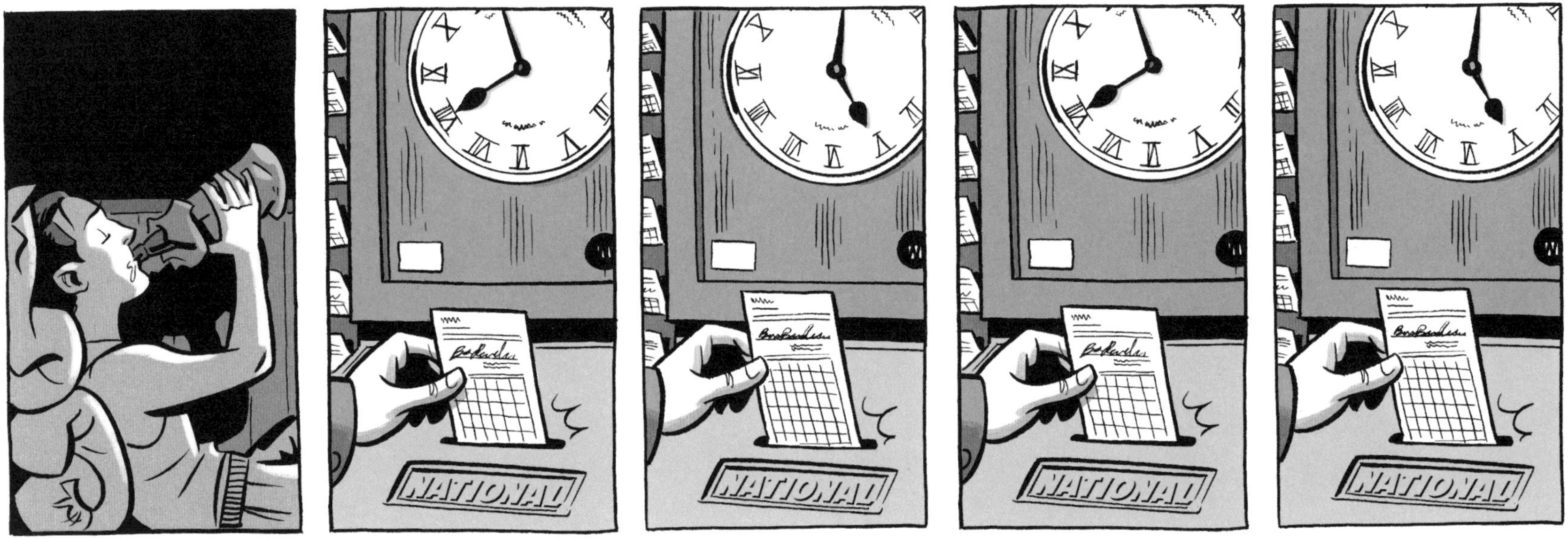
NATIONAL
NATIONAL
NATIONAL
NATIONAL

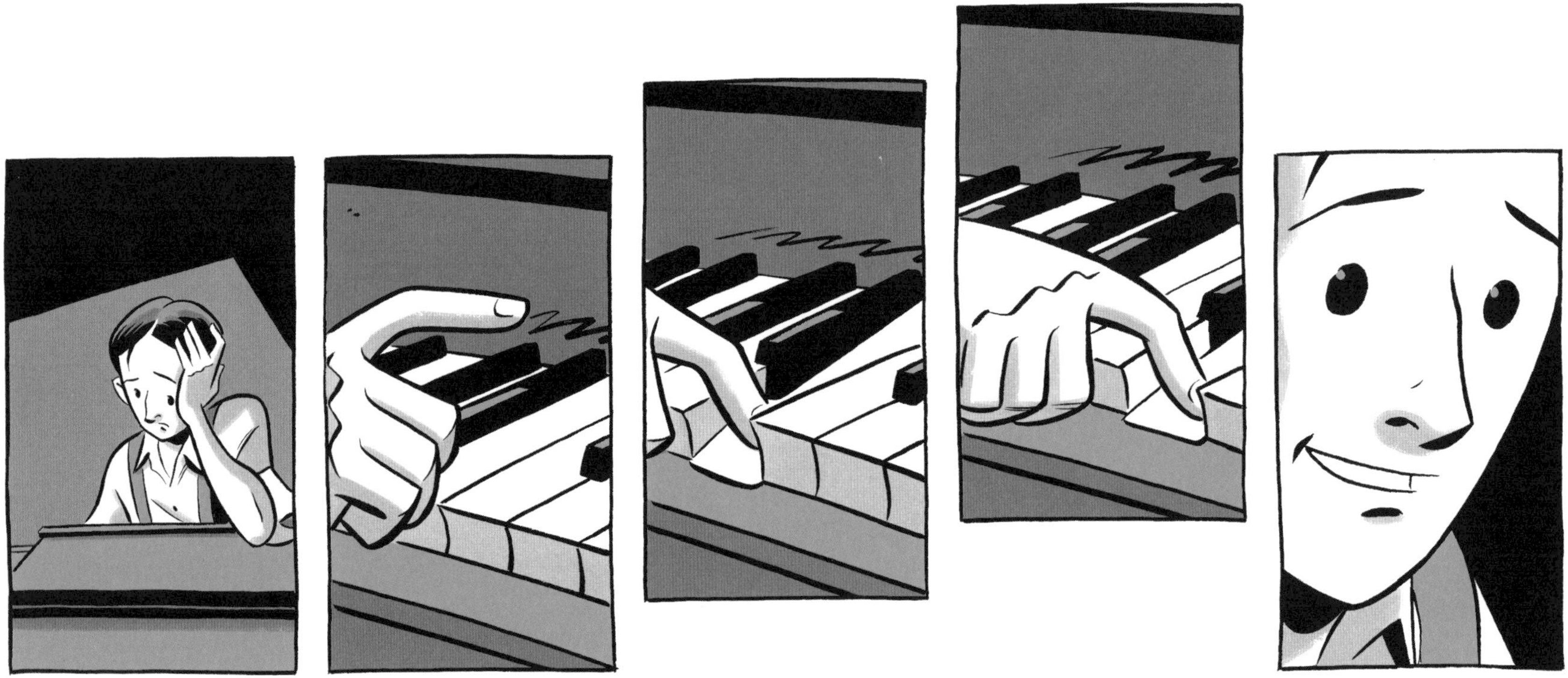

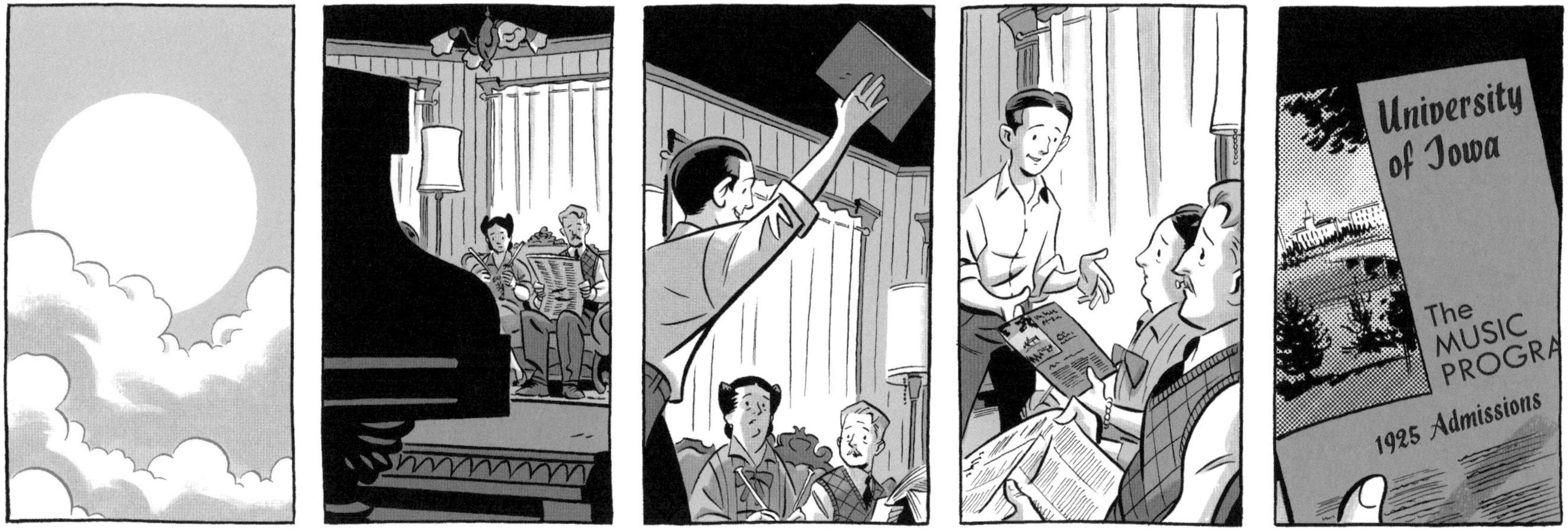
University of Iowa
The MUSIC PROGRA
1925 Admissions

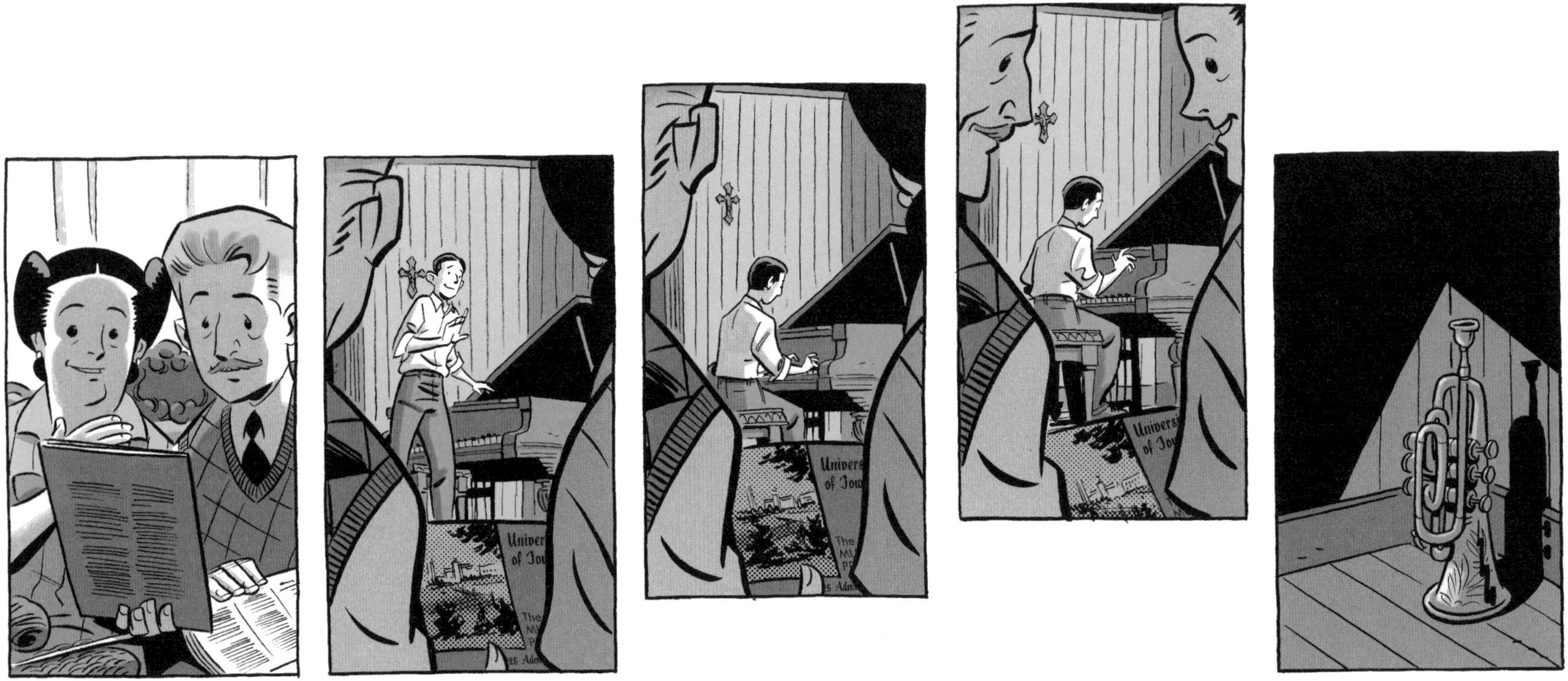

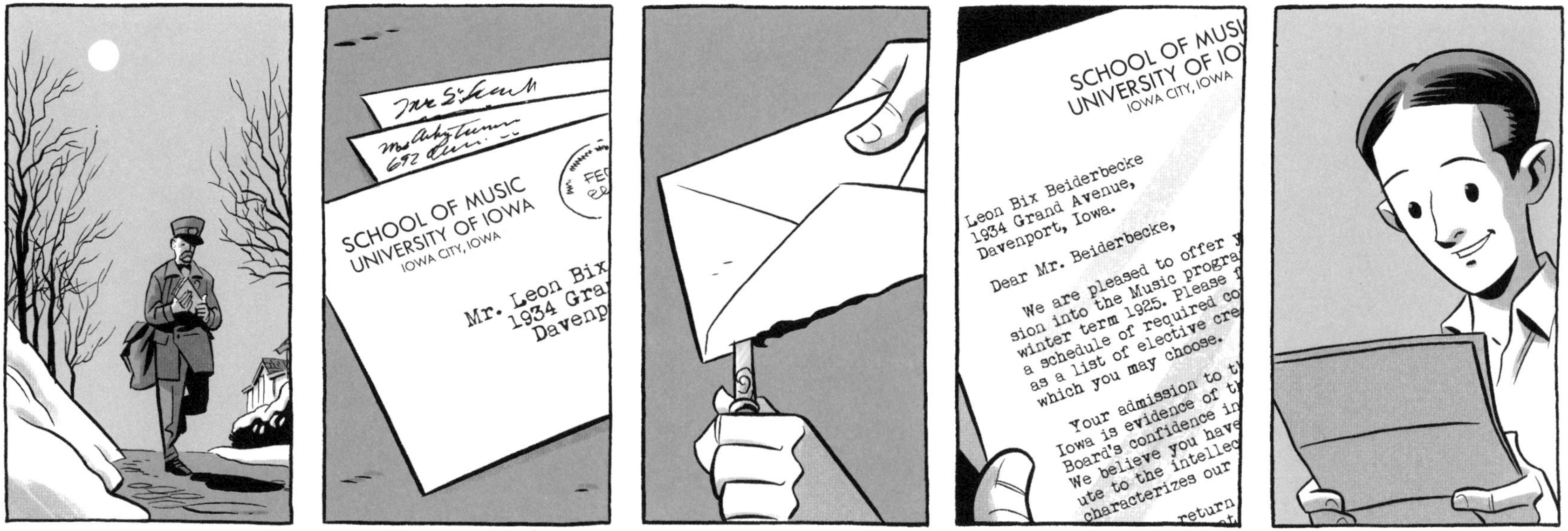
SCHOOL OF MUSIC
UNIVERSITY OF IOWA
IOWA CITY, IOWA
Mr. Leon Bix
1934 Gra
Davenp
SCHOOL OF MUSI
UNIVERSITY OF IO
IOWA CITY, IOWA
Leon Bix Beiderbecke
1934 Grand Avenue,
Davenport, Iowa.
Dear Mr. Beiderbecke,
We are pleased to offer y
sion into the Music progra
winter term 1925. Please f
a schedule of required co
as a list of elective cre
which you may choose.
Your admission to t
Iowa is evidence of t
Board's confidence in
We believe you have
ute to the intellec
characterizes our
return

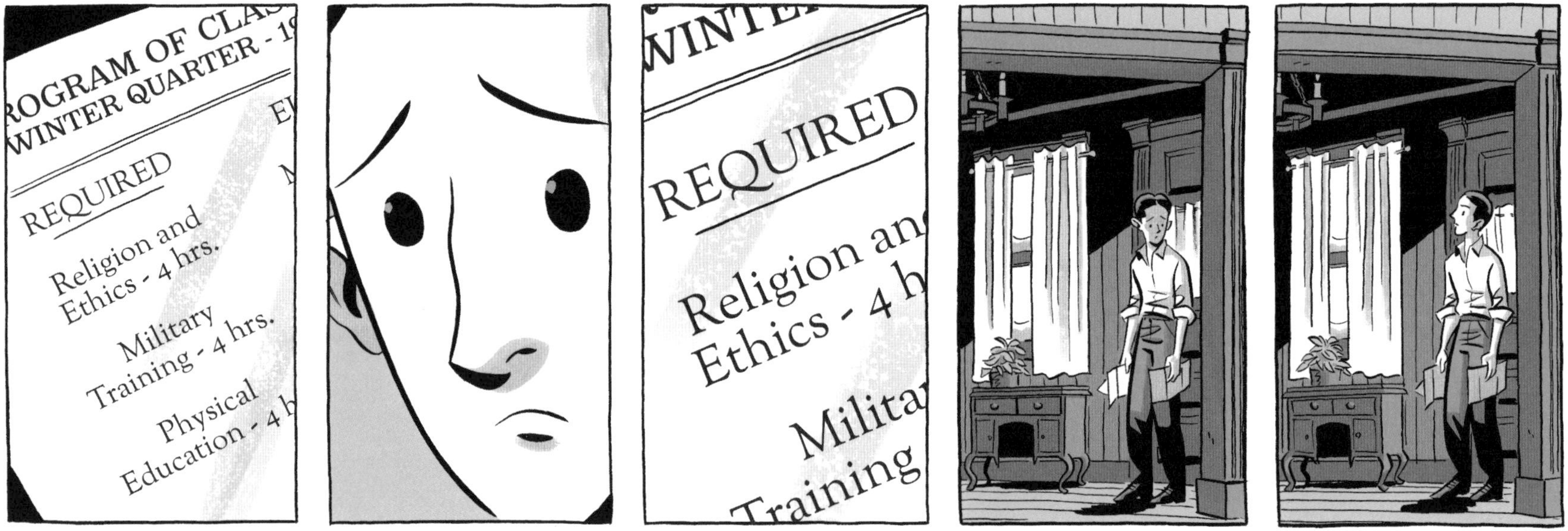
ROGRAM OF CLAS
WINTER QUARTER - 19
REQUIRED
Religion and
Ethics - 4 hrs.
Military
Training - 4 hrs.
Physical
Education - 4 h
WINTE
REQUIRED
Religion an
Ethics - 4 h
Milita
Training

YOU ARE NOW LEAVING
IOWA
THE HAWKEYE STATE

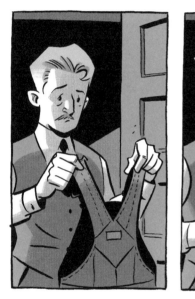

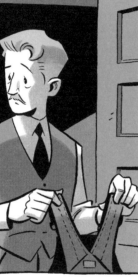

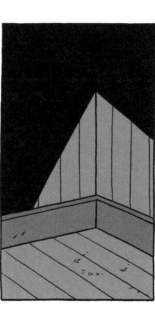

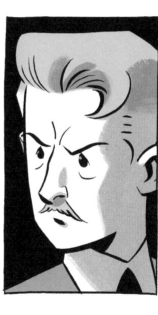

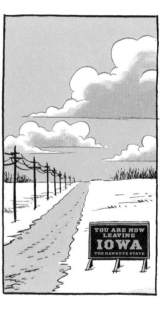

Part Two

JUST ONE MORE KISS

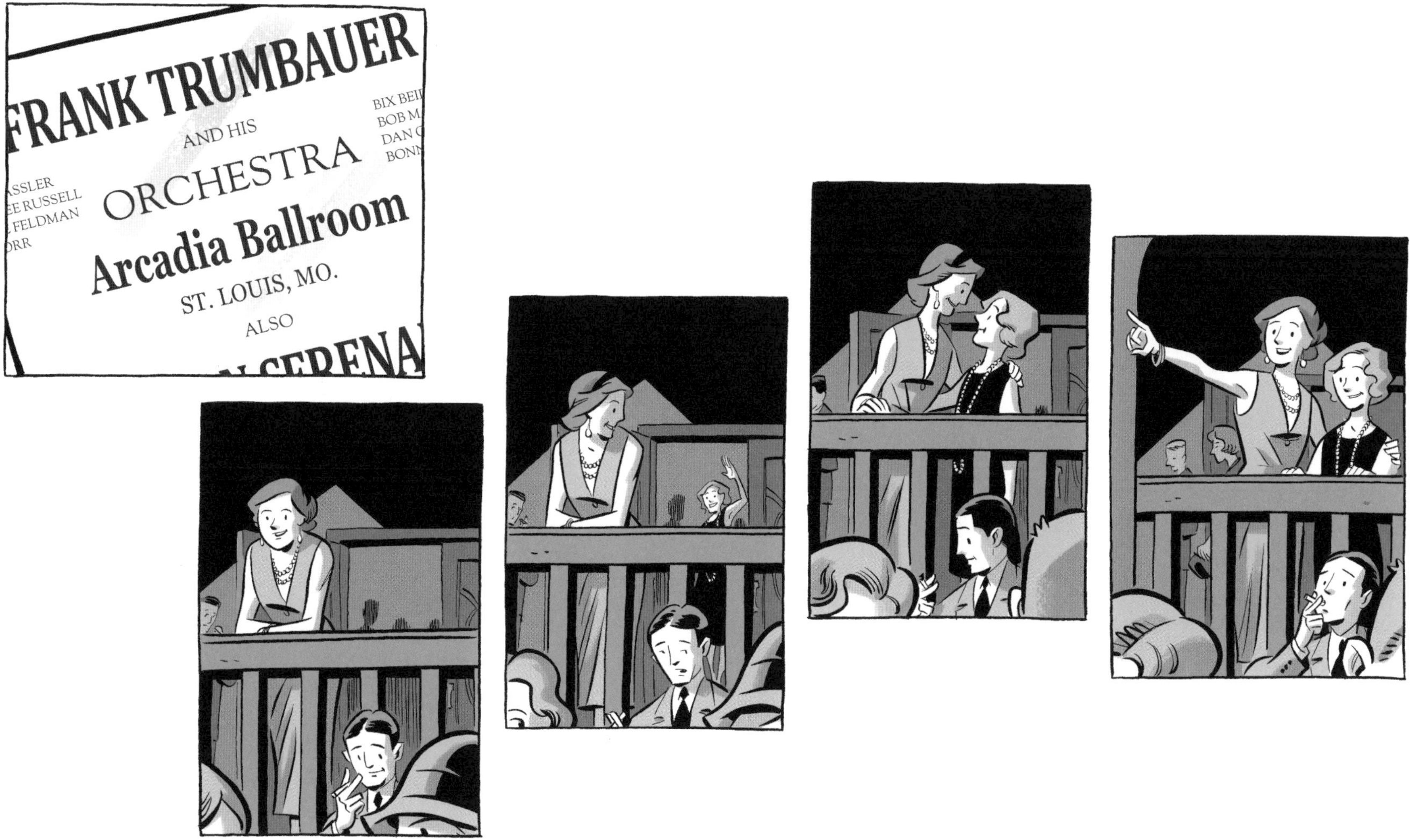
FRANK TRUMBAUER
AND HIS
ORCHESTRA
Arcadia Ballroom
ST. LOUIS, MO.
ALSO

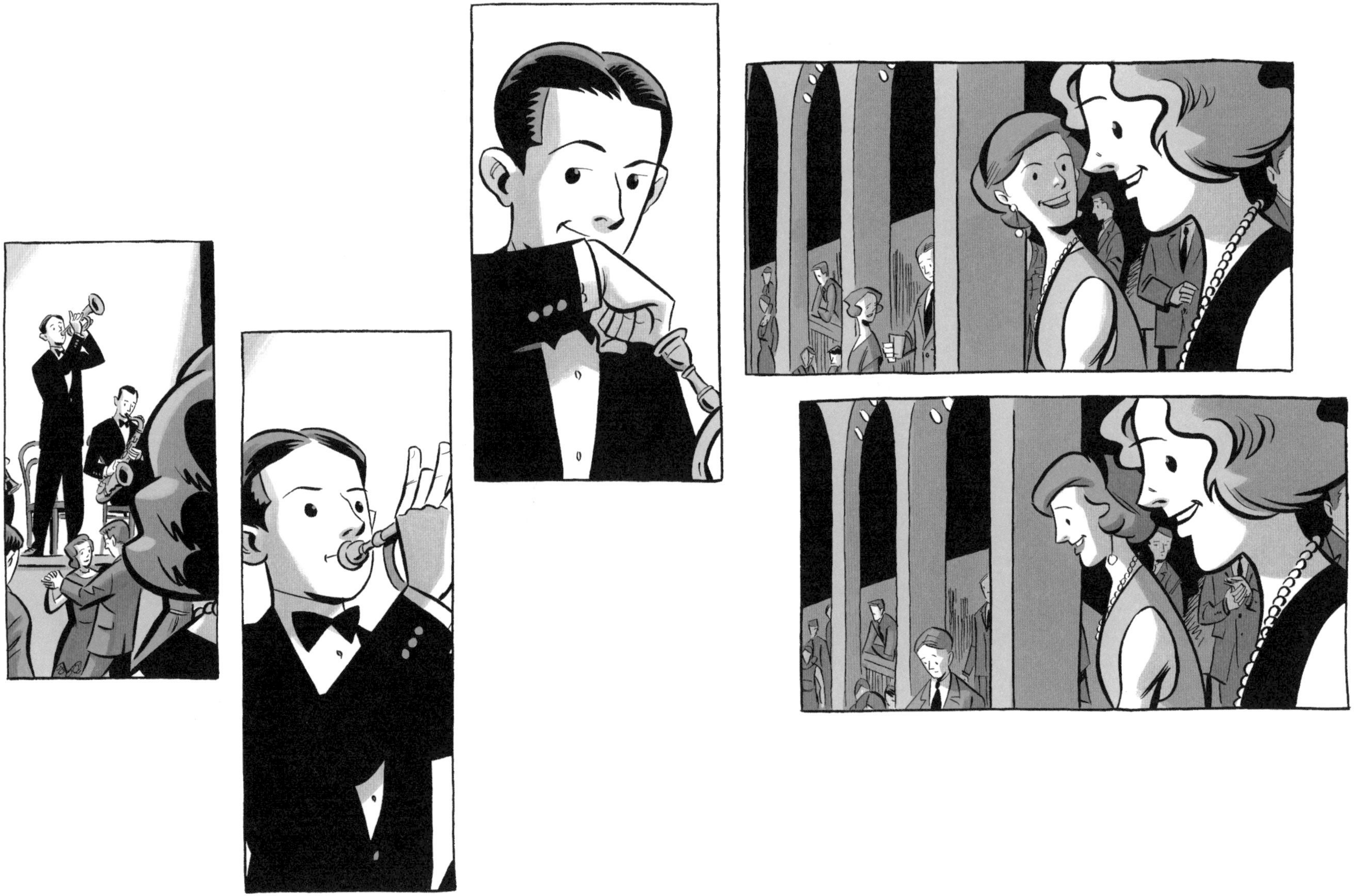

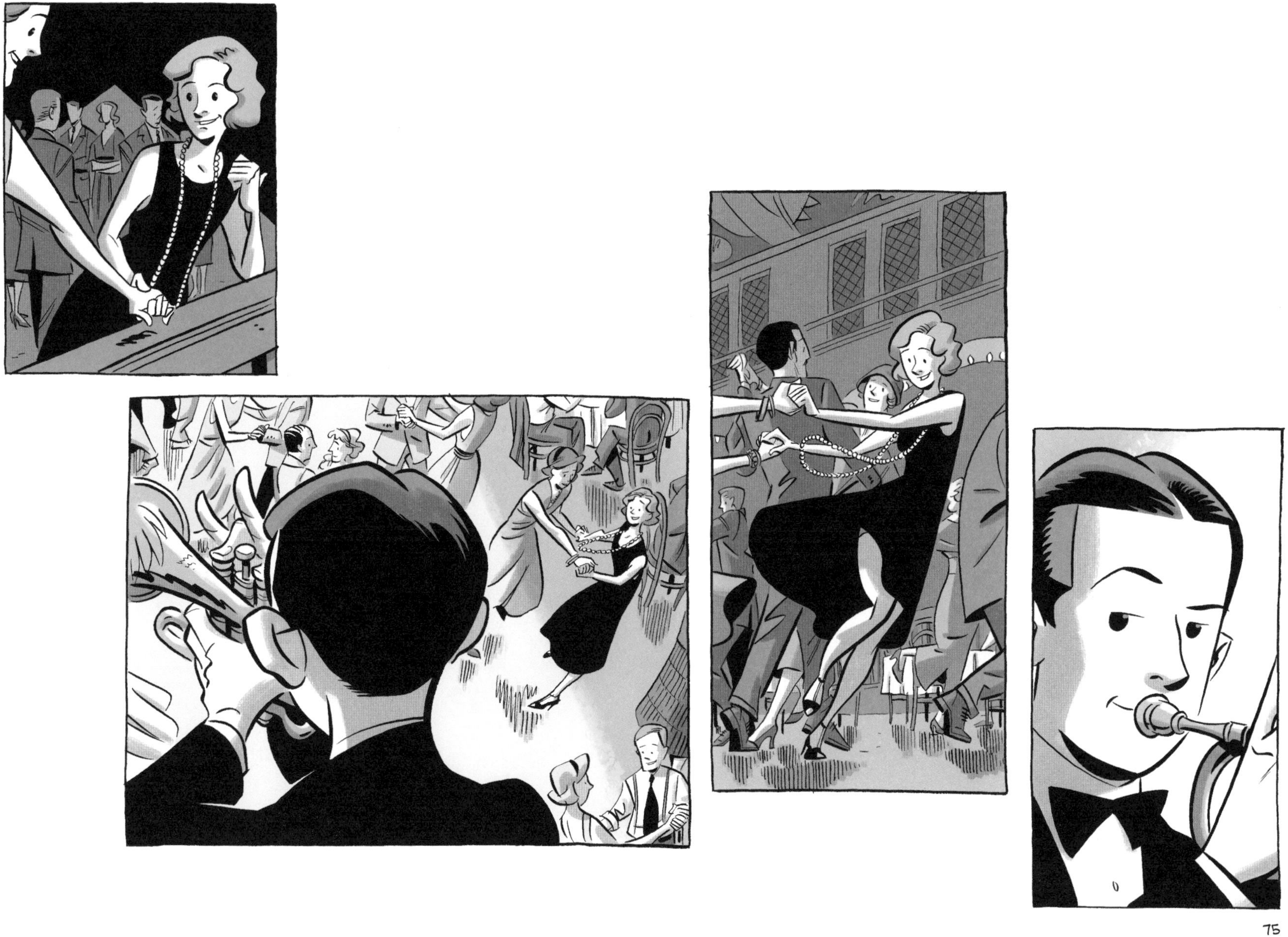

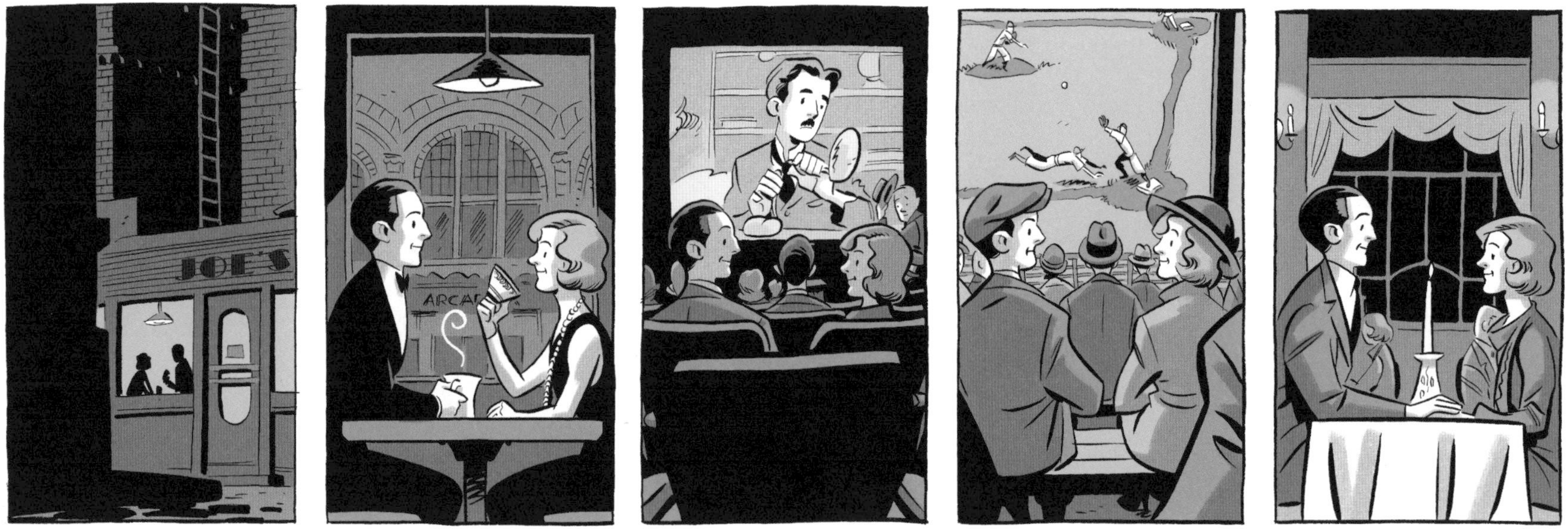
JOE'S

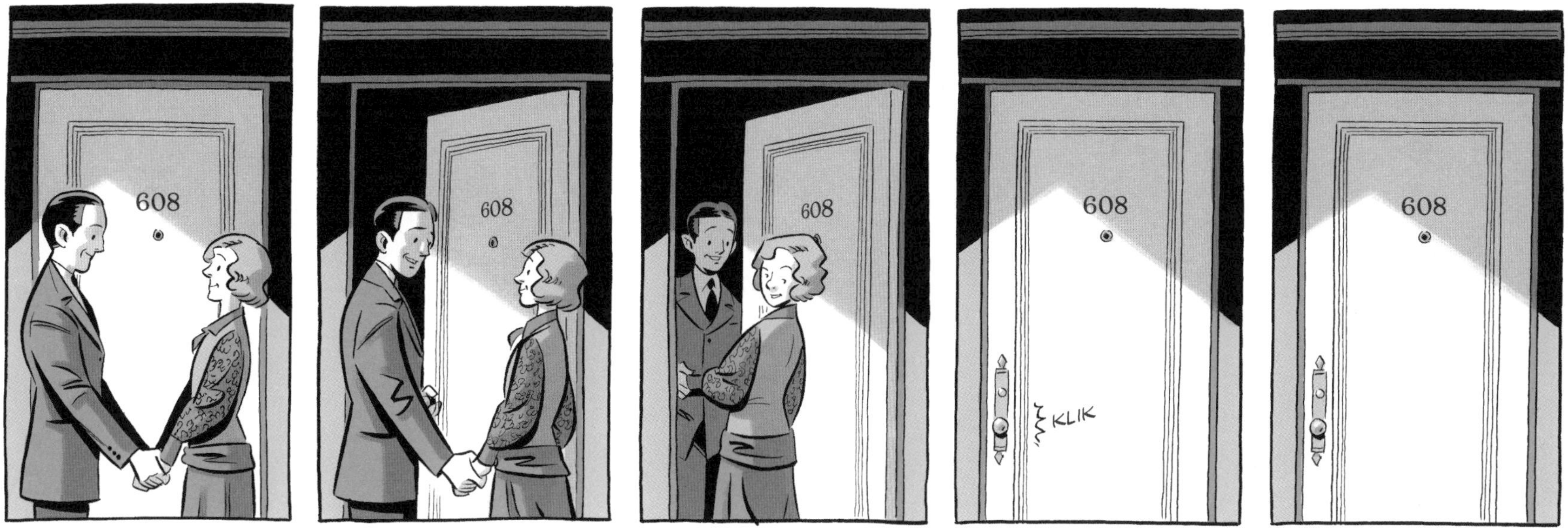
608
608
608
608
KLIK
608

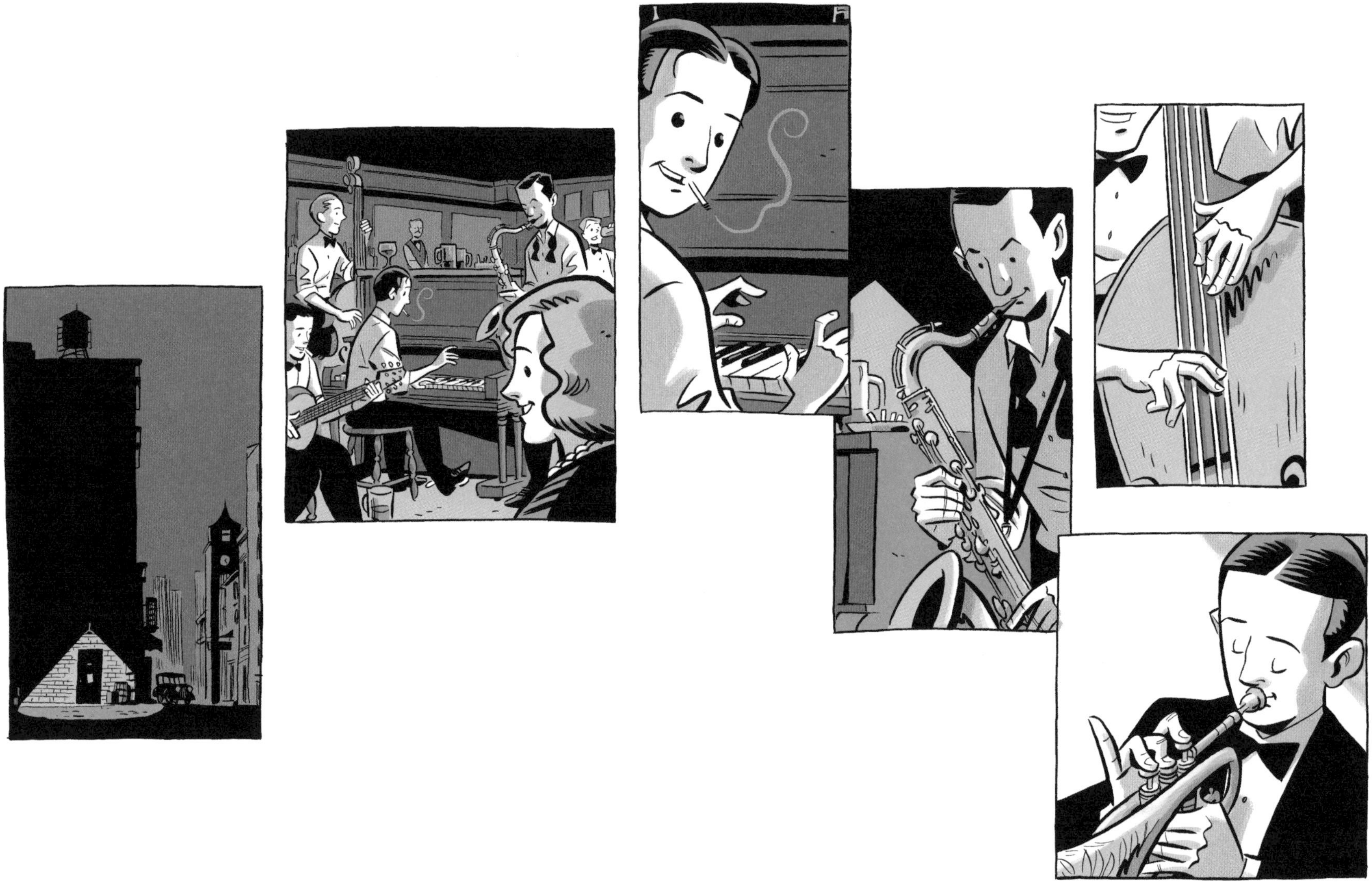

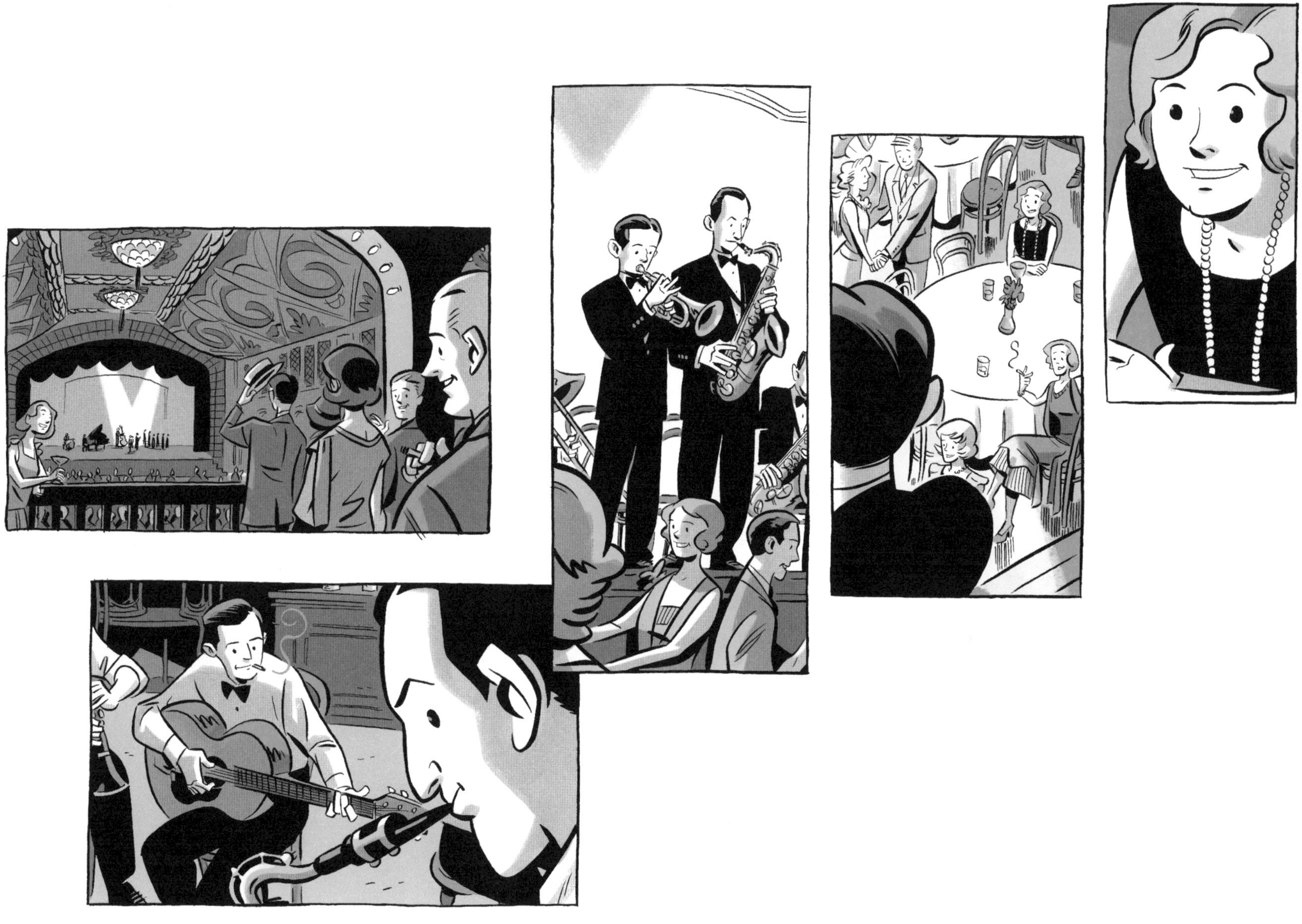

608
BIX?

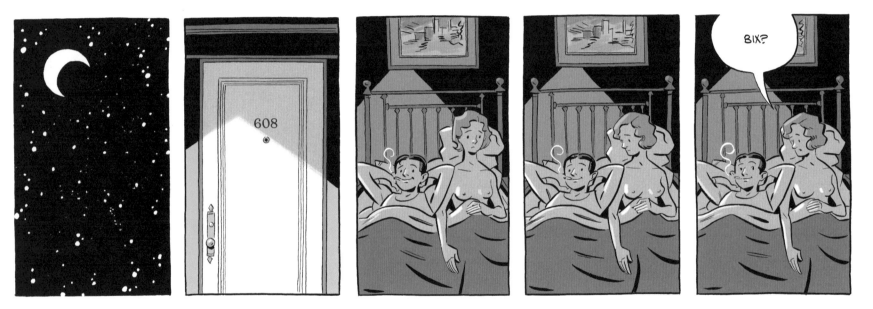

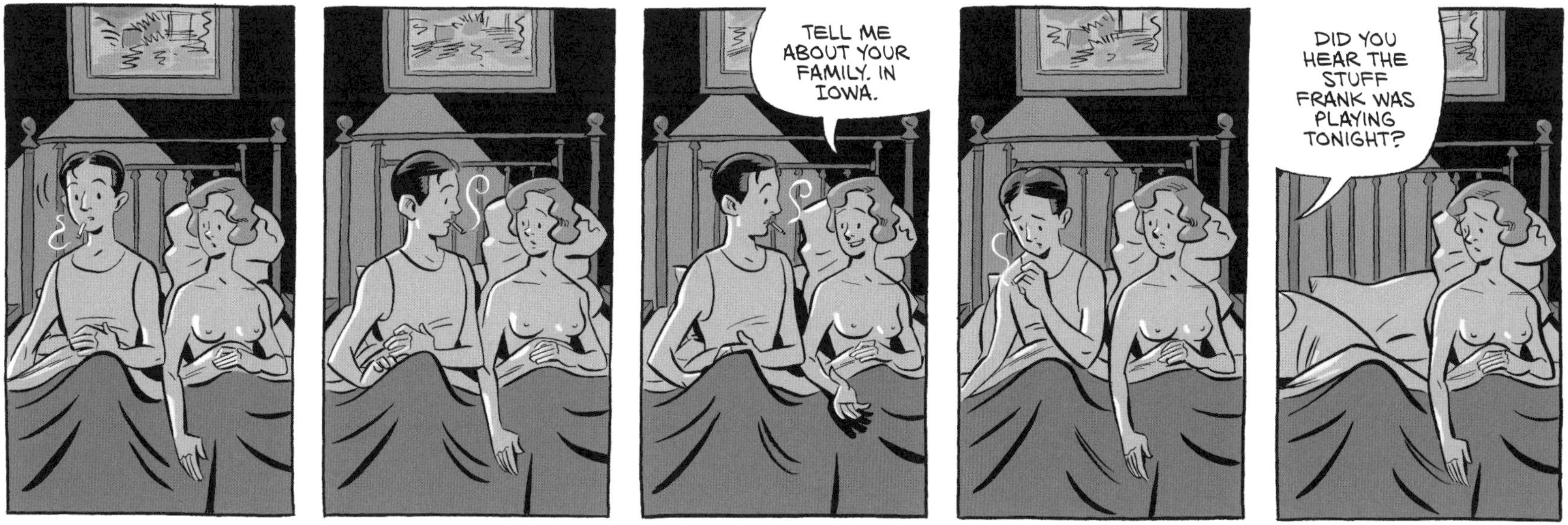
TELL ME ABOUT YOUR FAMILY. IN IOWA.
DID YOU HEAR THE STUFF FRANK WAS PLAYING TONIGHT?

THAT WAS THE REAL THING, RIGHT THERE. HE REALLY LISTENS.

HE SHOULD BE PLAYING WITH PAUL WHITEMAN OR SOMEBODY. WE **BOTH** SHOULD.

DID YOU HEAR HOW HE AND I WERE RESPONDING TO EACH OTHER'S SOLOS?

LIKE LOUIS ARMSTRONG AND KING OLIVER DO.

YOU TWO PLAY VERY WELL TOGETHER. BUT DIDN'T YOU HEAR ME?

I ASKED ABOUT YOUR FAMILY.

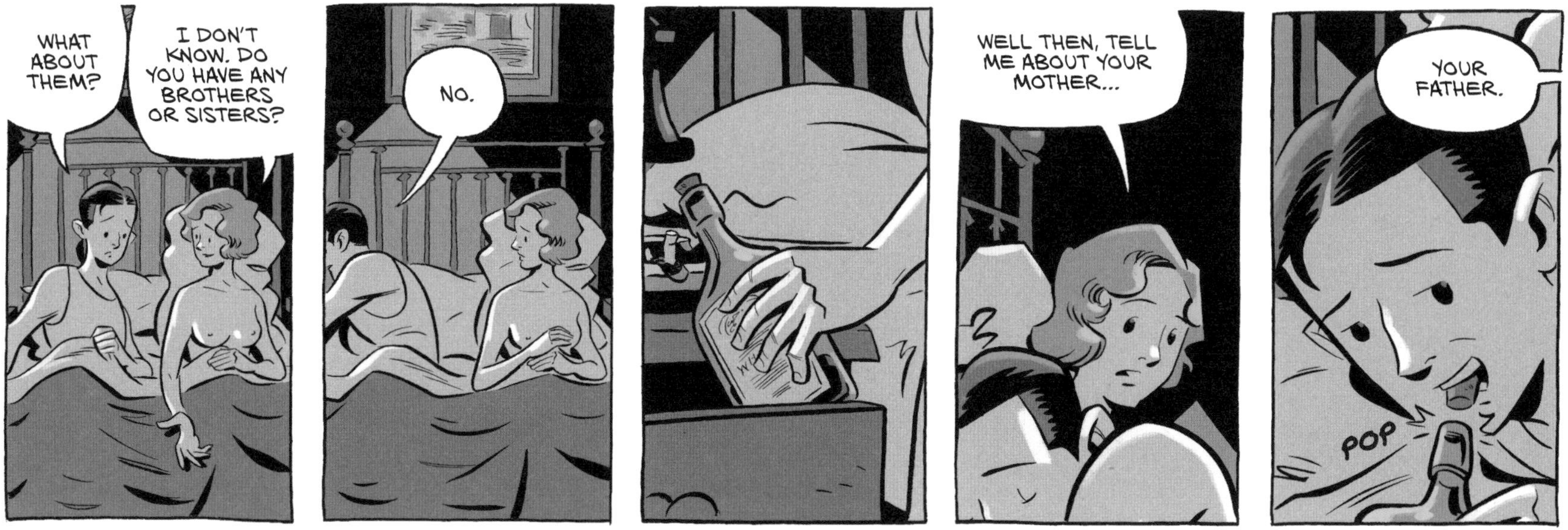
WHAT ABOUT THEM?
I DON'T KNOW. DO YOU HAVE ANY BROTHERS OR SISTERS?
NO.
WELL THEN, TELL ME ABOUT YOUR MOTHER...
YOUR FATHER.
POP

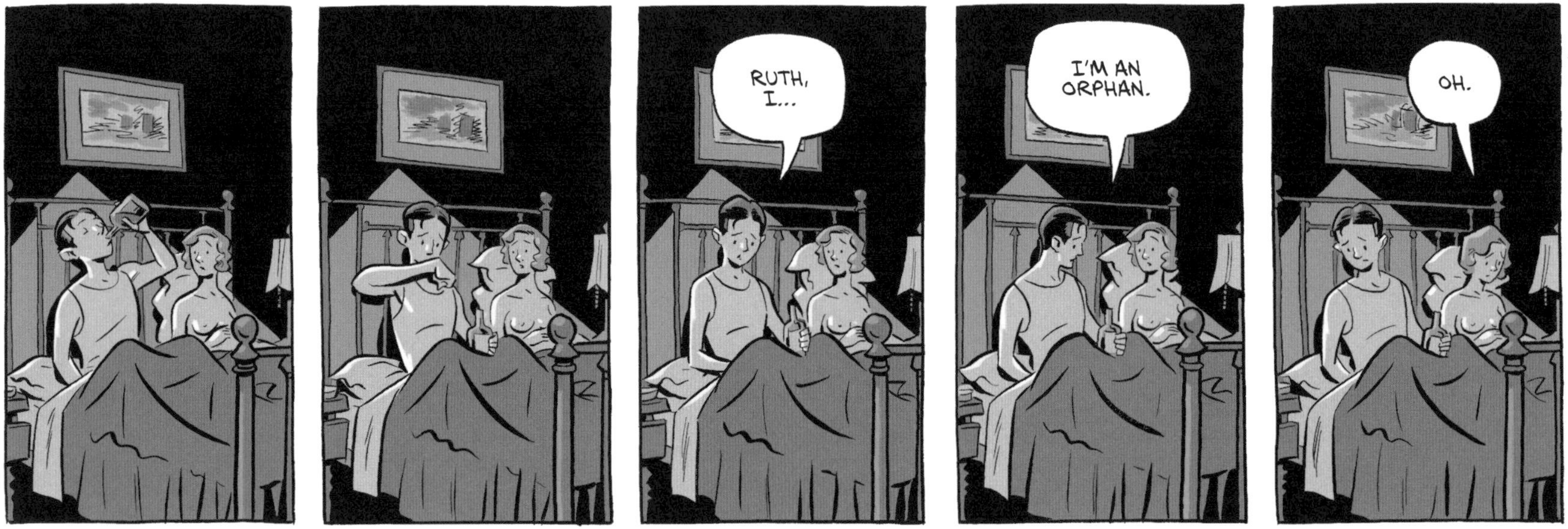
RUTH, I...
I'M AN ORPHAN.
OH.

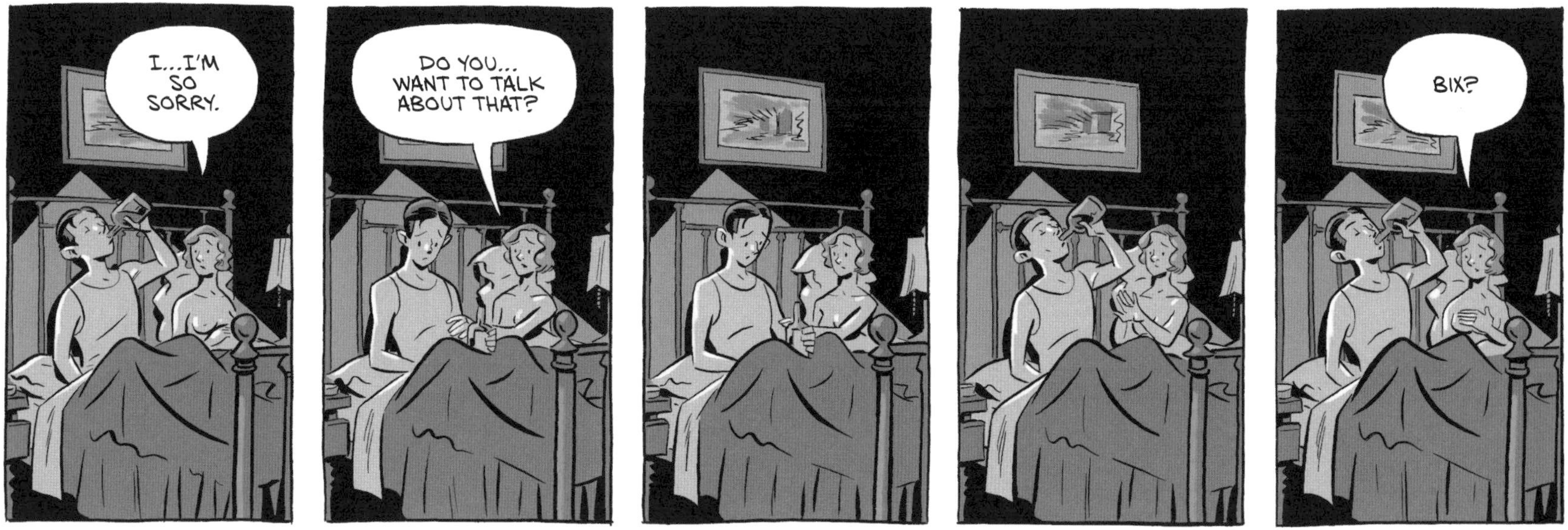
I...I'M SO SORRY.
DO YOU... WANT TO TALK ABOUT THAT?
BIX?

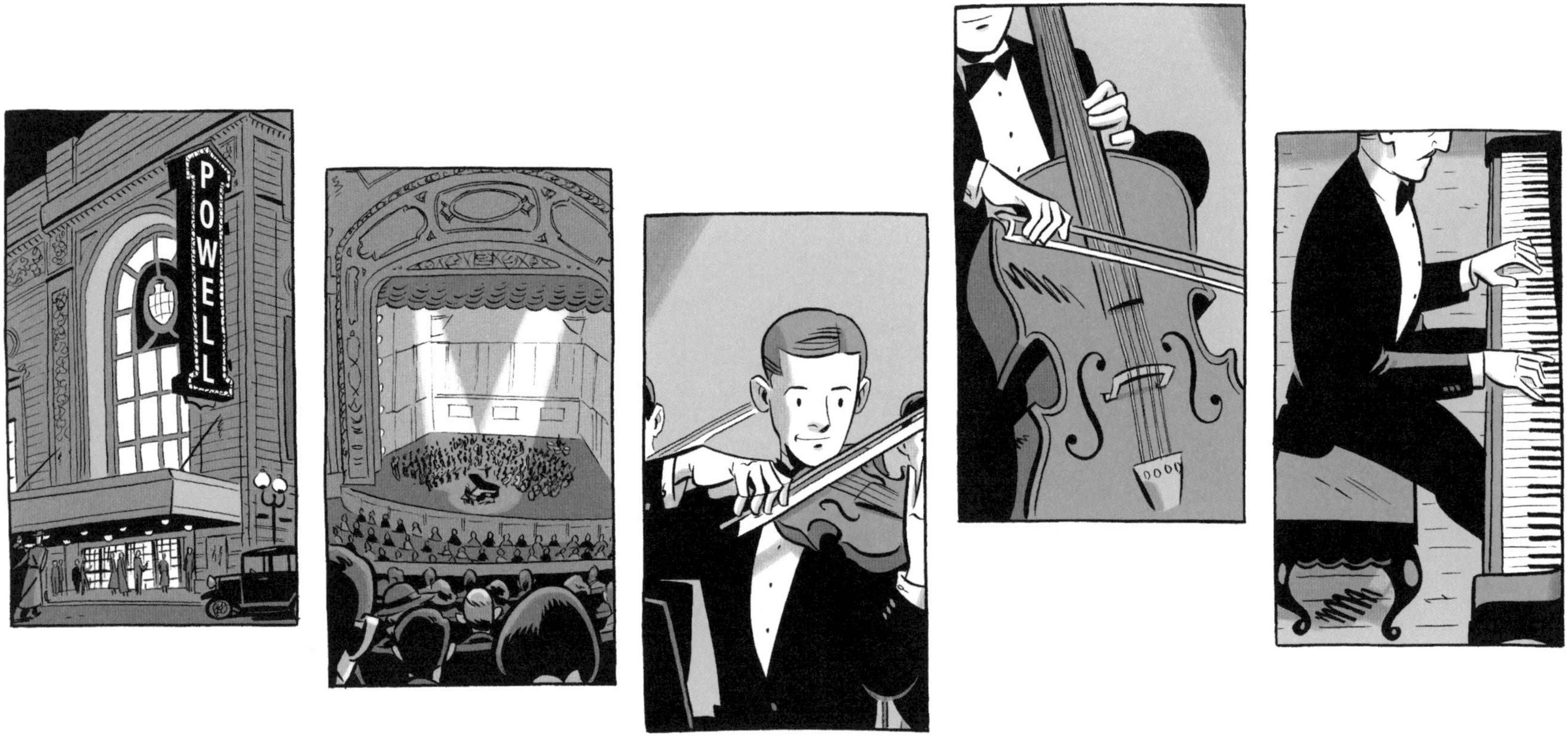
POWELL

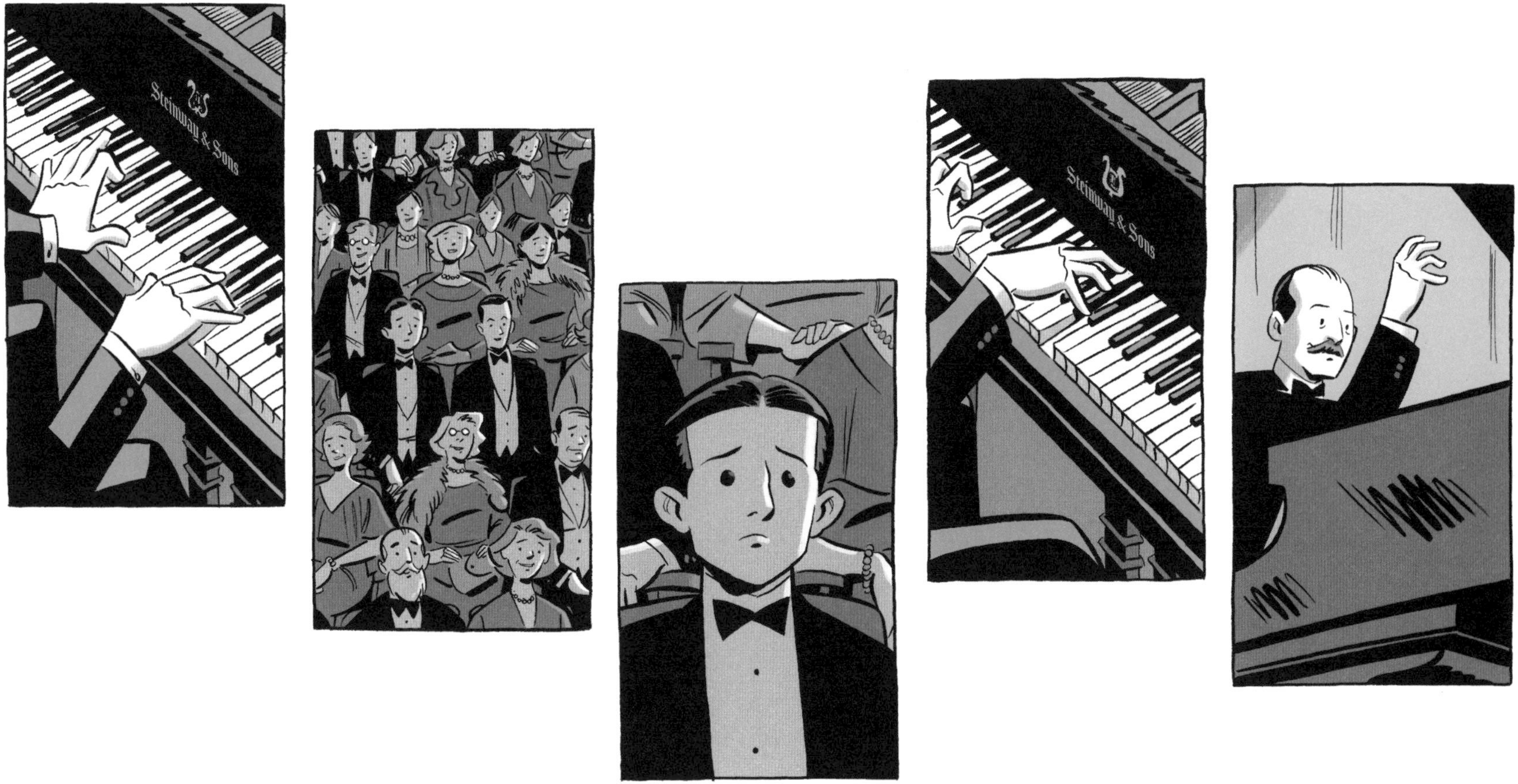
Steinway & Sons
Steinway & Sons

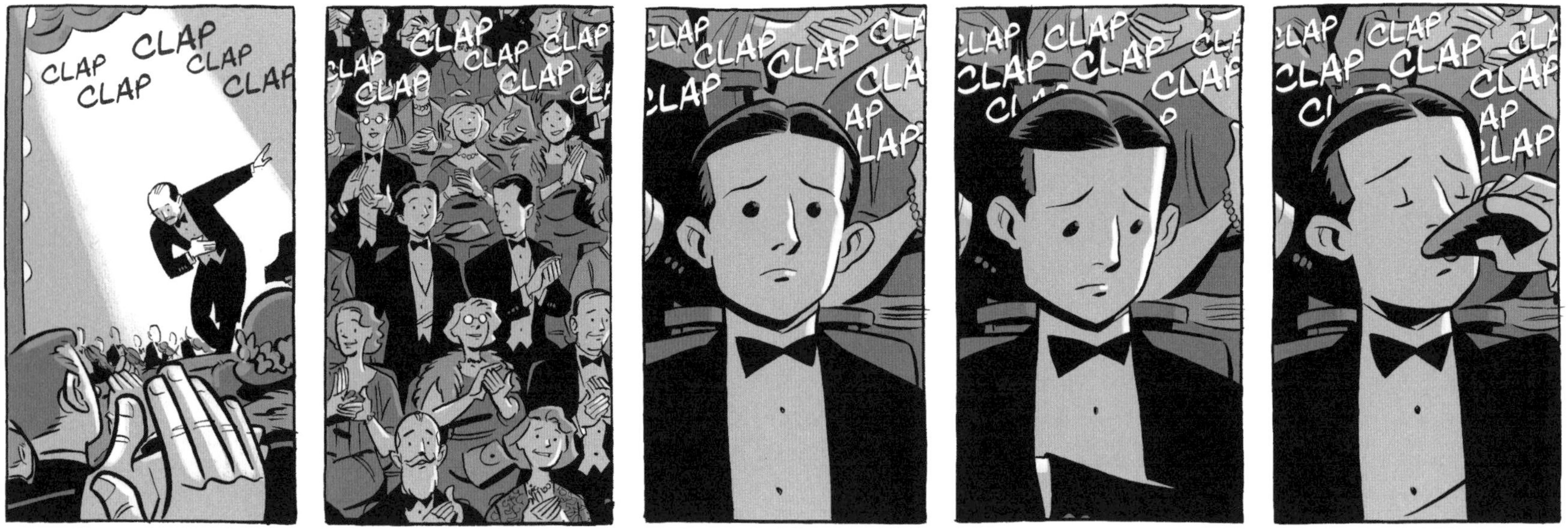
CLAP
CLAP
CLAP
CLAP
CLAP
CLAP
CLAP
CLAP
CLAP
CLAP
CLAP
CLAP
CLAP
CLAP
CLAP
CLAP
CLAP
CLAP

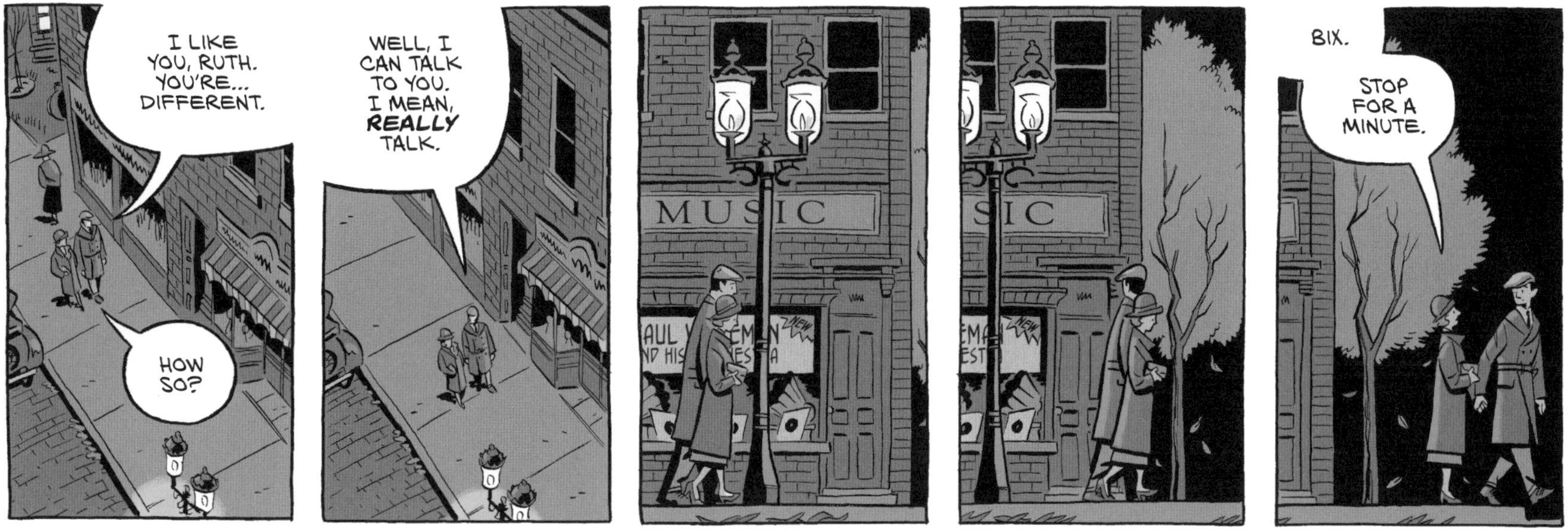
I LIKE YOU, RUTH. YOU'RE... DIFFERENT.
HOW SO?
WELL, I CAN TALK TO YOU. I MEAN, **REALLY** TALK.
MUSIC
NEW
BIX.
STOP FOR A MINUTE.

IT'S NOTHING.
LET'S KEEP WALKING.
I'M LATE, BIX.

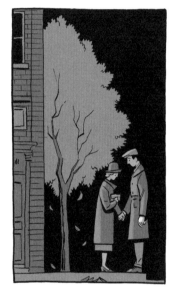

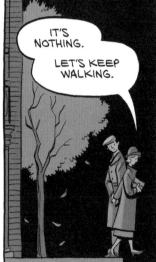

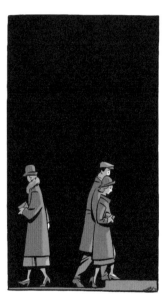

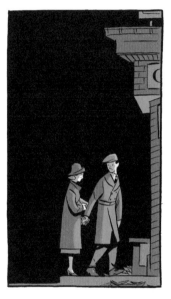

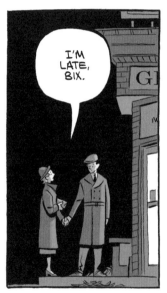

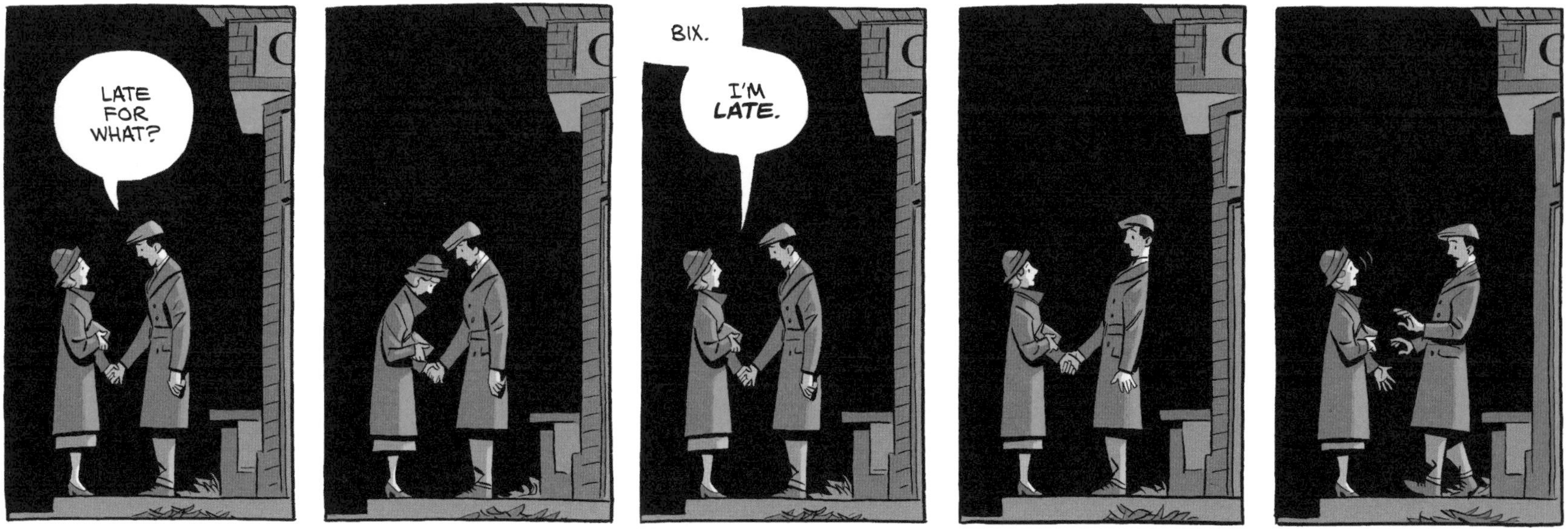
LATE FOR WHAT?
BIX.
I'M LATE.

HOW LATE?

MORE THAN A WEEK.

<SOB!>

TRY NOT TO WORRY ABOUT IT.

LET'S GIVE IT A FEW MORE DAYS.

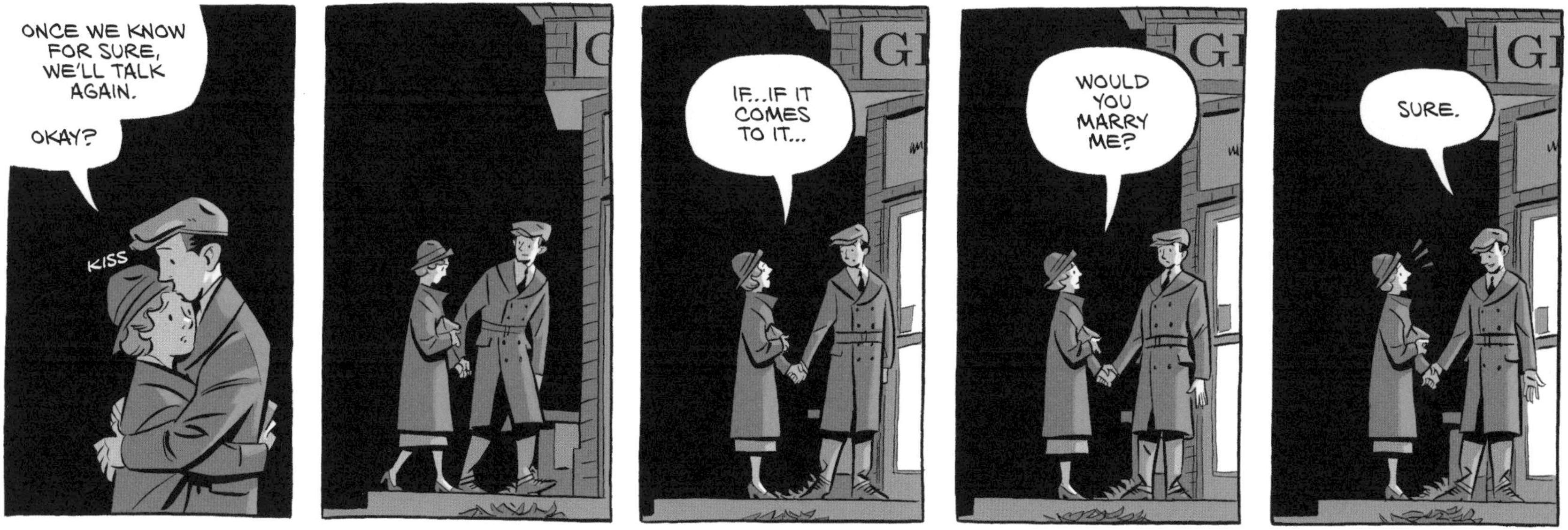
ONCE WE KNOW FOR SURE, WE'LL TALK AGAIN.
OKAY?
KISS
IF...IF IT COMES TO IT...
WOULD YOU MARRY ME?
SURE.

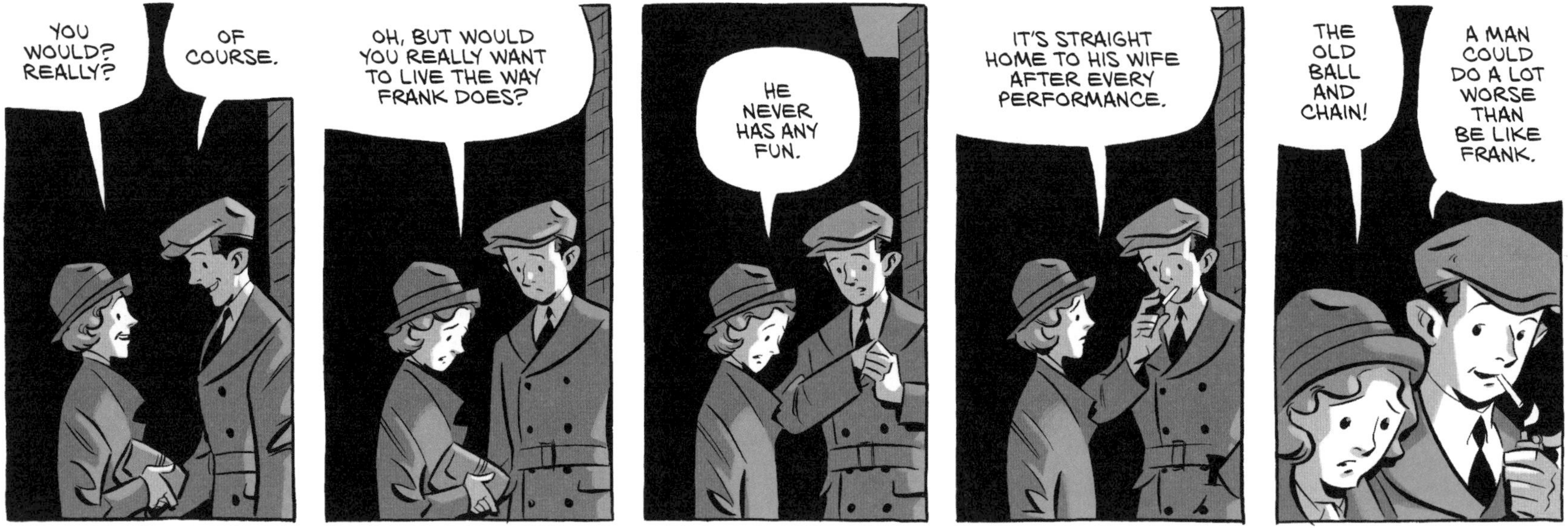
YOU WOULD? REALLY?
OF COURSE.
OH, BUT WOULD YOU REALLY WANT TO LIVE THE WAY FRANK DOES?
HE NEVER HAS ANY FUN.
IT'S STRAIGHT HOME TO HIS WIFE AFTER EVERY PERFORMANCE.
THE OLD BALL AND CHAIN!
A MAN COULD DO A LOT WORSE THAN BE LIKE FRANK.

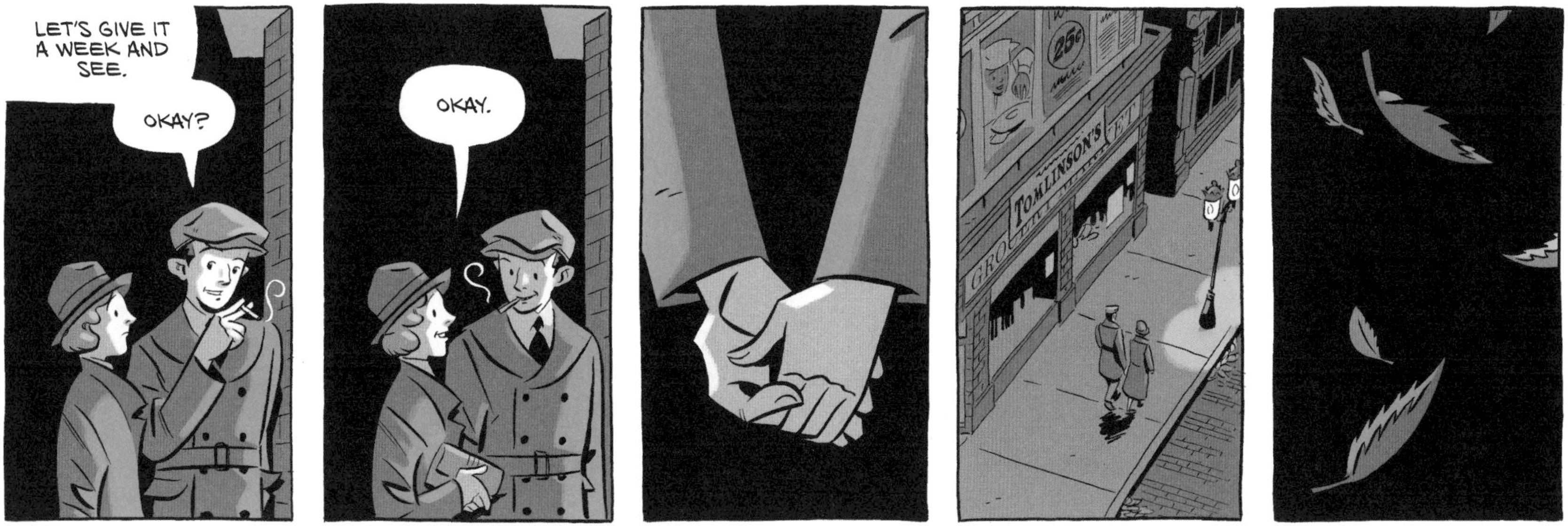
LET'S GIVE IT A WEEK AND SEE.
OKAY?
OKAY.
25¢
TOMLINSON'S

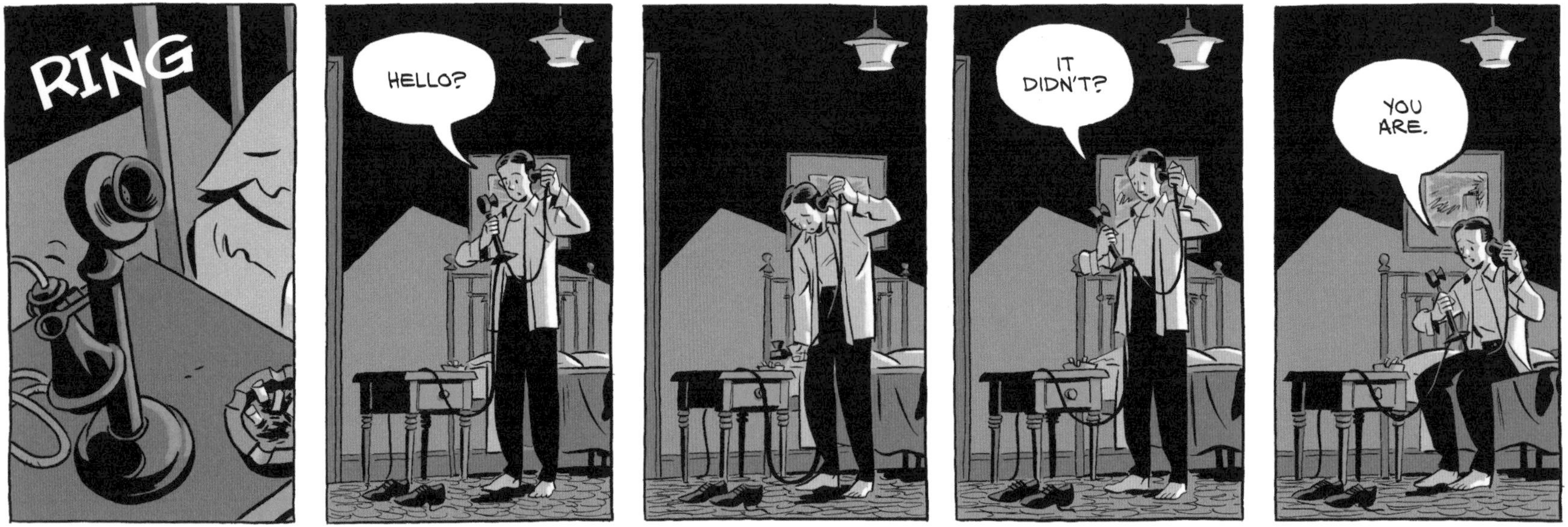
RING
HELLO?
IT DIDN'T?
YOU ARE.

IT'S OKAY.
IT JUST MEANS WE'RE MEANT TO BE TOGETHER.
RUTH?
AW, DON'T CRY, RUTHIE.

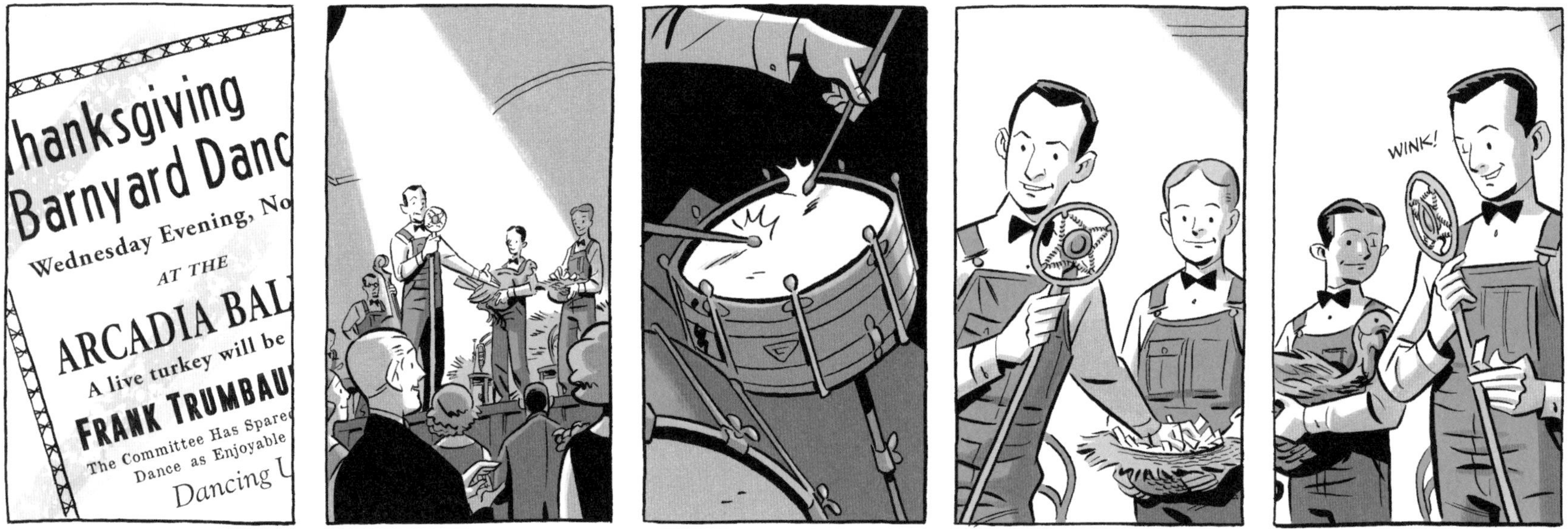
hanksgiving
Barnyard Danc
Wednesday Evening, No
AT THE
ARCADIA BAL
A live turkey will be
FRANK TRUMBAU
The Committee Has Spare
Dance as Enjoyable
Dancing U
WINK!

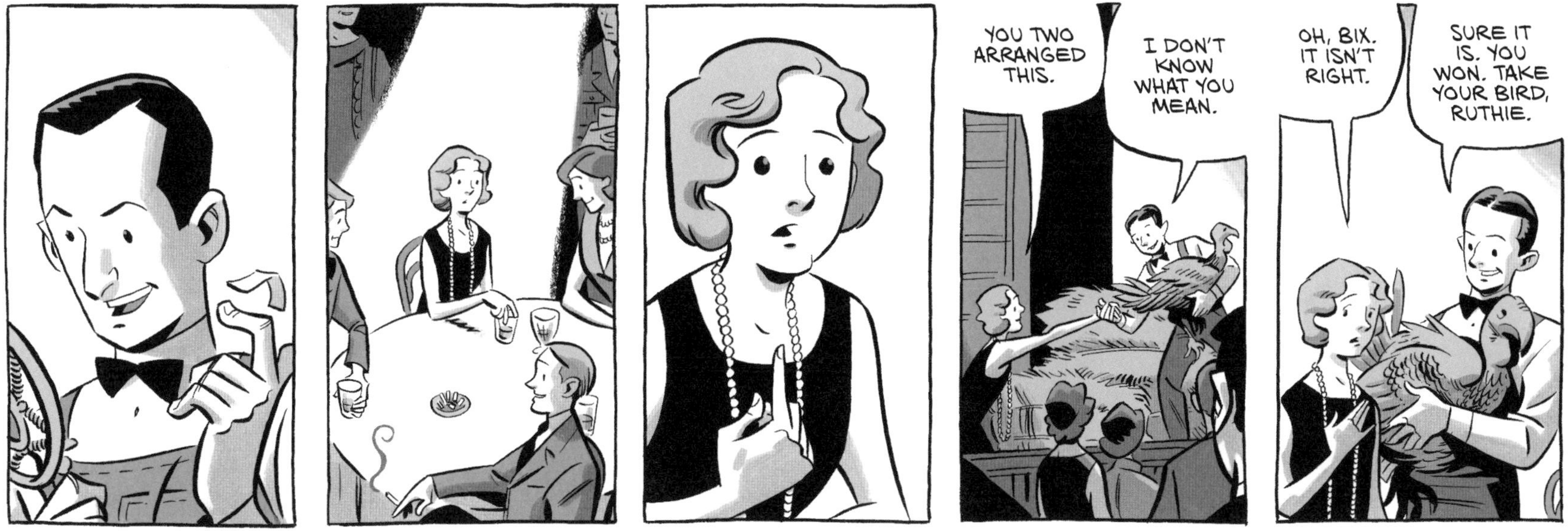
YOU TWO ARRANGED THIS.
I DON'T KNOW WHAT YOU MEAN.
OH, BIX. IT ISN'T RIGHT.
SURE IT IS. YOU WON. TAKE YOUR BIRD, RUTHIE.

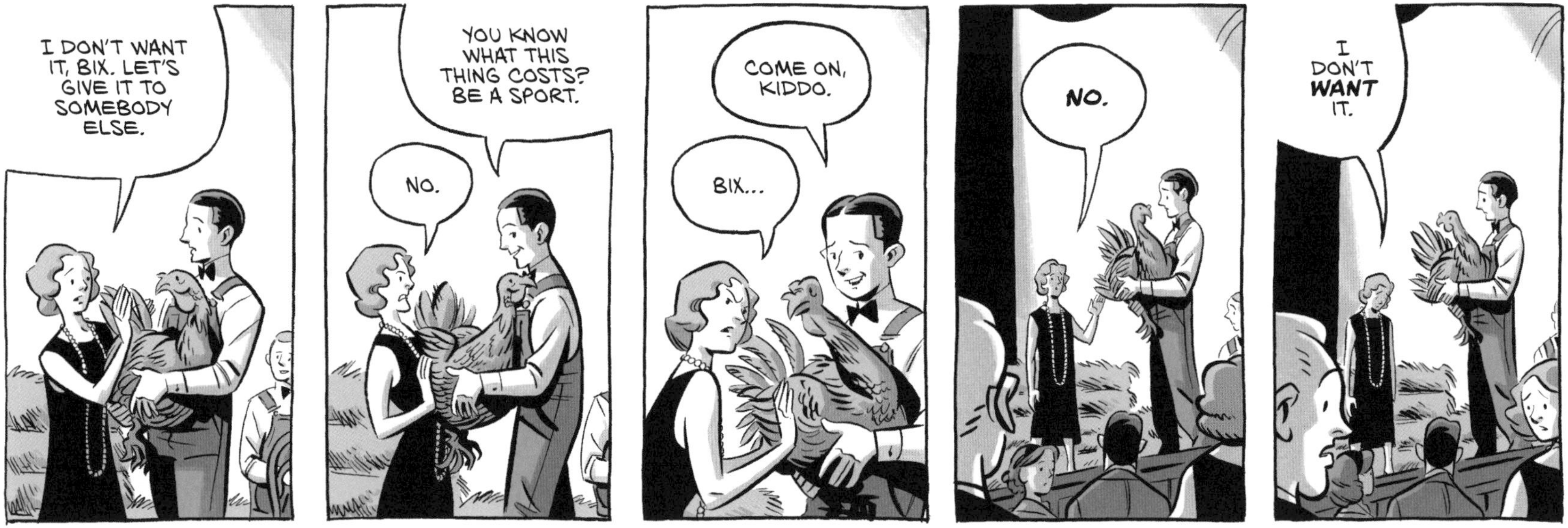
I DON'T WANT IT, BIX. LET'S GIVE IT TO SOMEBODY ELSE.
YOU KNOW WHAT THIS THING COSTS? BE A SPORT.
NO.
COME ON, KIDDO.
BIX...
NO.
I DON'T **WANT** IT.

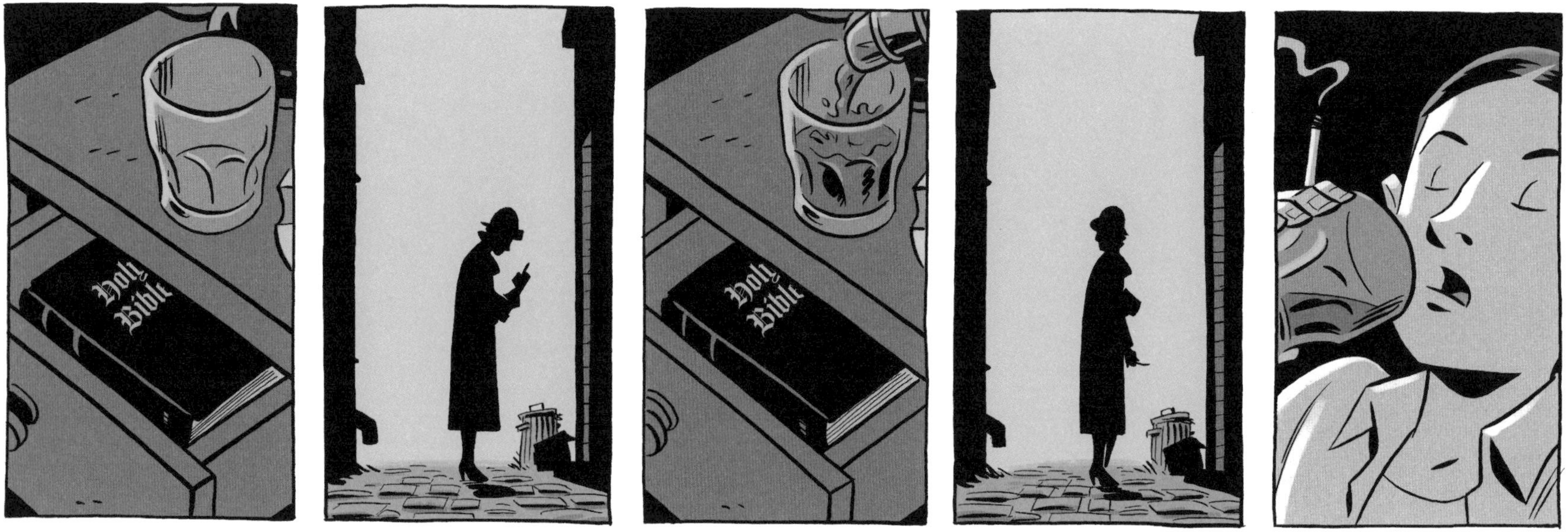
Holy Bible
Holy Bible

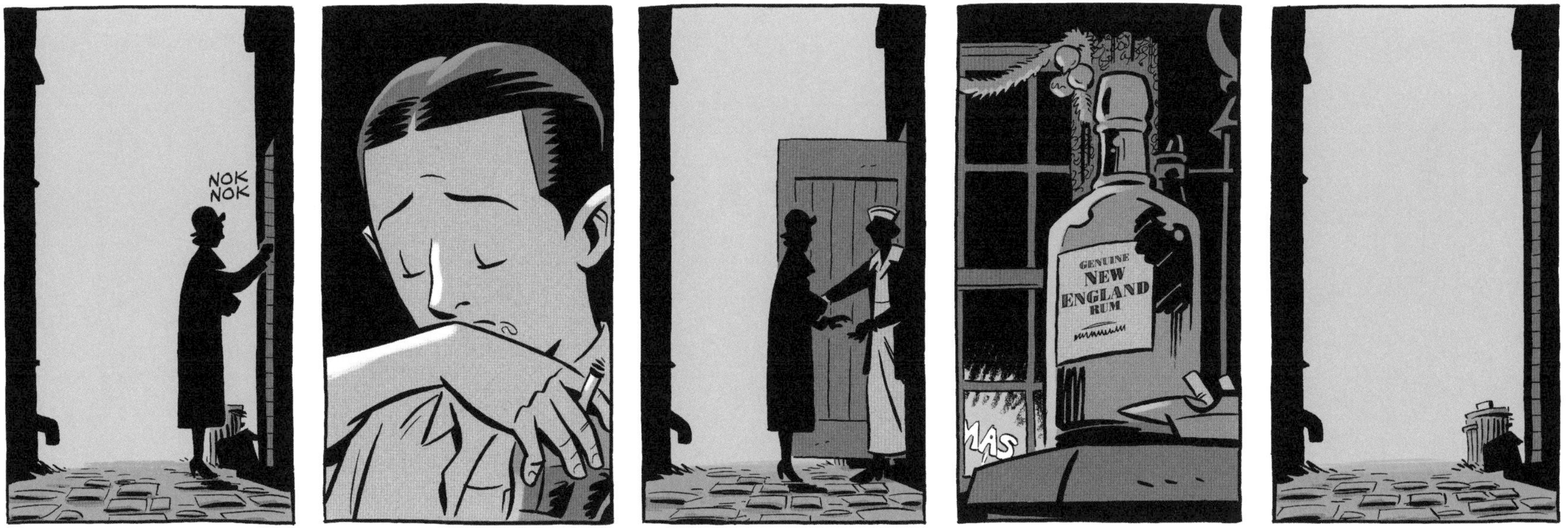
NOK
NOK
GENUINE
NEW
ENGLAND
RUM
MAS

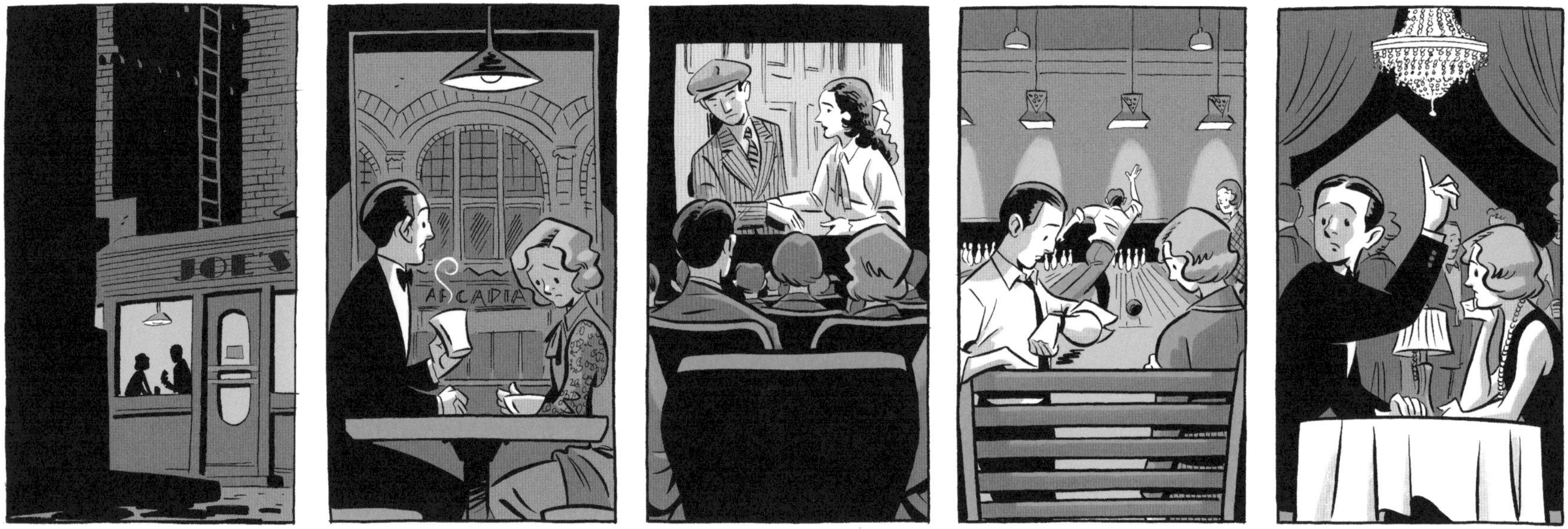
JOE'S
ARCADIA

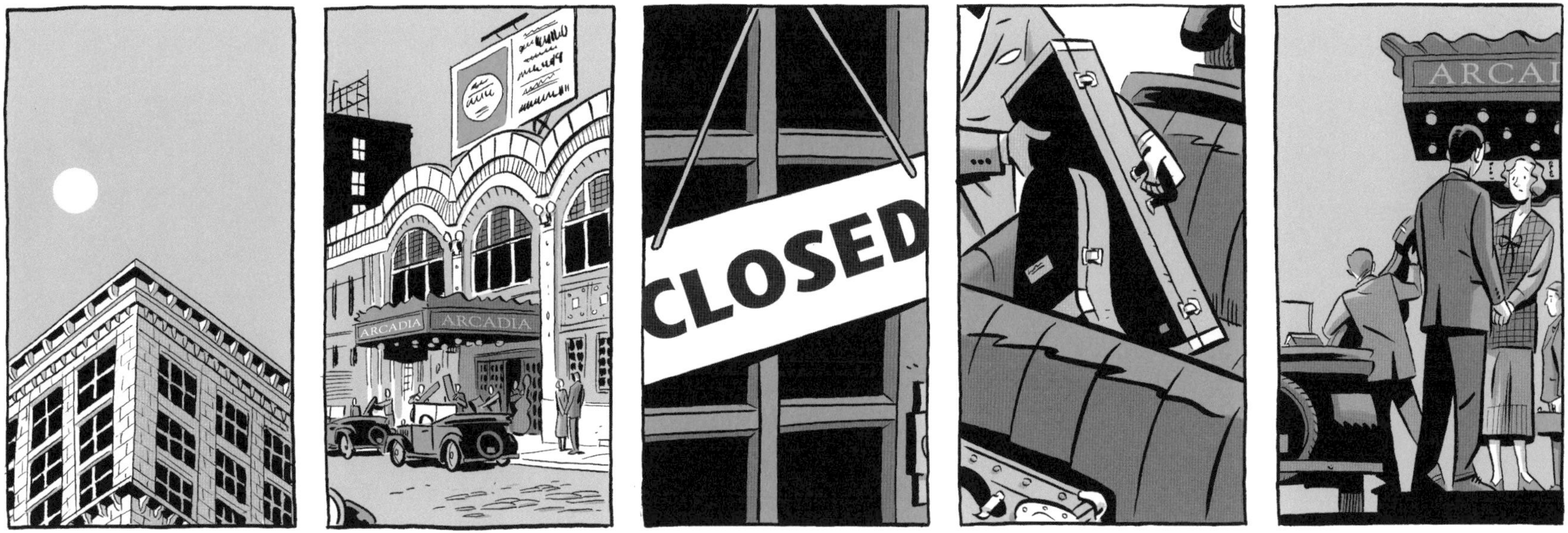
ARCADIA
ARCADIA
CLOSED

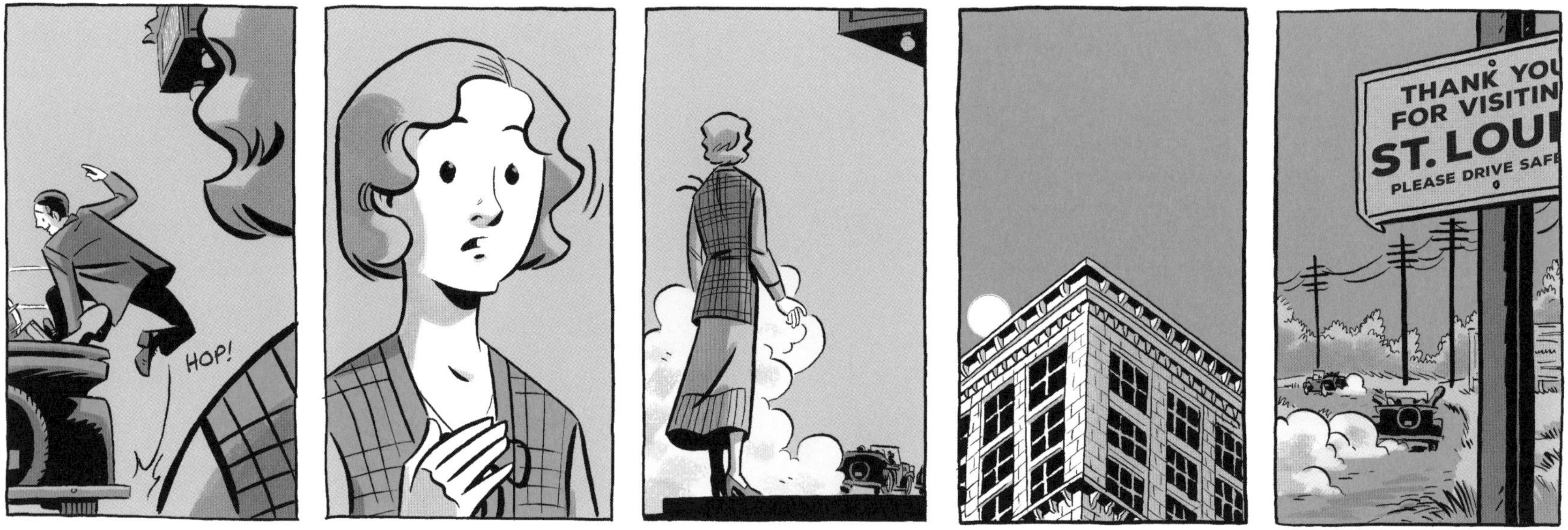
HOP!
THANK YOU
FOR VISITIN
ST. LOU
PLEASE DRIVE SAFE

Part Three

SINGIN' THE BLUES

Victor
Talking Machine Co.

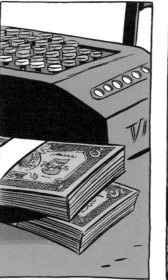

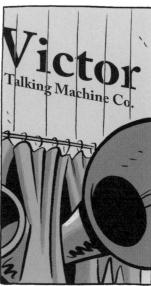

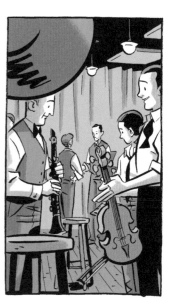

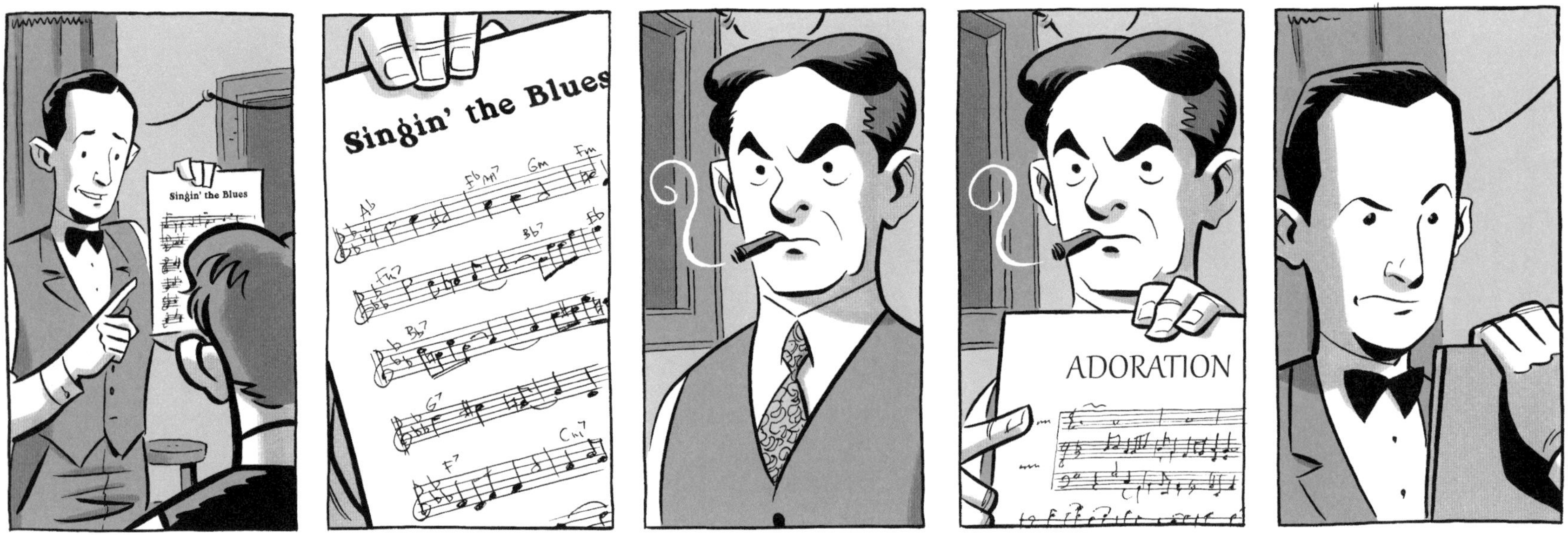
Singin' the Blues
Singin' the Blues
ADORATION

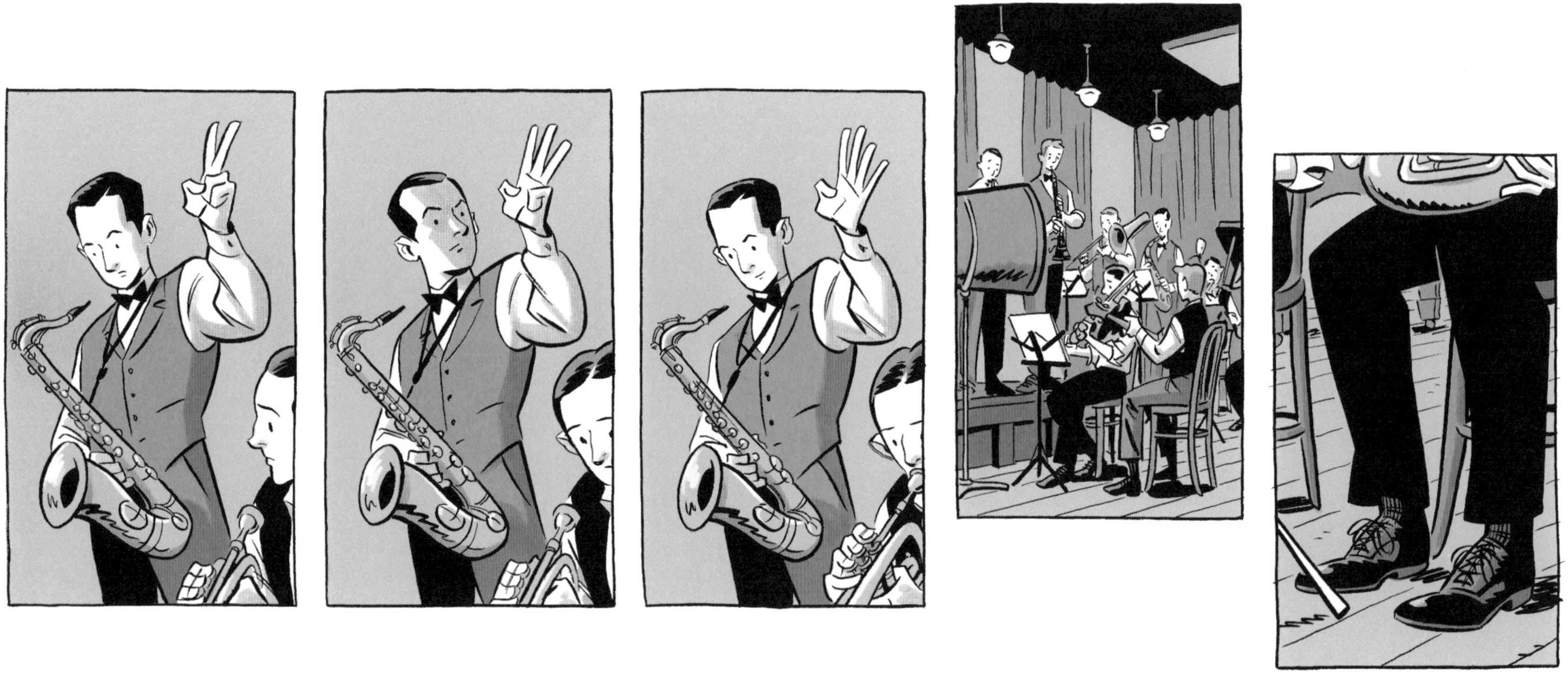

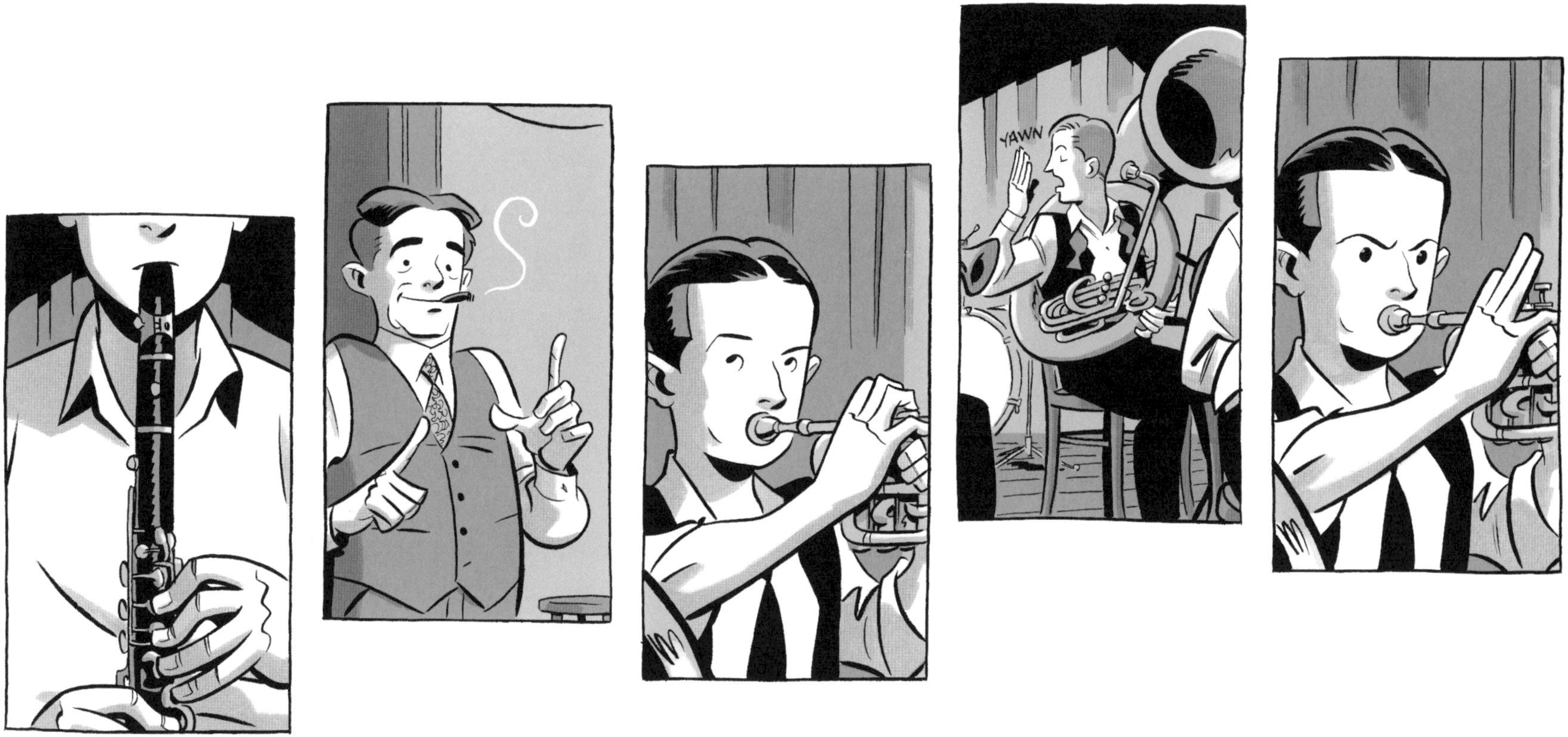
YAWN

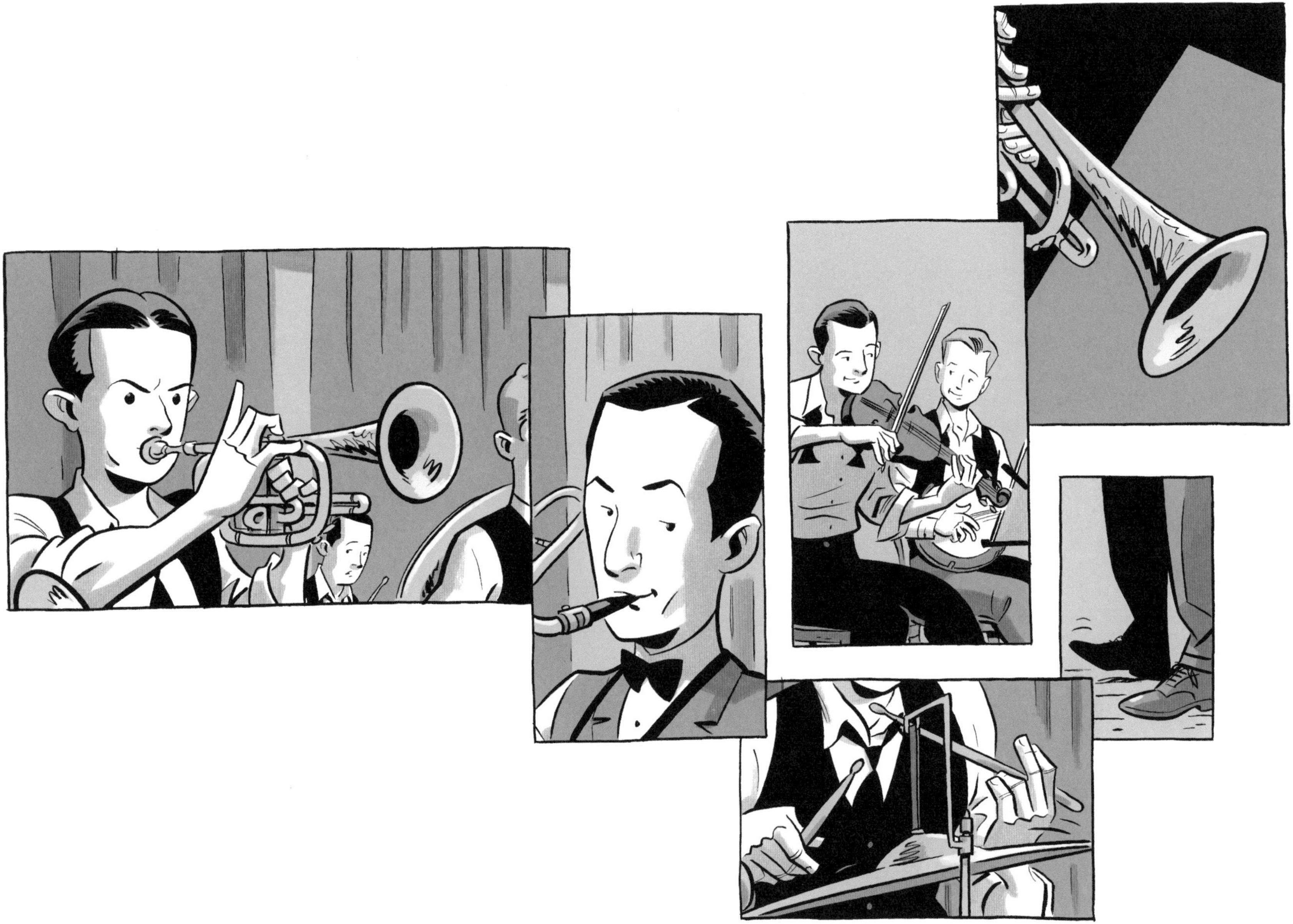

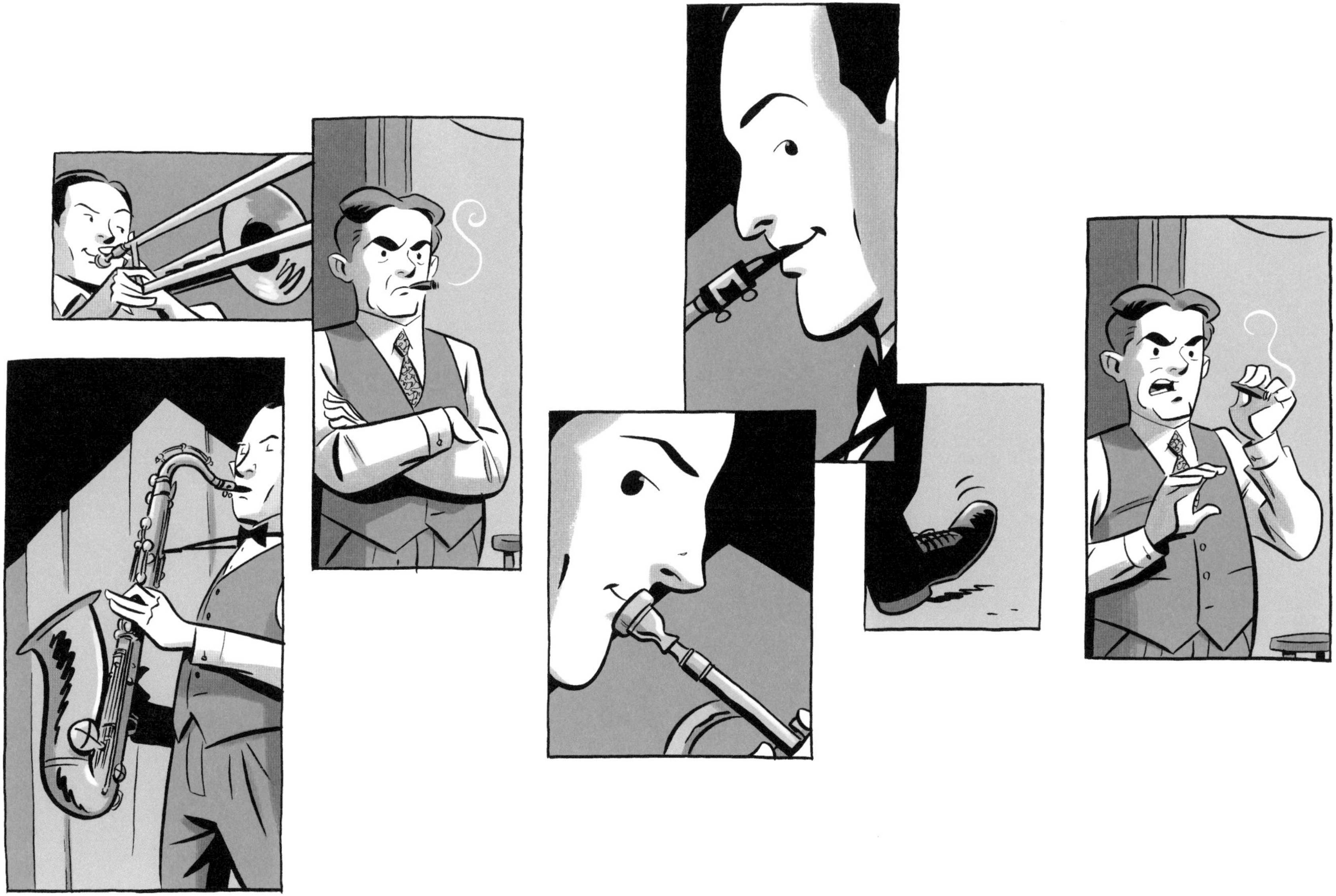

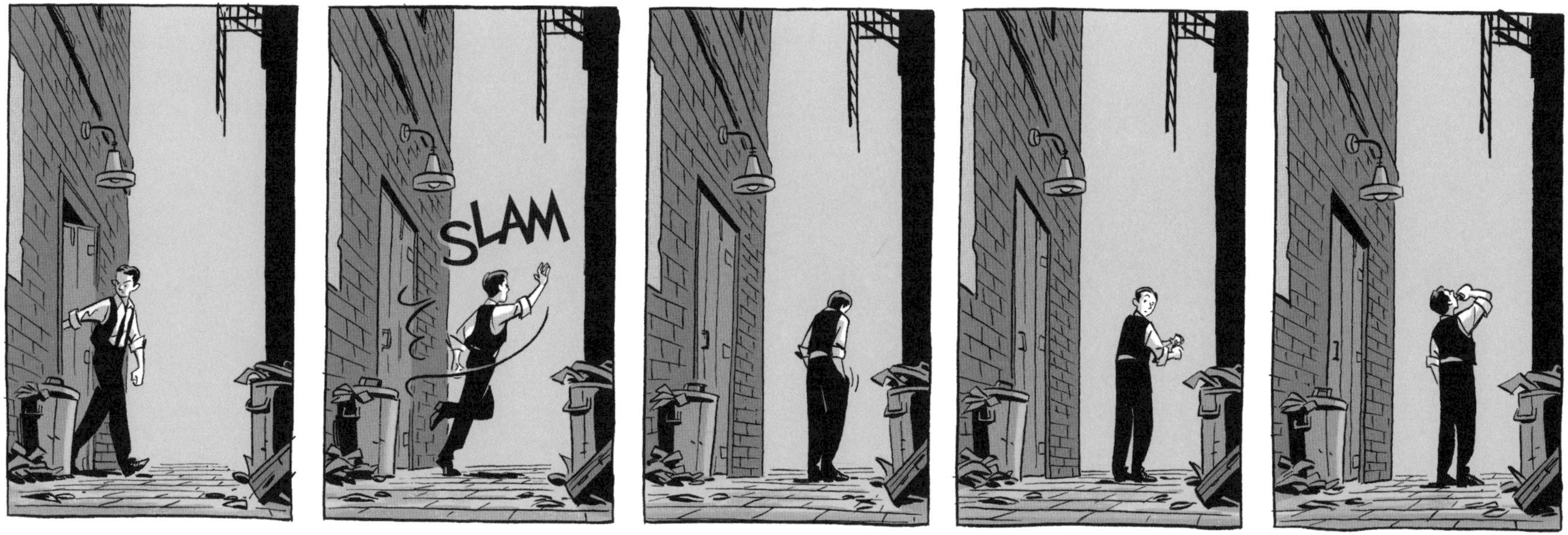
SLAM

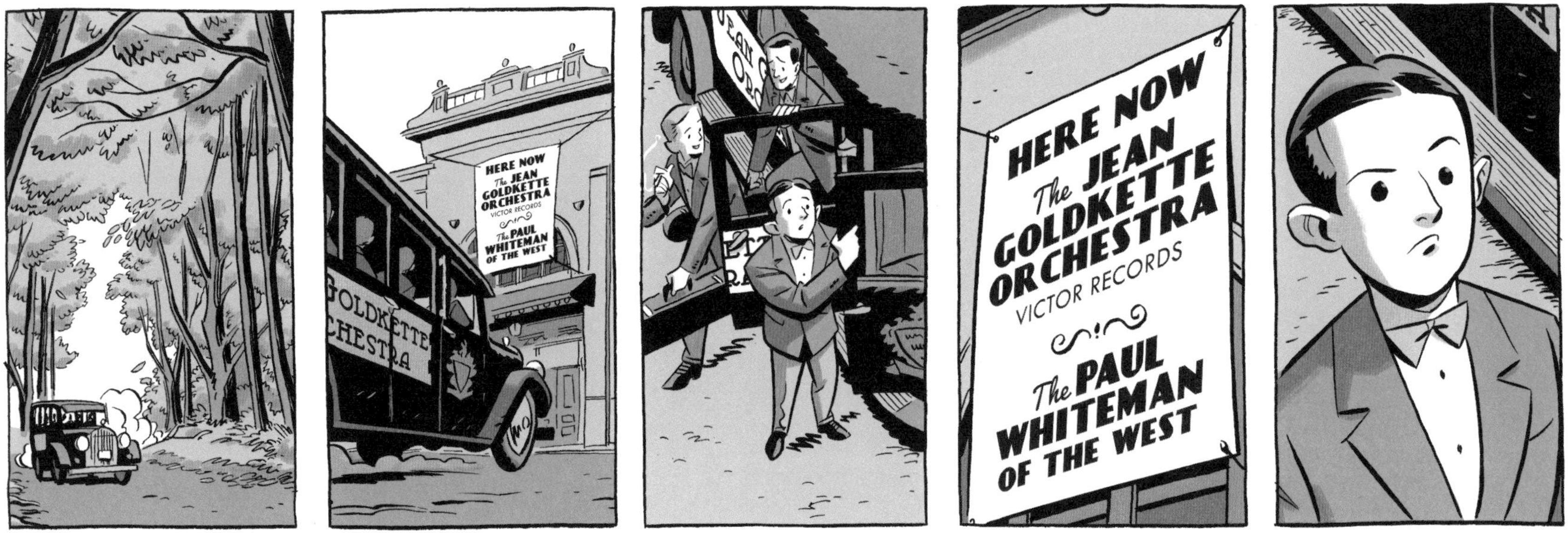
HERE NOW
The JEAN GOLDKETTE ORCHESTRA
VICTOR RECORDS
The PAUL WHITEMAN OF THE WEST
GOLDKETTE
CHESTRA
HERE NOW
The JEAN GOLDKETTE ORCHESTRA
VICTOR RECORDS
The PAUL WHITEMAN OF THE WEST

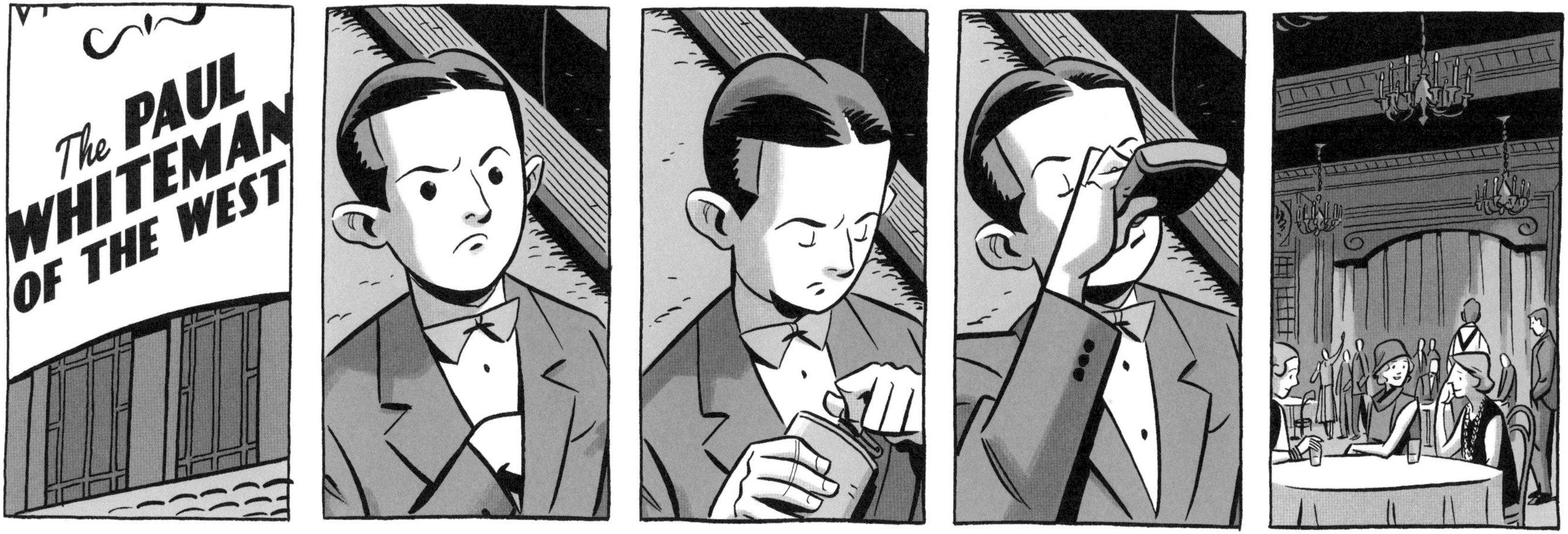
The PAUL WHITEMAN OF THE WEST

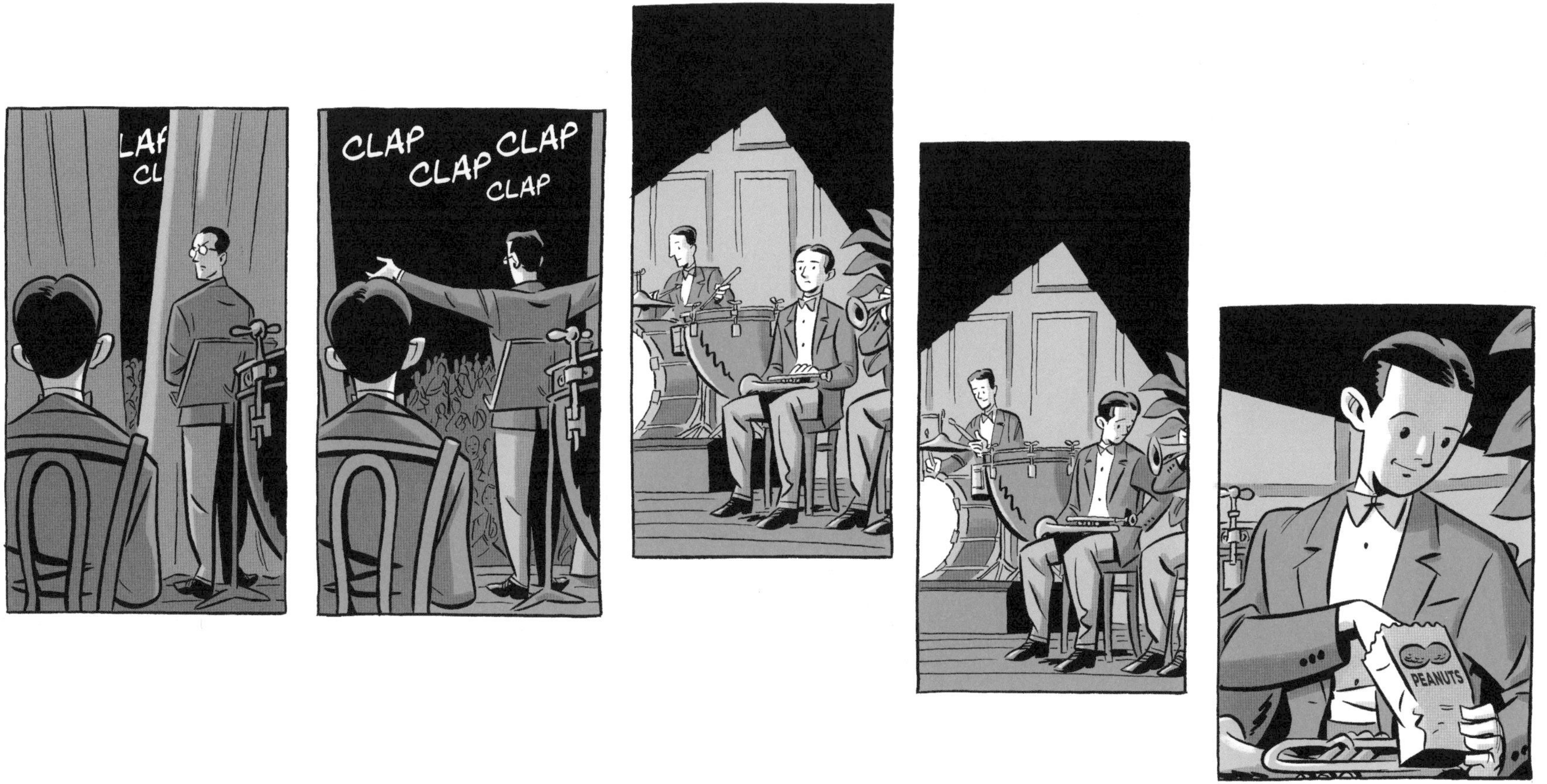
LAP
CL
CLAP
CLAP
CLAP
CLAP
PEANUTS

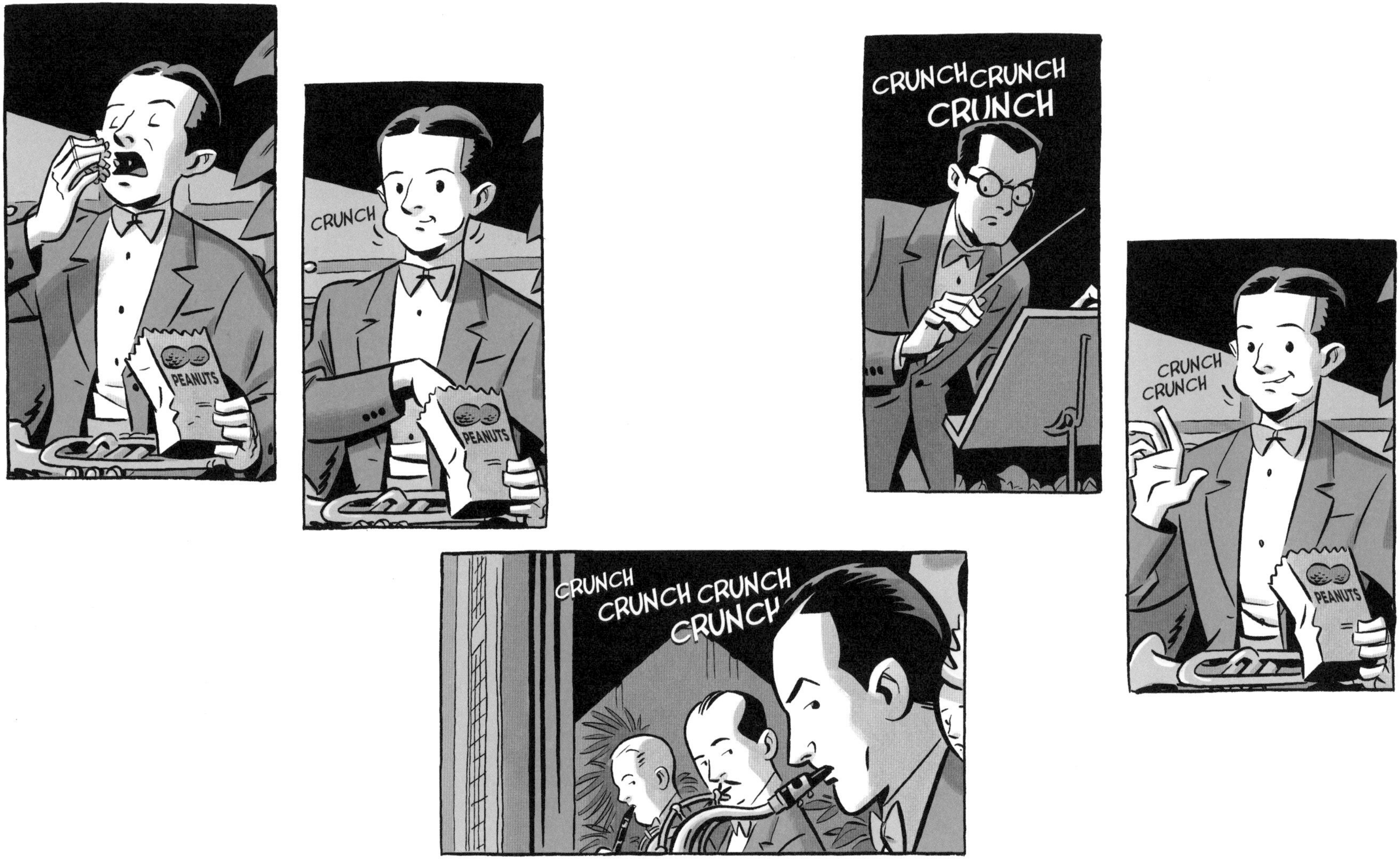
PEANUTS
CRUNCH
PEANUTS
CRUNCH
CRUNCH CRUNCH
CRUNCH
CRUNCH CRUNCH
CRUNCH
CRUNCH
CRUNCH
PEANUTS

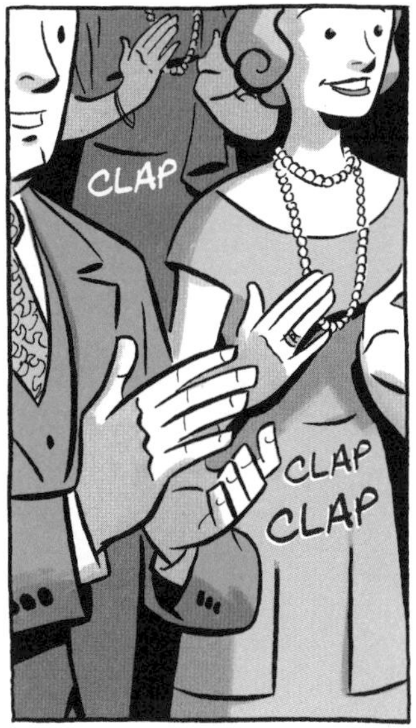
CLAP
CLAP
CLAP
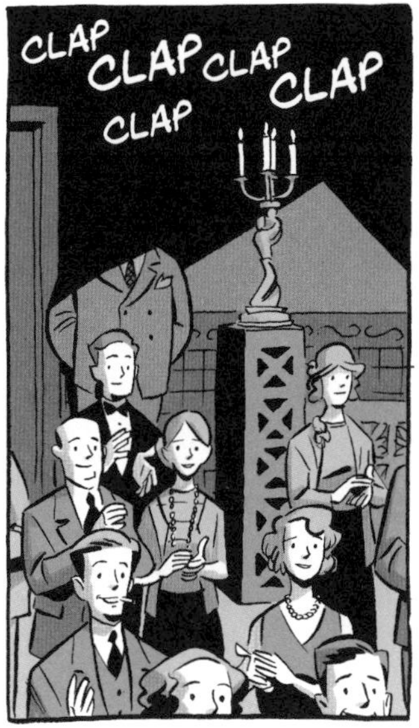
CLAP
CLAP
CLAP
CLAP
CLAP
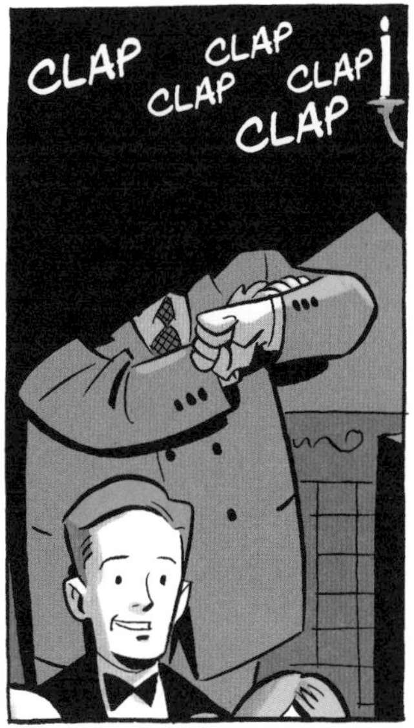
CLAP
CLAP
CLAP
CLAP
CLAP
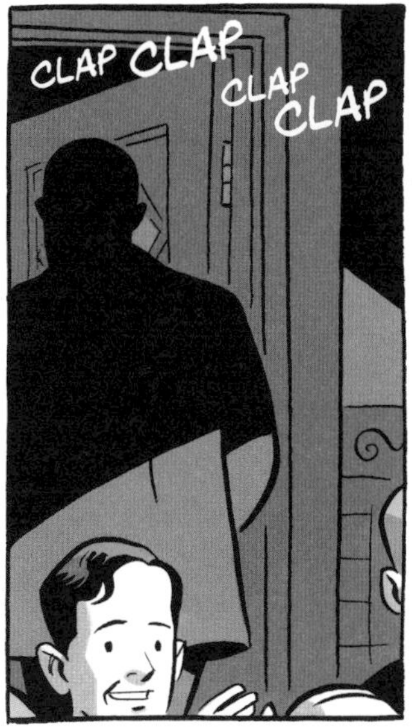
CLAP
CLAP
CLAP
CLAP
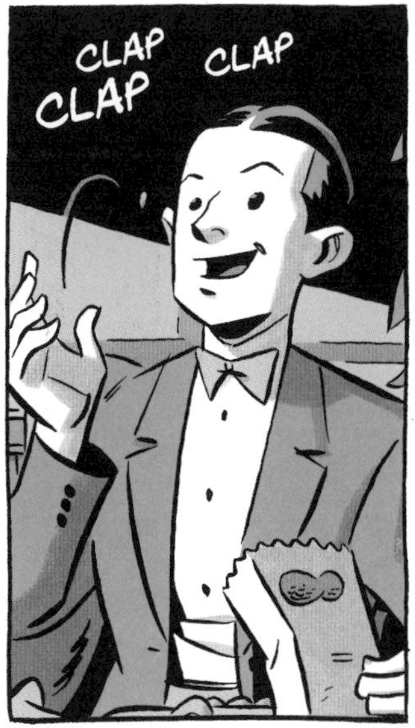
CLAP
CLAP
CLAP

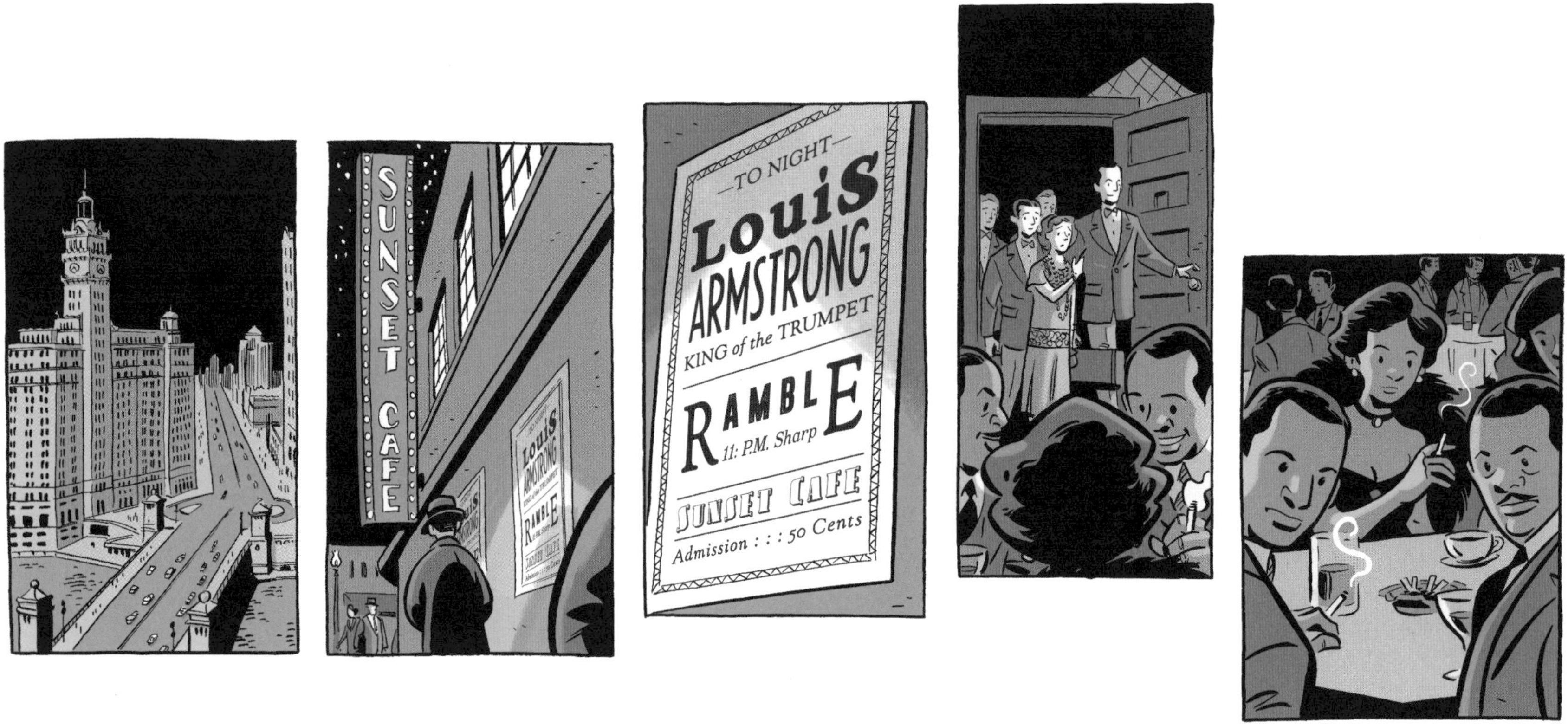
SUNSET CAFE
—TO NIGHT—
Louis
ARMSTRONG
KING of the TRUMPET
RAMBLE
11: P.M. Sharp
SUNSET CAFE
Admission : : : 50 Cents

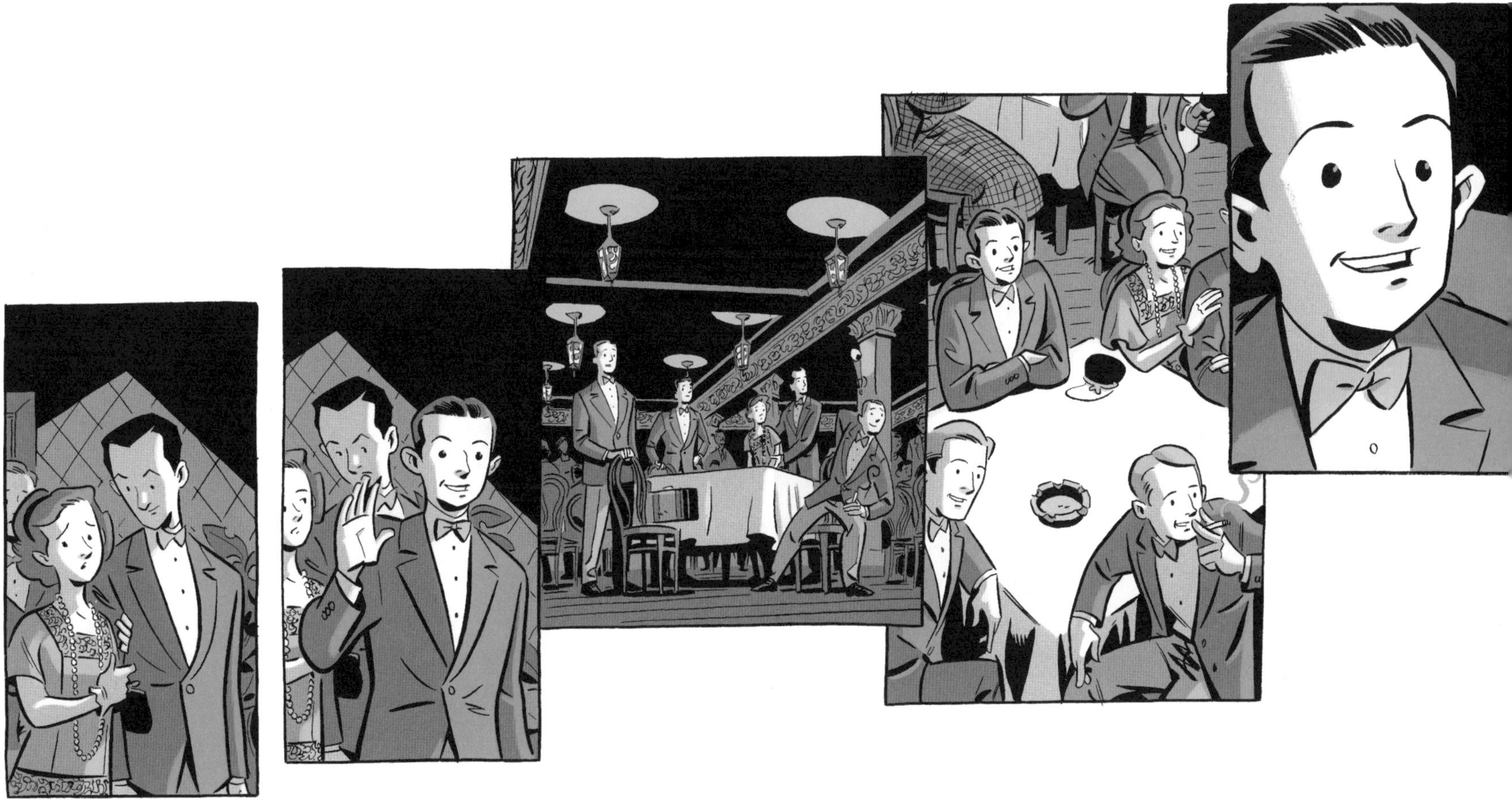

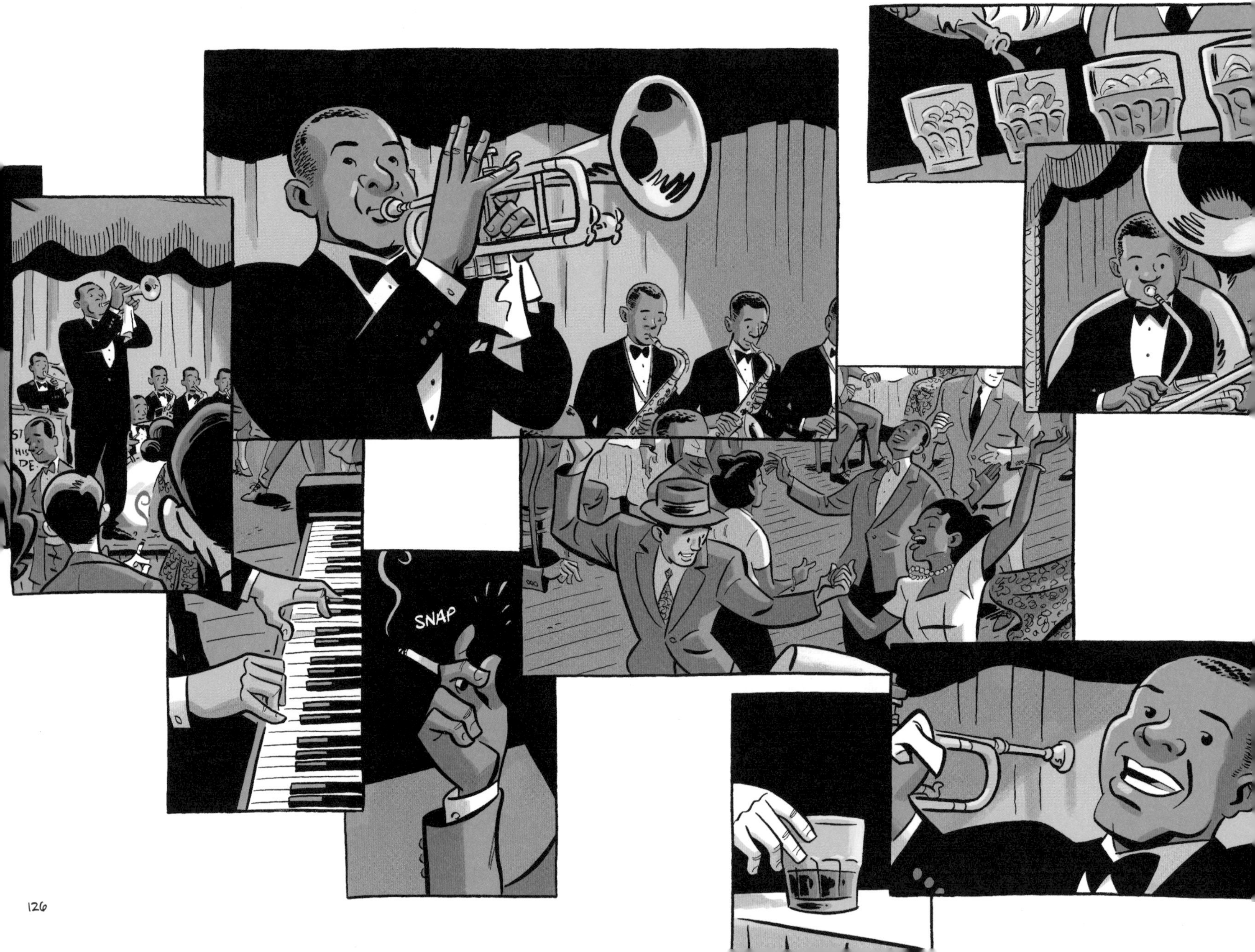
SNAP

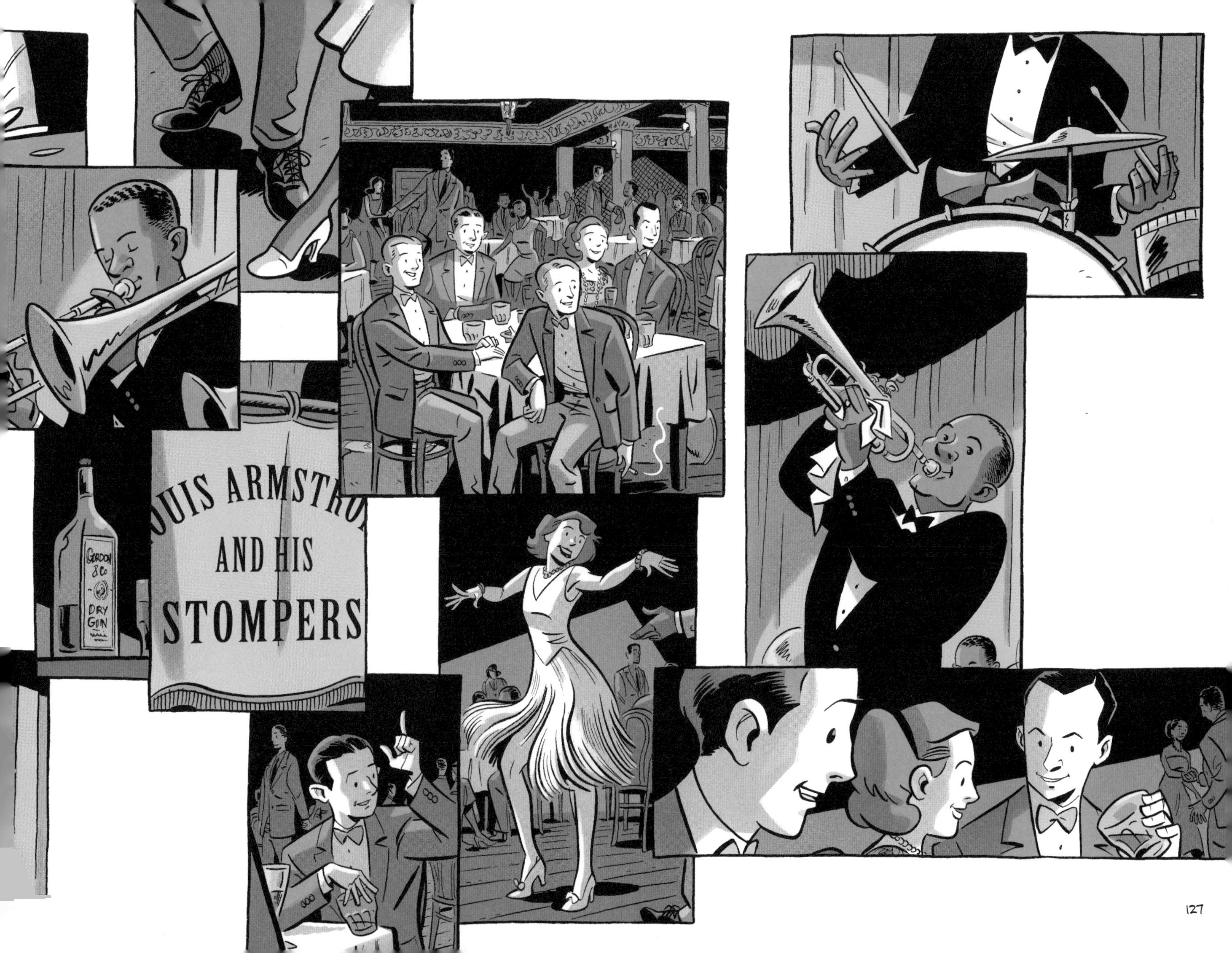
OUIS ARMSTRO
AND HIS
STOMPERS
GORDON & Co
DRY GIN

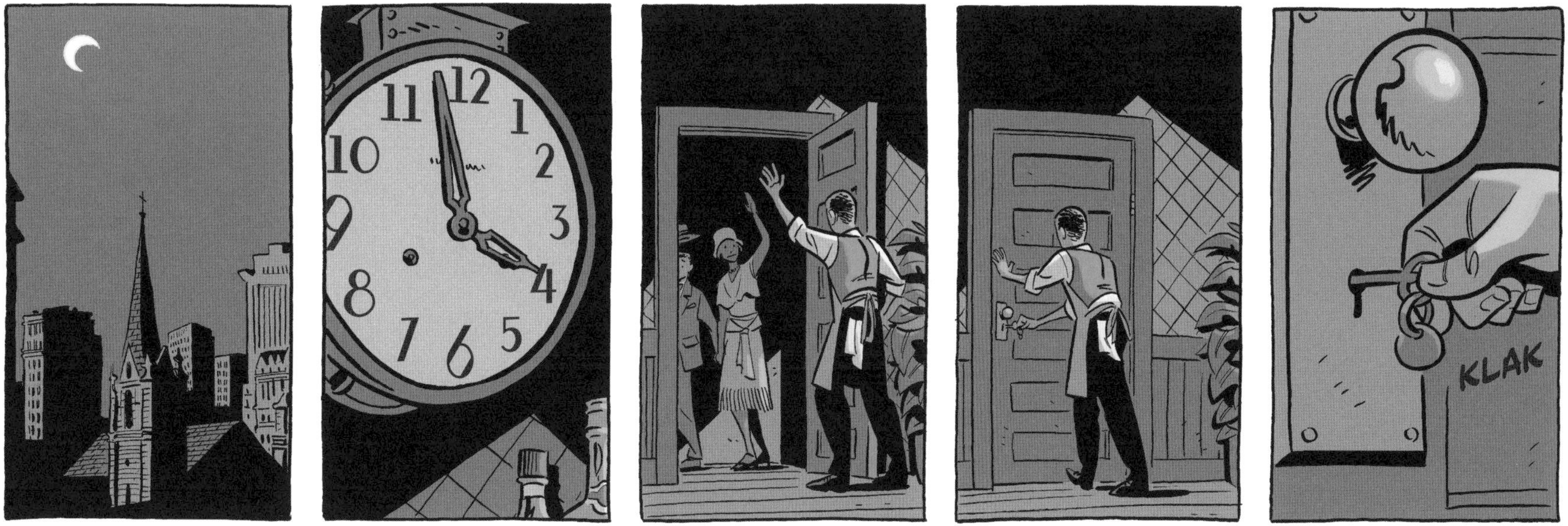
KLAK

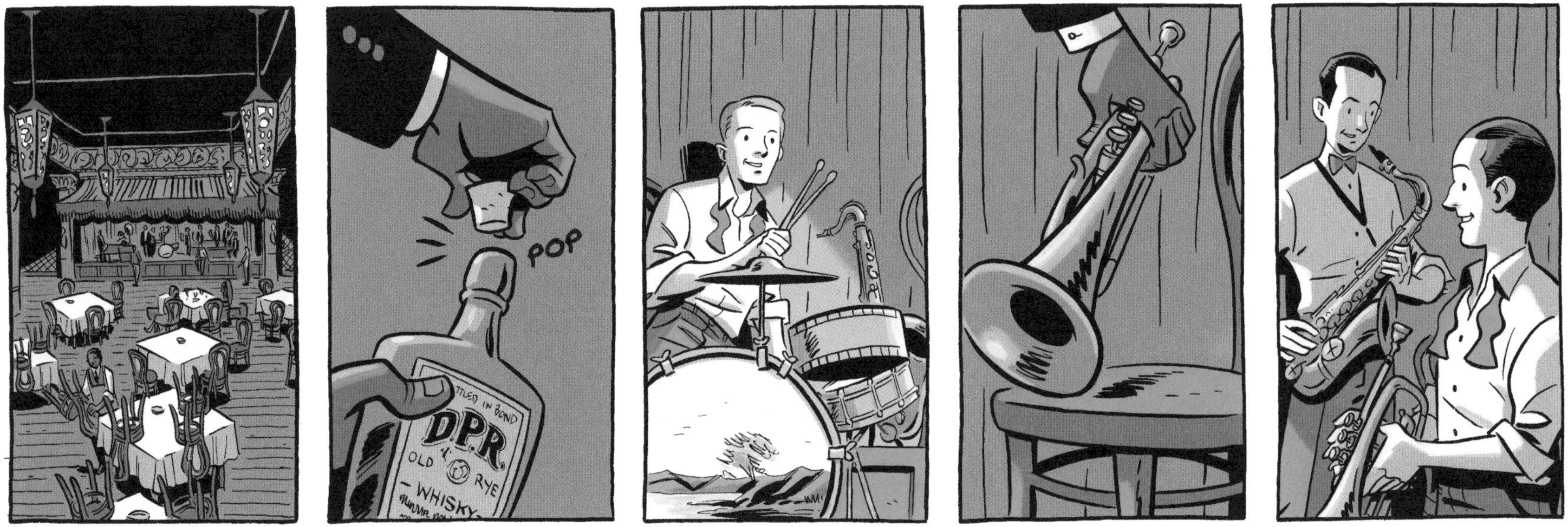
POP
D.P.R.
OLD RYE
WHISKY

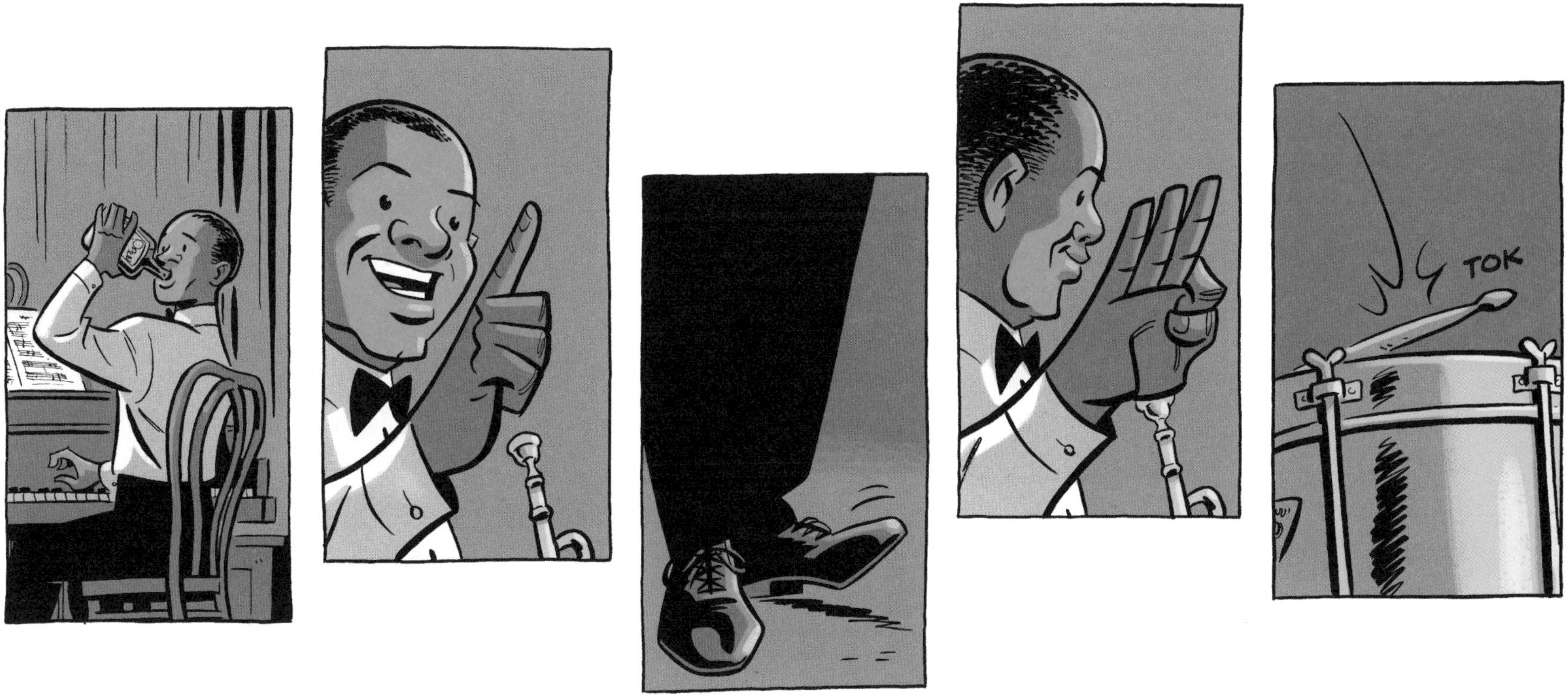
TOK

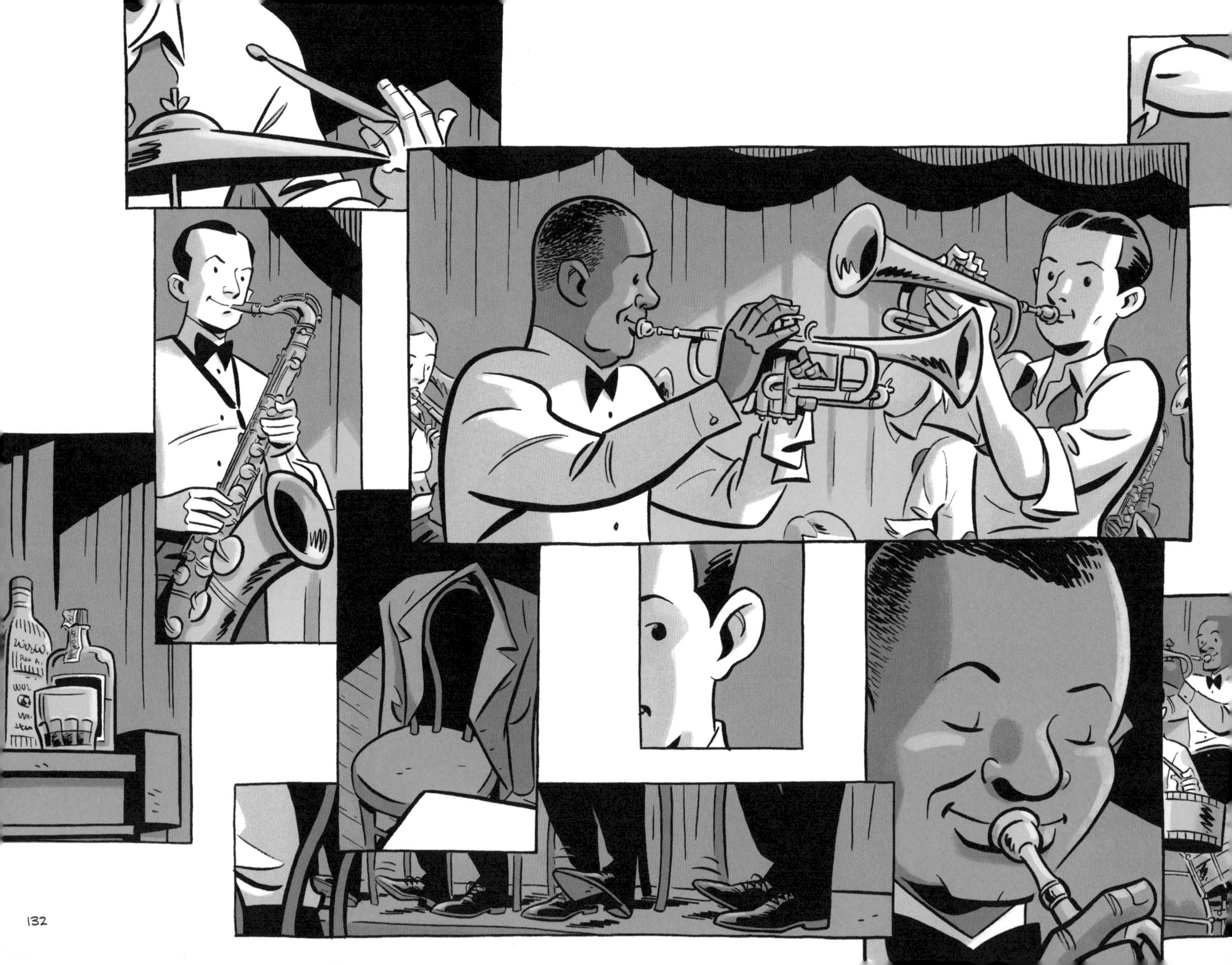

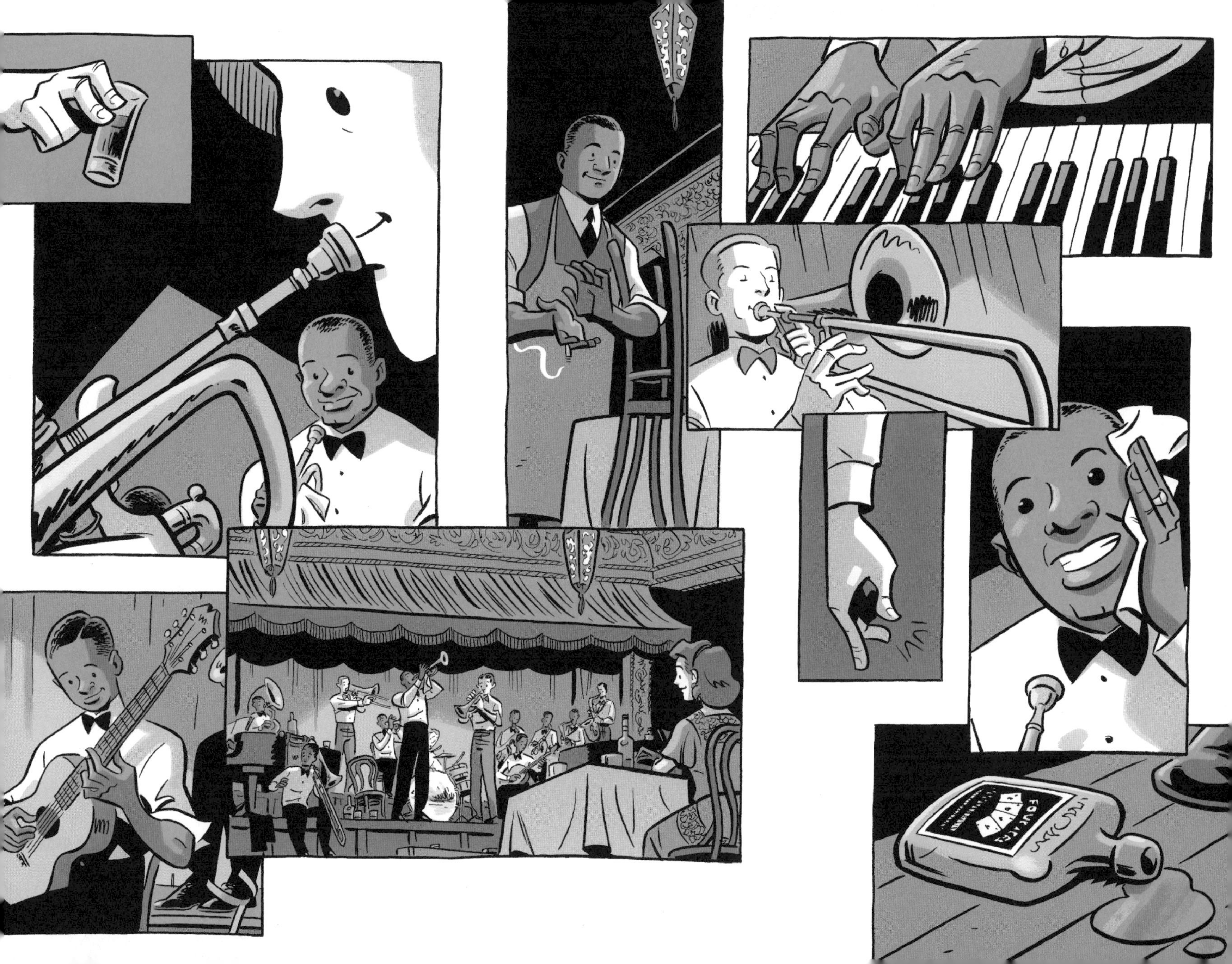
FOUR ACES

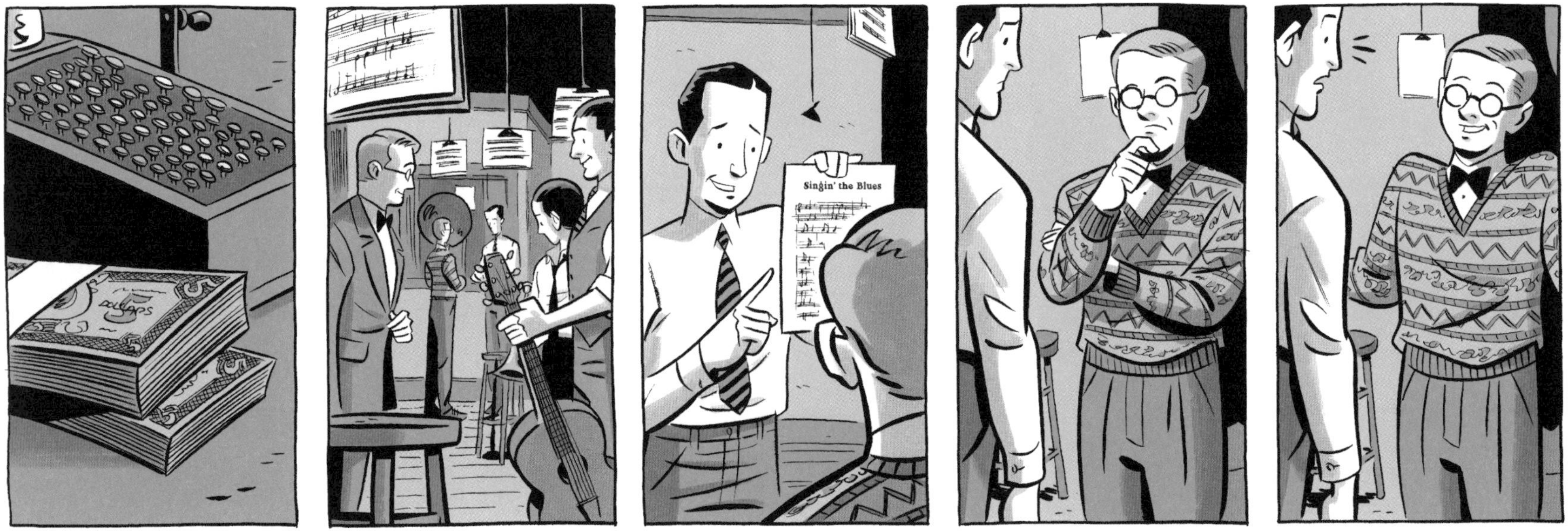
Singin' the Blues

OKeh
ELECTRIC
72-B
SINGIN' THE BLUES
(Robinson - Conrad)
FRANKIE TRUMBAUER & HIS
ORCHESTRA WITH BIX
AND LANG
Fox Trot

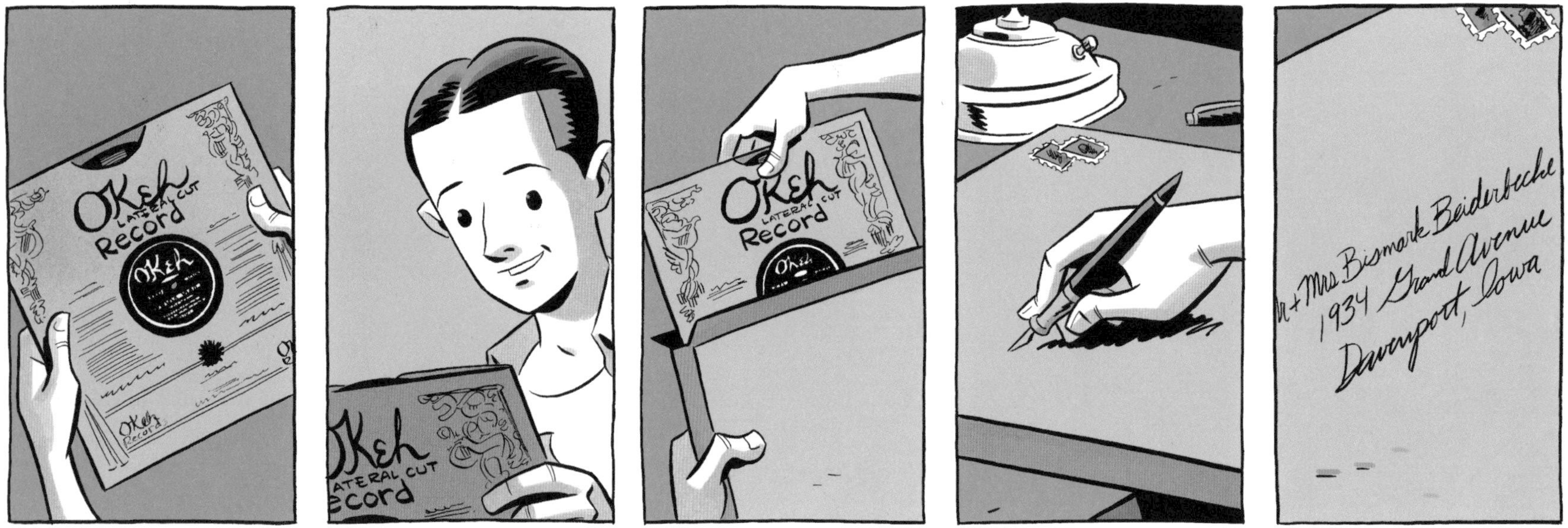
OKeh
LATERAL CUT
Record
OKeh
LATERAL CUT
Record
OKeh
LATERAL CUT
Record
r+Mrs Bismark Beiderbecke
1934 Grand Avenue
Davenport, Iowa

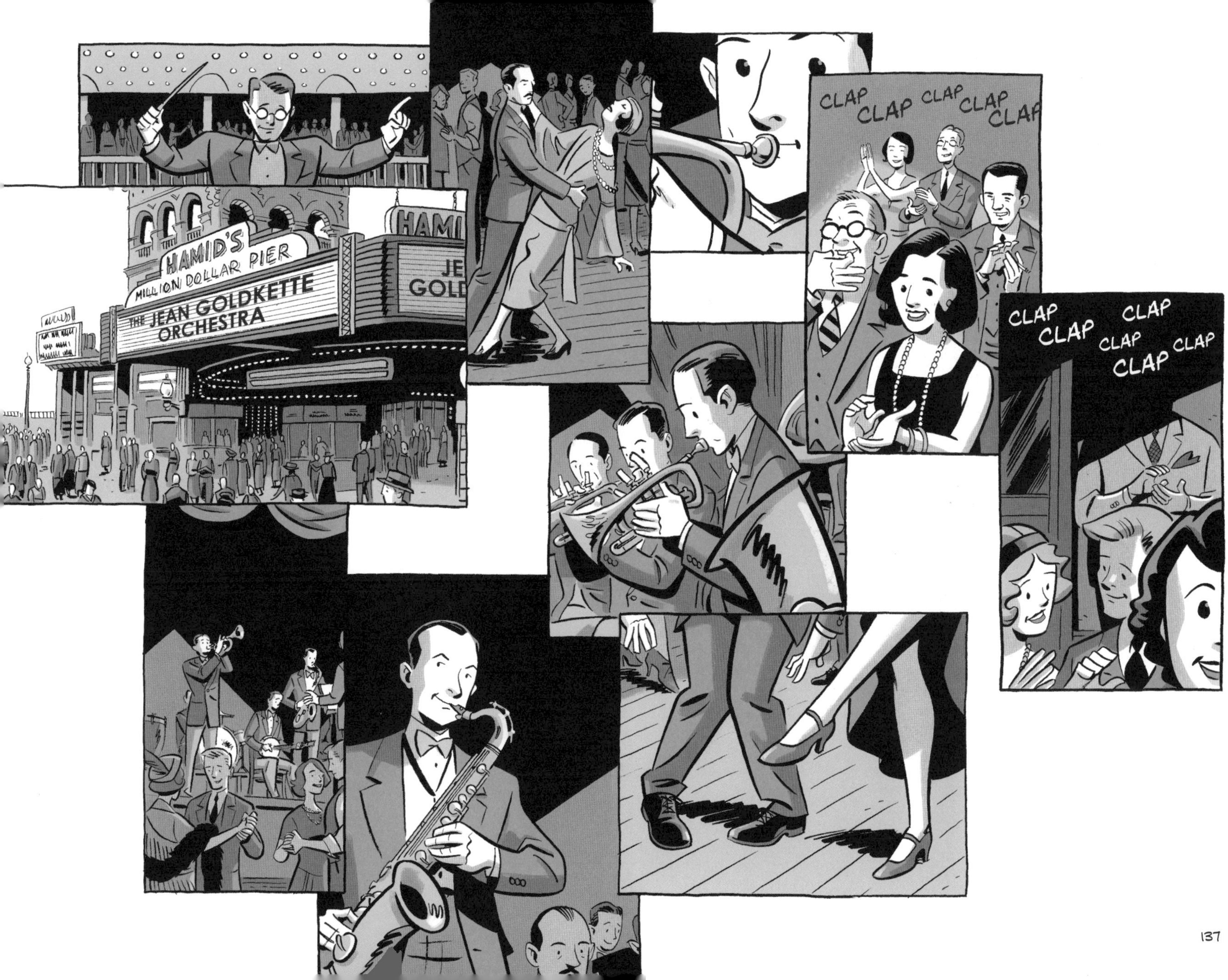
HAMID'S
MILLION DOLLAR PIER
THE JEAN GOLDKETTE ORCHESTRA
HAMI
JE
GOLD
CLAP CLAP CLAP CLAP CLAP
CLAP CLAP CLAP CLAP CLAP CLAP

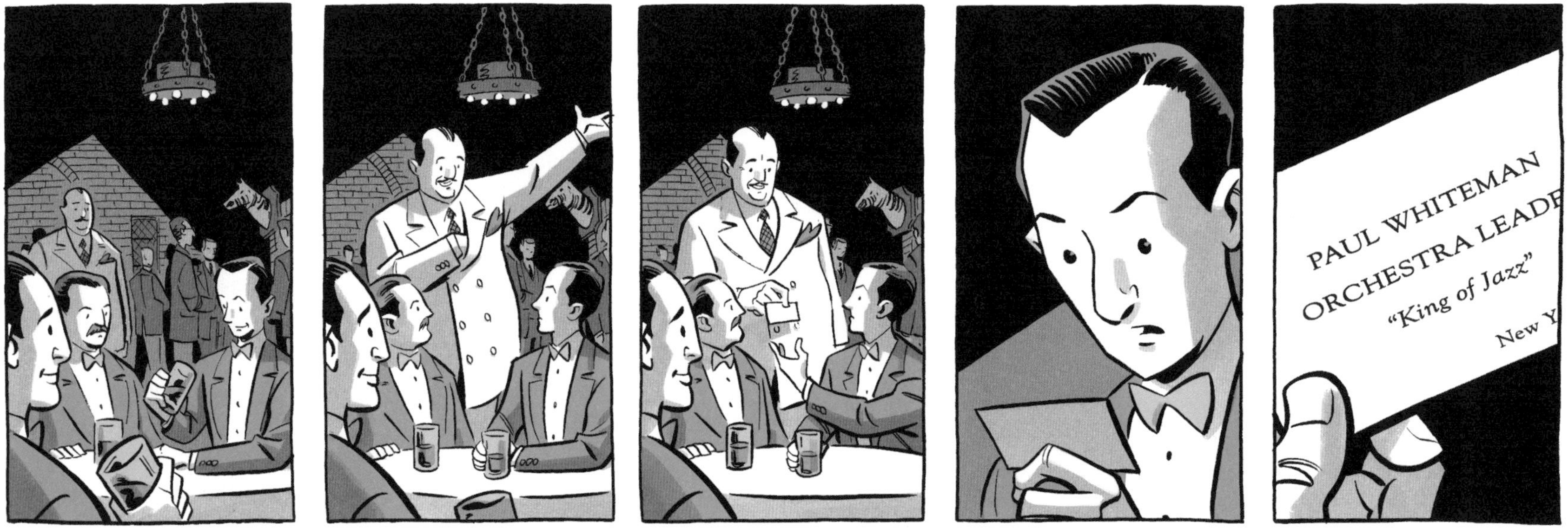
PAUL WHITEMAN
ORCHESTRA LEADE
"King of Jazz"
New Y

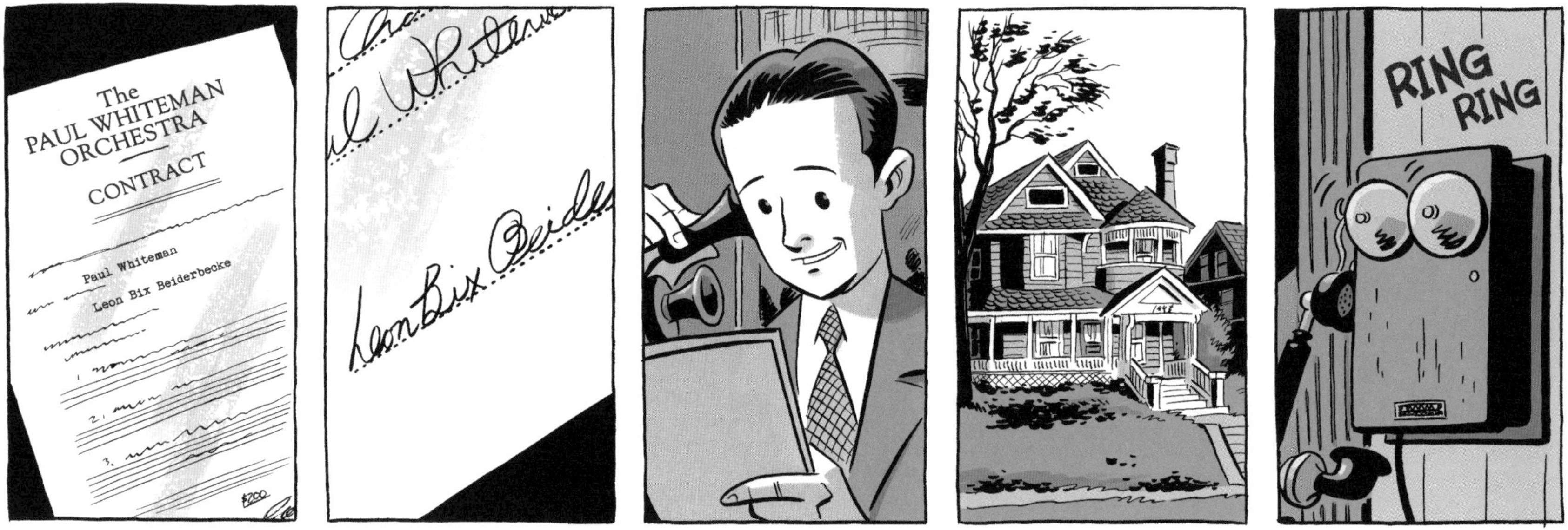
The
PAUL WHITEMAN
ORCHESTRA
CONTRACT
Paul Whiteman
Leon Bix Beiderbecke
1.
2.
3.
$200
RING
RING

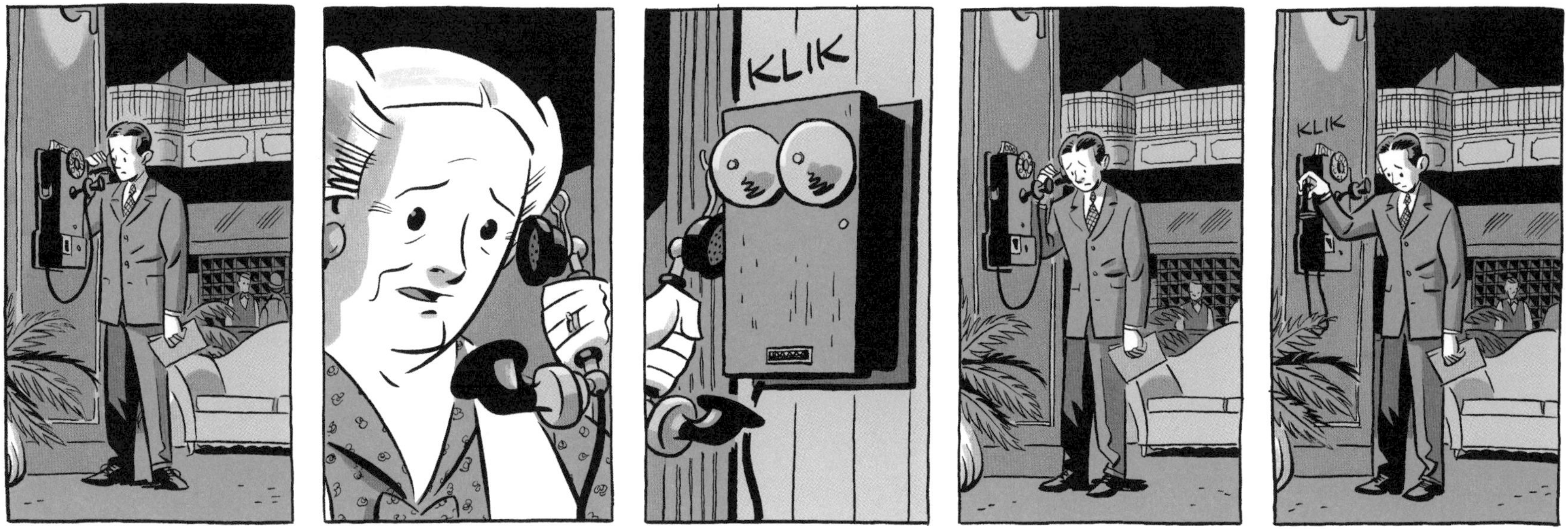
KLIK
KLIK

Part Four

IN A MIST

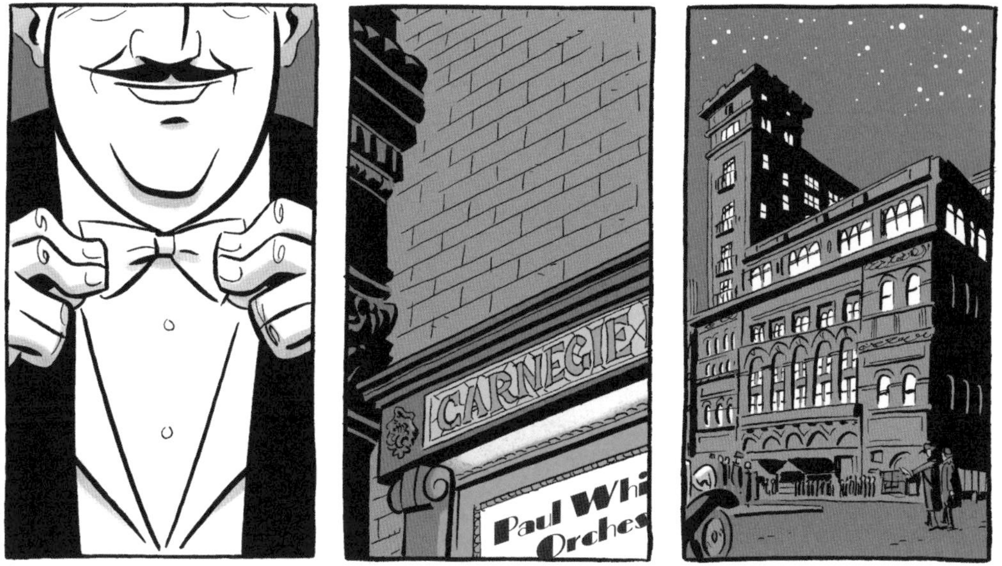
CARNEGIE
Paul Whi
Orches

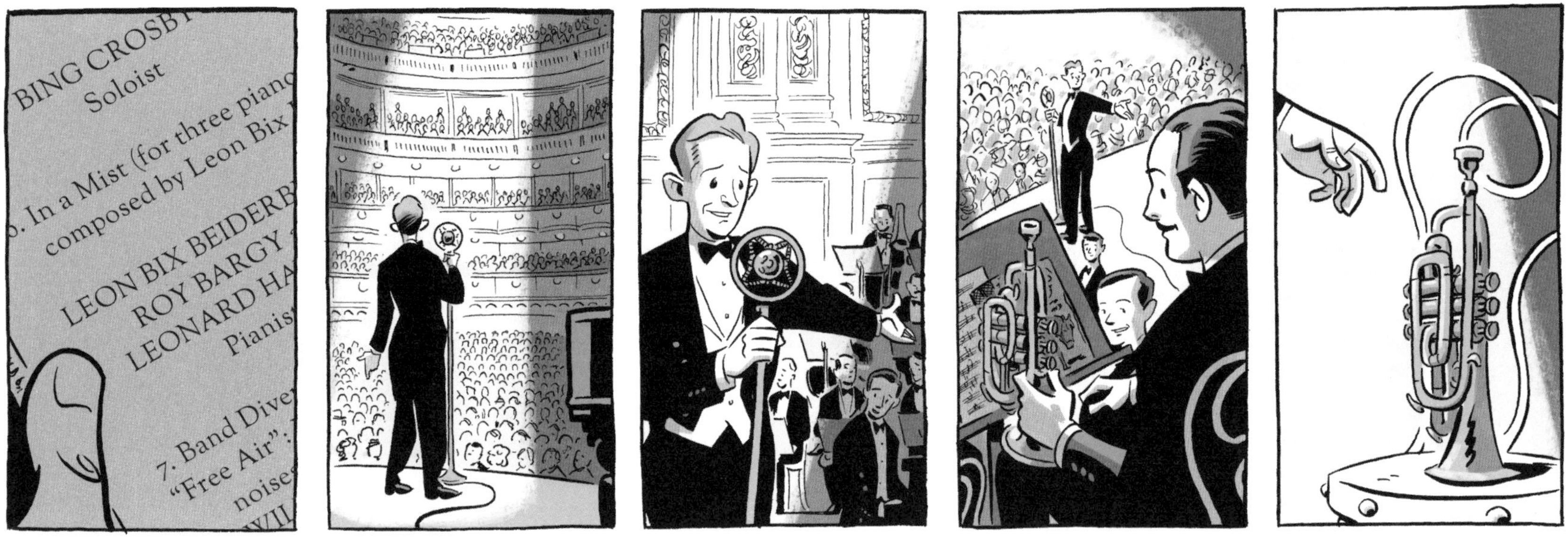
BING CROSB
Soloist
. In a Mist (for three pian
composed by Leon Bix
LEON BIX BEIDERB
ROY BARGY
LEONARD HA
Pianist
7. Band Dive
“Free Air”:
noises

Steinway & Sons

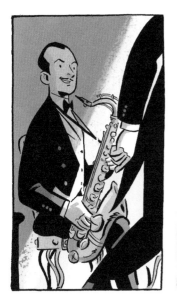

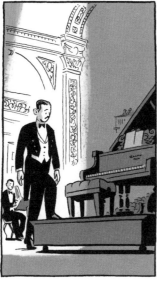

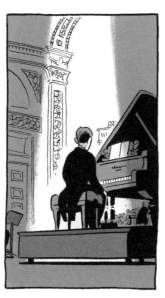

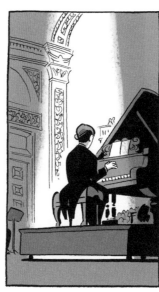

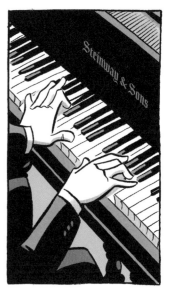

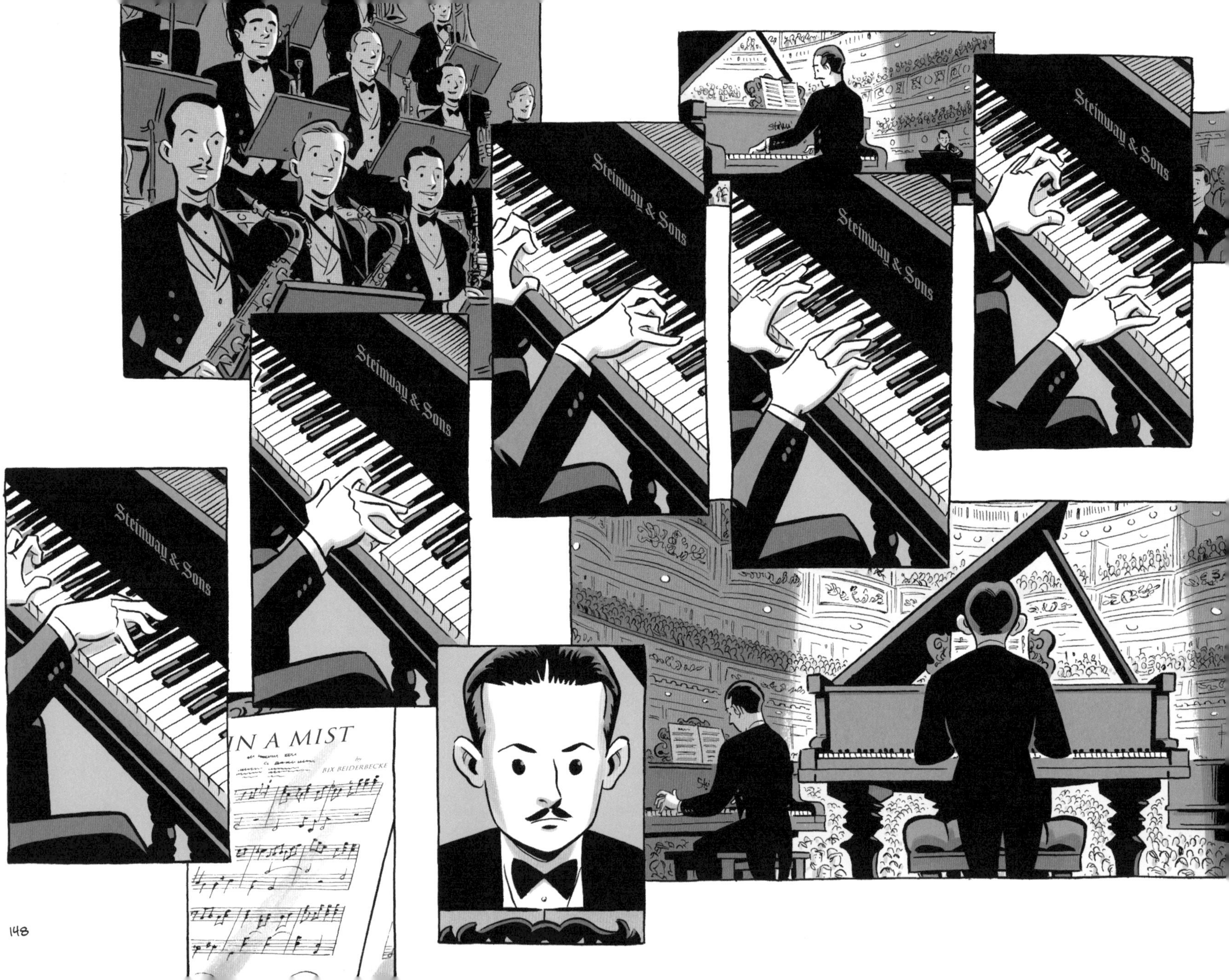
Steinway & Sons
Steinway & Sons
Steinway & Sons
Steinway & Sons
Steinway & Sons
IN A MIST
by
BIX BEIDERBECKE

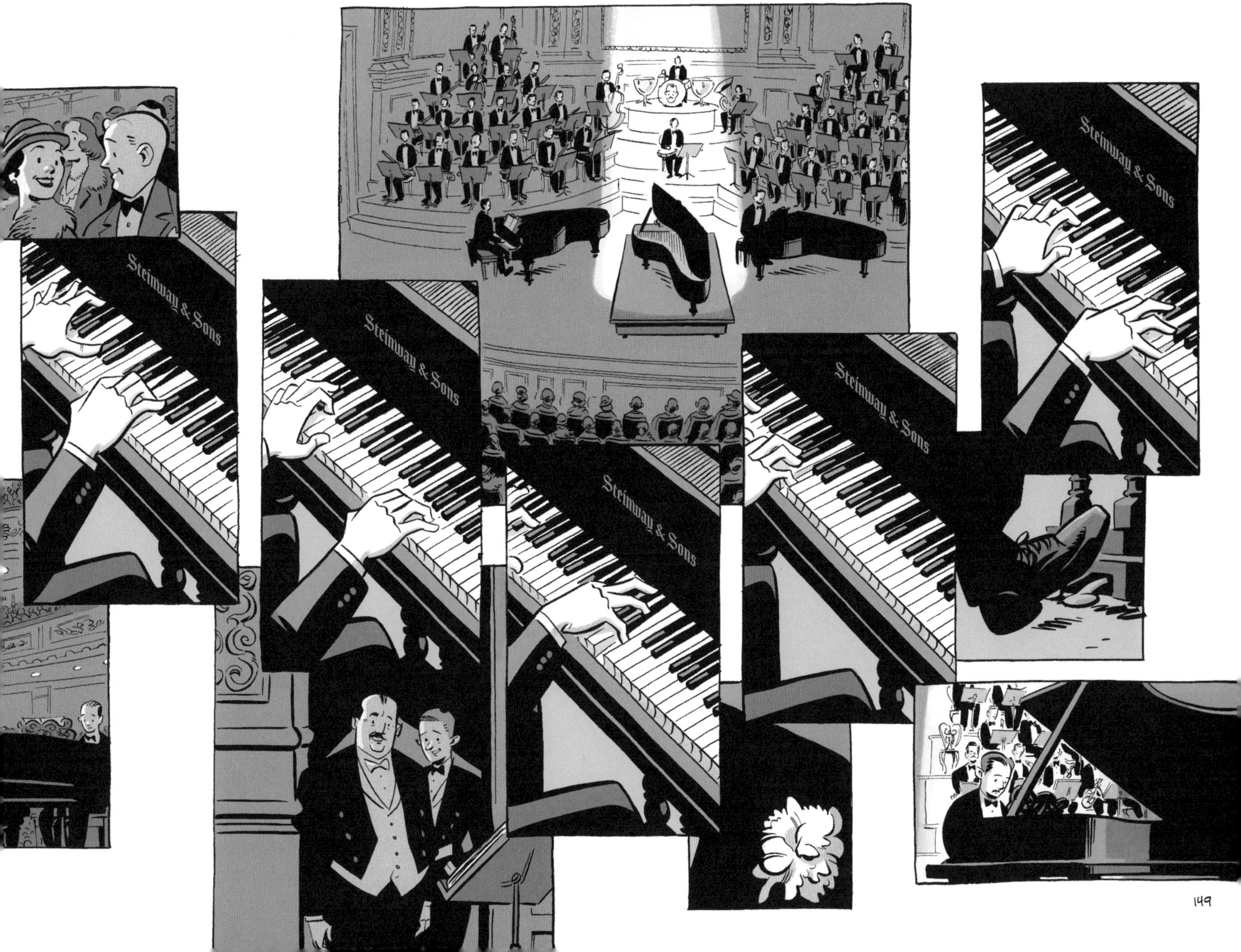
Steinway & Sons
Steinway & Sons
Steinway & Sons
Steinway & Sons
Steinway & Sons

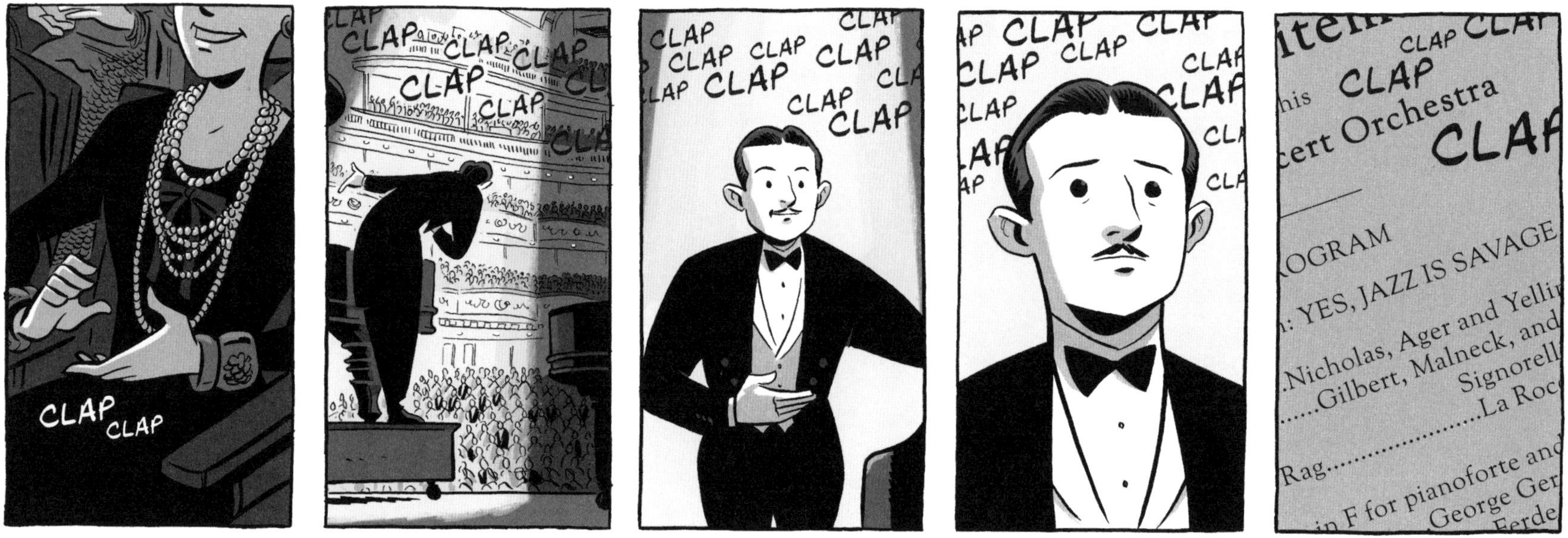
CLAP CLAP
CLAP CLAP CLAP CLAP CLAP
CLAP CLAP CLAP CLAP CLAP CLAP CLAP CLAP
CLAP CLAP CLAP CLAP CLAP CLAP CLAP
his CLAP
cert Orchestra
CLAP CLAP
OGRAM
: YES, JAZZ IS SAVAGE
.Nicholas, Ager and Yelli
.....Gilbert, Malneck, and
Signorell
......................La Roc
Rag...........................
in F for pianoforte and
George Ger
Ferde

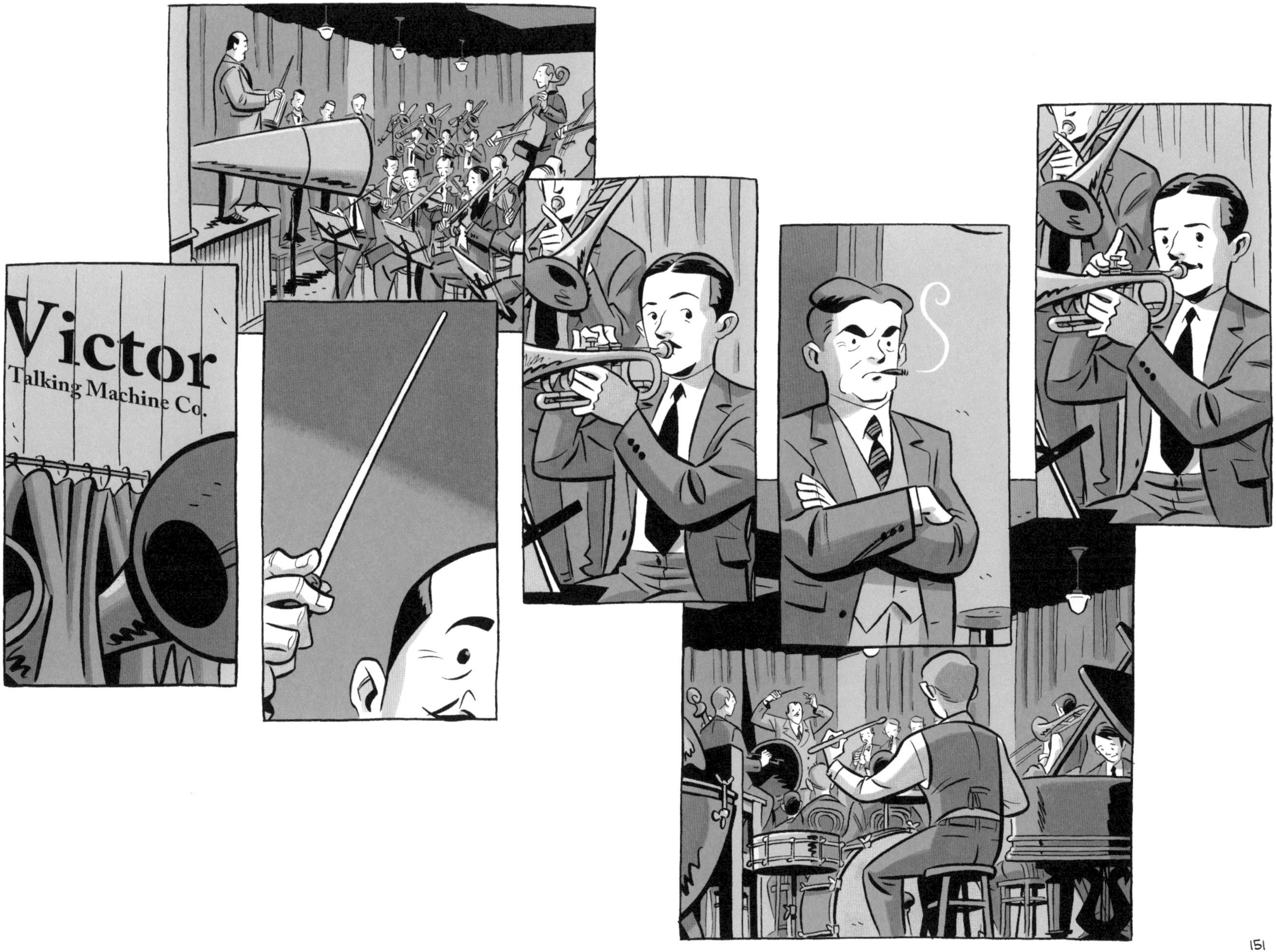
Victor
Talking Machine Co.

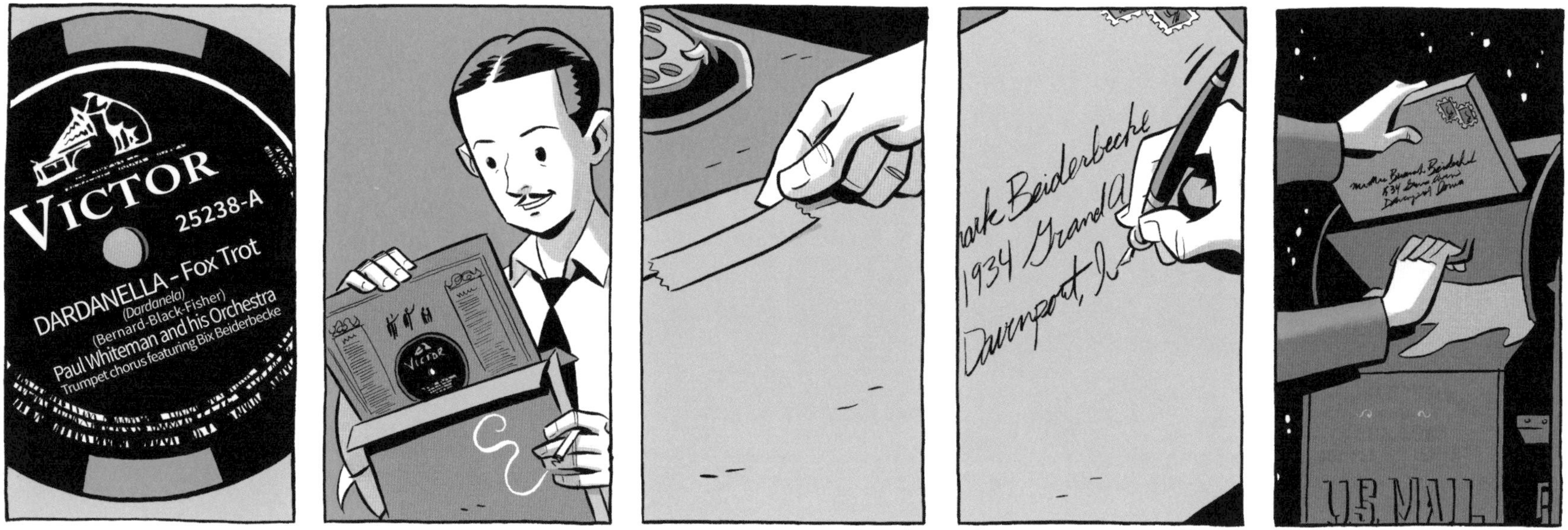
VICTOR
25238-A
DARDANELLA - Fox Trot
(Dardanela)
(Bernard-Black-Fisher)
Paul Whiteman and his Orchestra
Trumpet chorus featuring Bix Beiderbecke
ark Beiderbecke
1934 Grand A
Davenport, I
U.S. MAIL

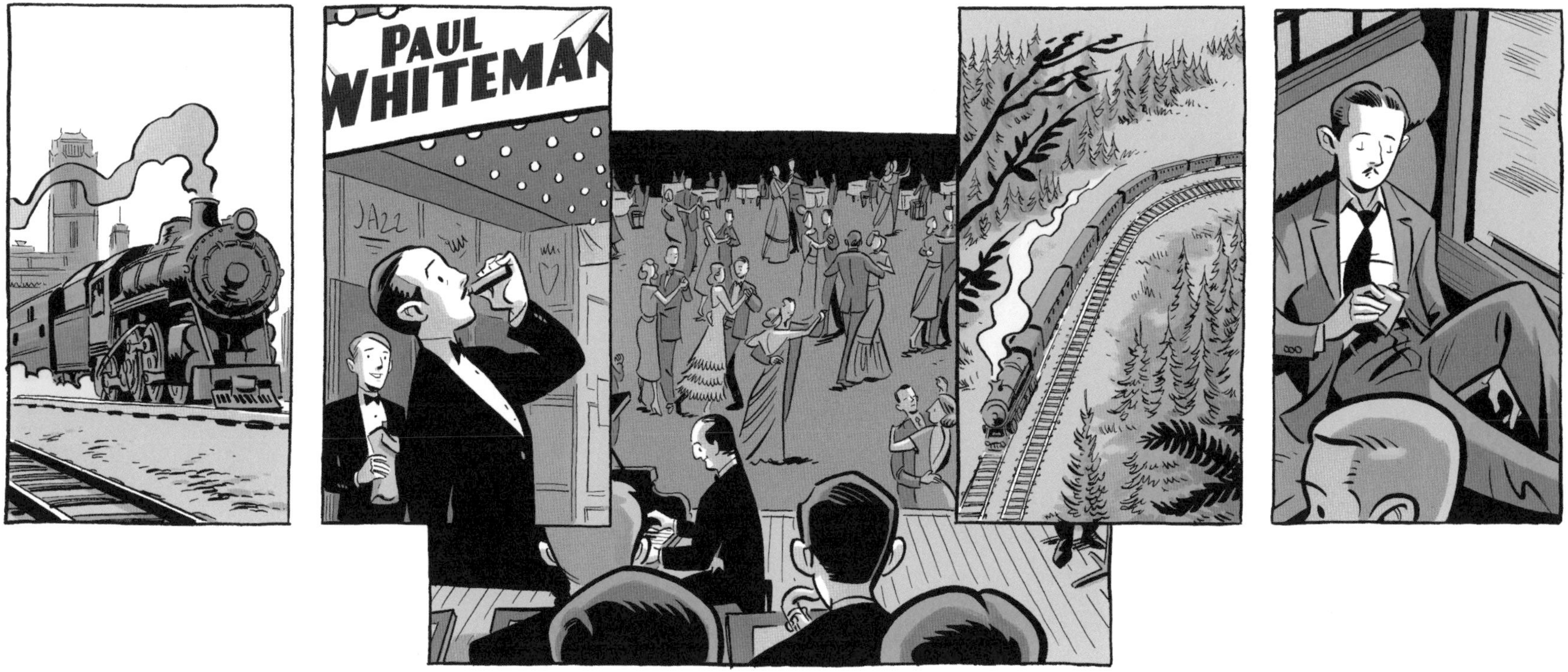
PAUL
WHITEMA
JAZZ

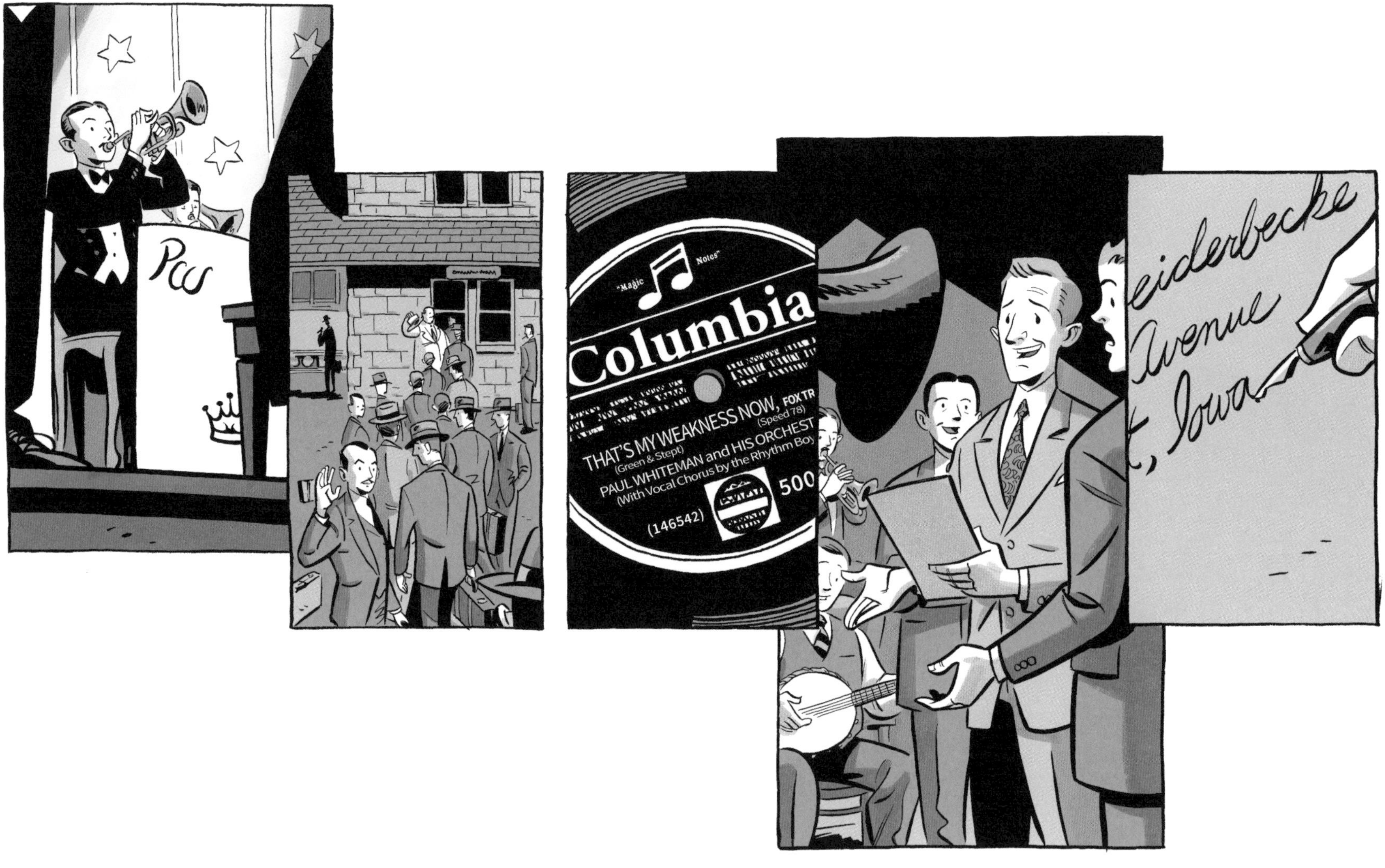
"Magic Notes"
Columbia
THAT'S MY WEAKNESS NOW, FOX TR
(Green & Stept)
(Speed 78)
PAUL WHITEMAN and HIS ORCHEST
(With Vocal Chorus by the Rhythm Boy
500
(146542)
eiderbecke
Avenue
, Iowa

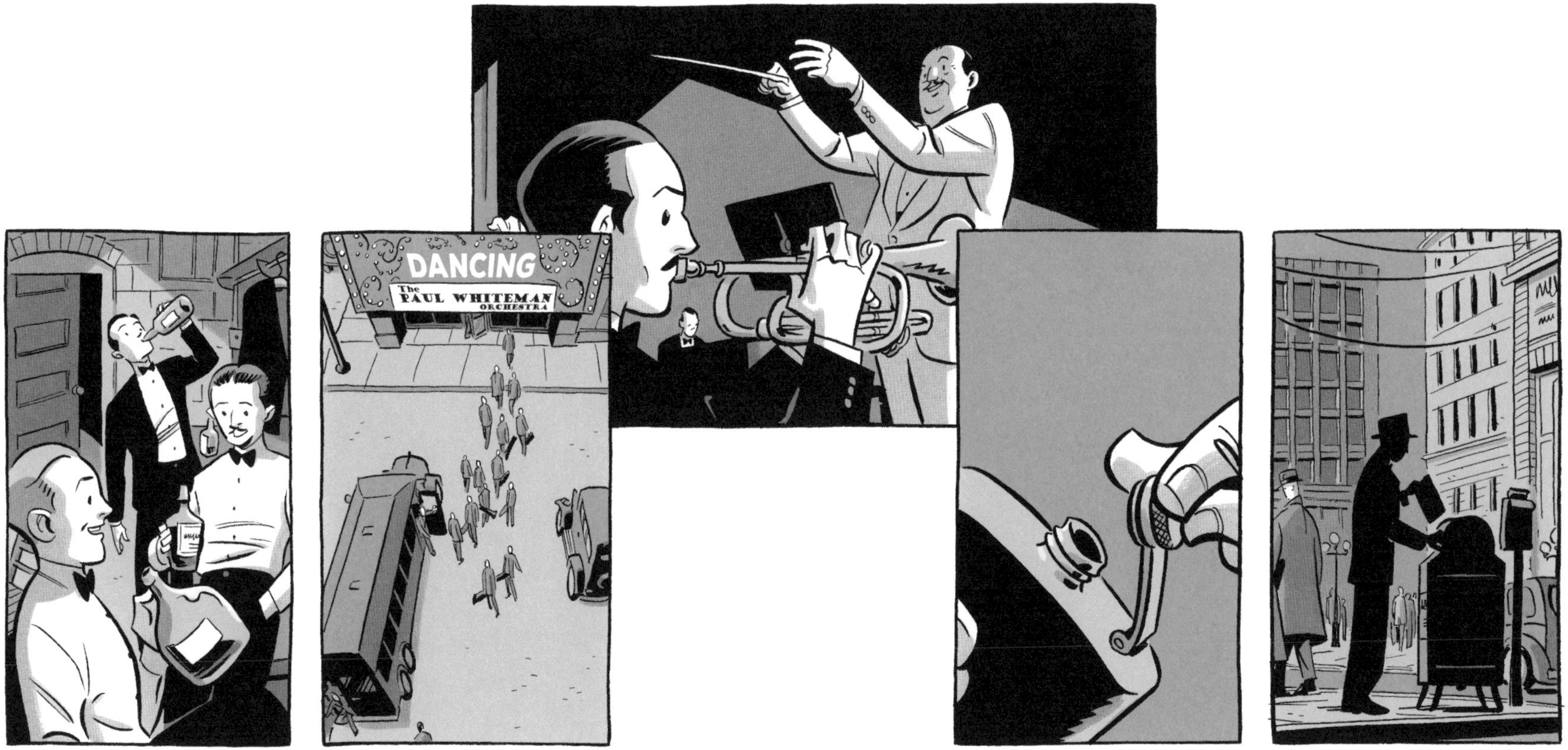
DANCING
The PAUL WHITEMAN ORCHESTRA

WHITE PATRONS ONLY

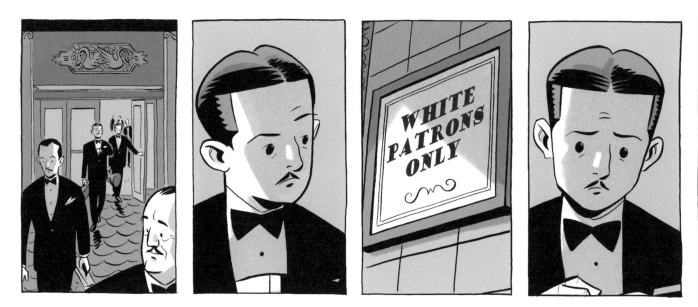

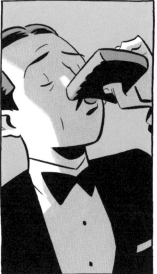

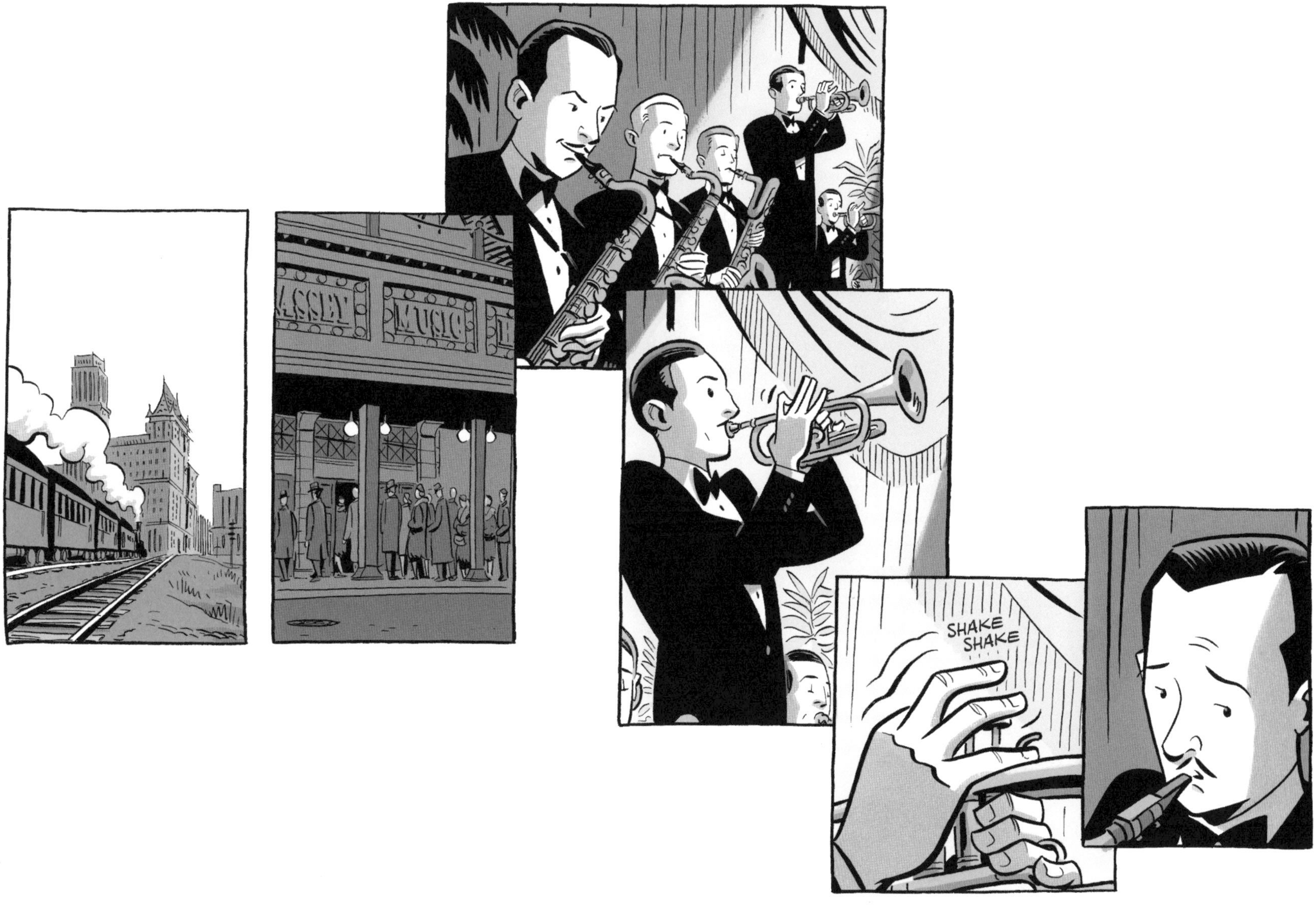
ASSEY
MUSIC
SHAKE
SHAKE

TULSA
CKETS

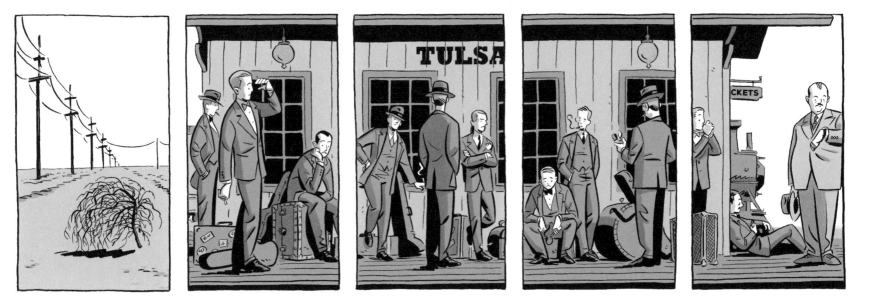

11 NOV 28
CHEAP SINGLE TICKET
TULSA TO
PONCA CITY
3959

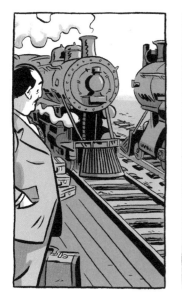

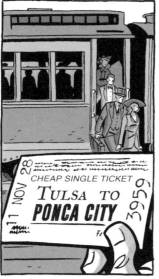

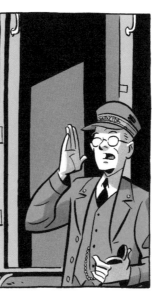

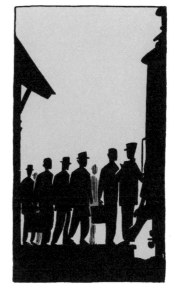

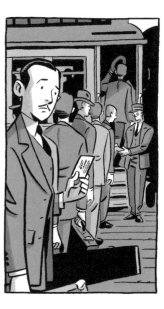

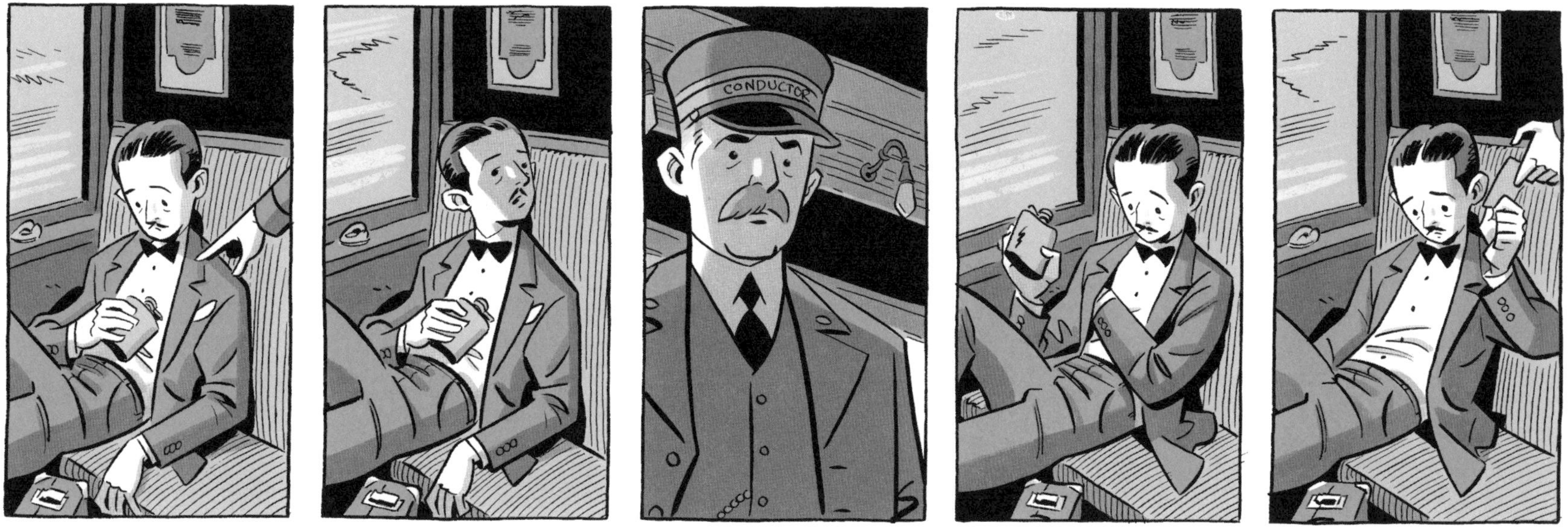
CONDUCTOR

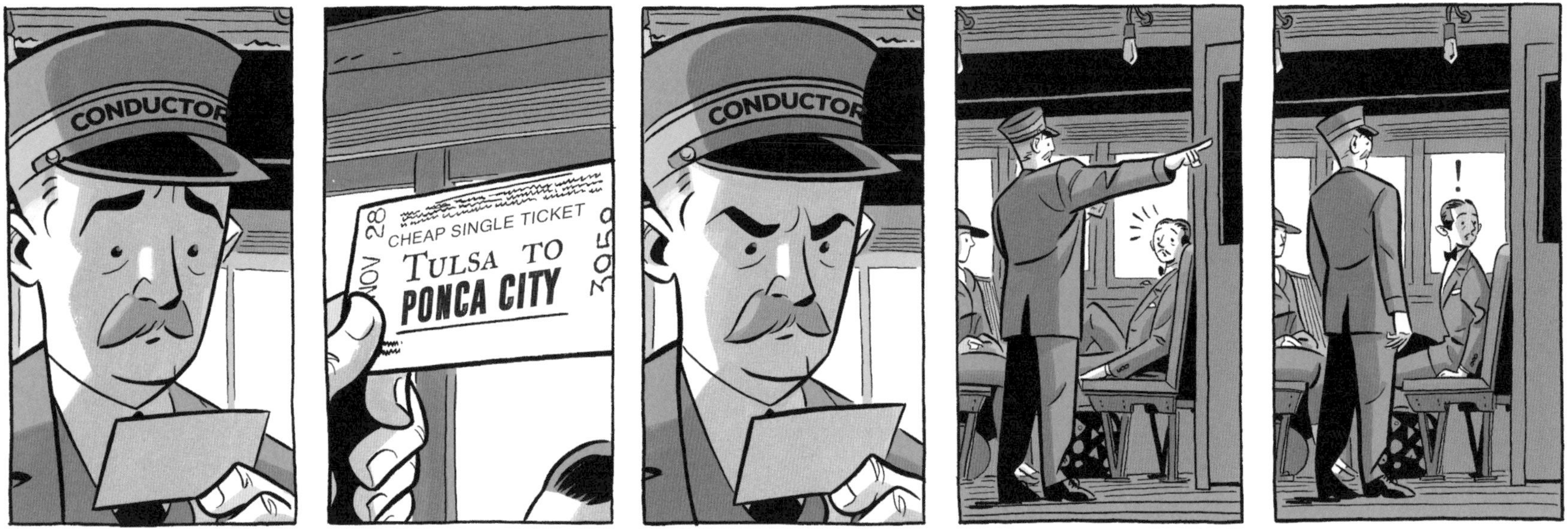
CONDUCTOR
CHEAP SINGLE TICKET
NOV 28
TULSA TO
PONCA CITY
3959
CONDUCTOR
!

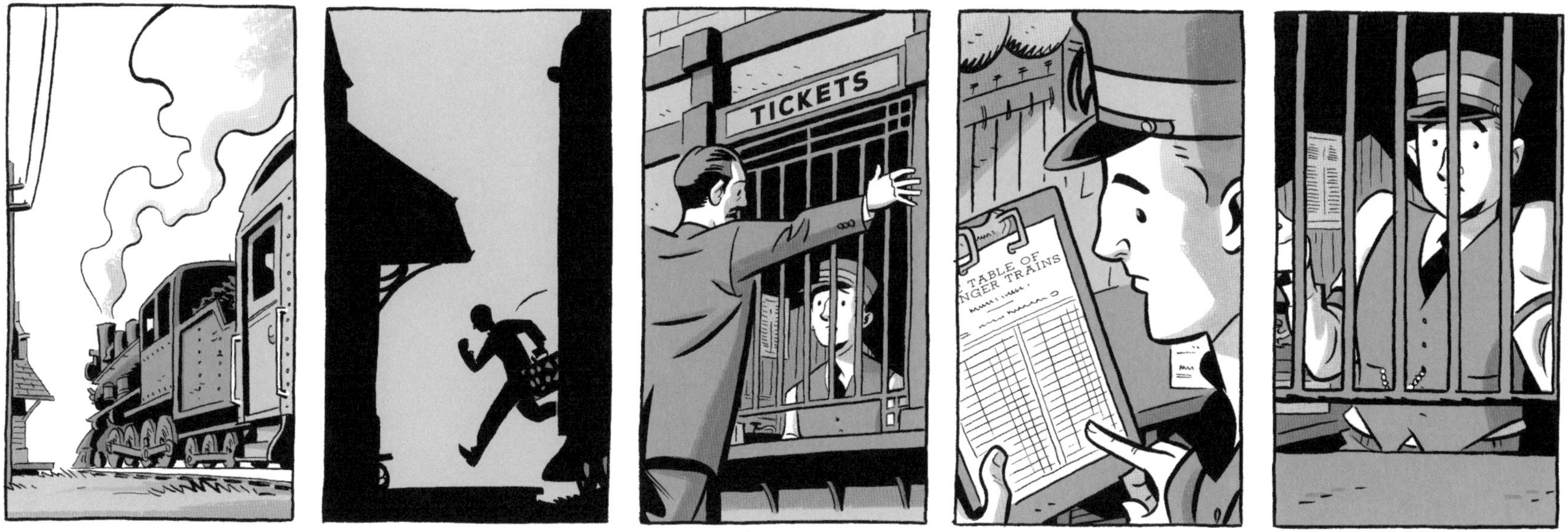
TICKETS
TABLE OF
TRAINS

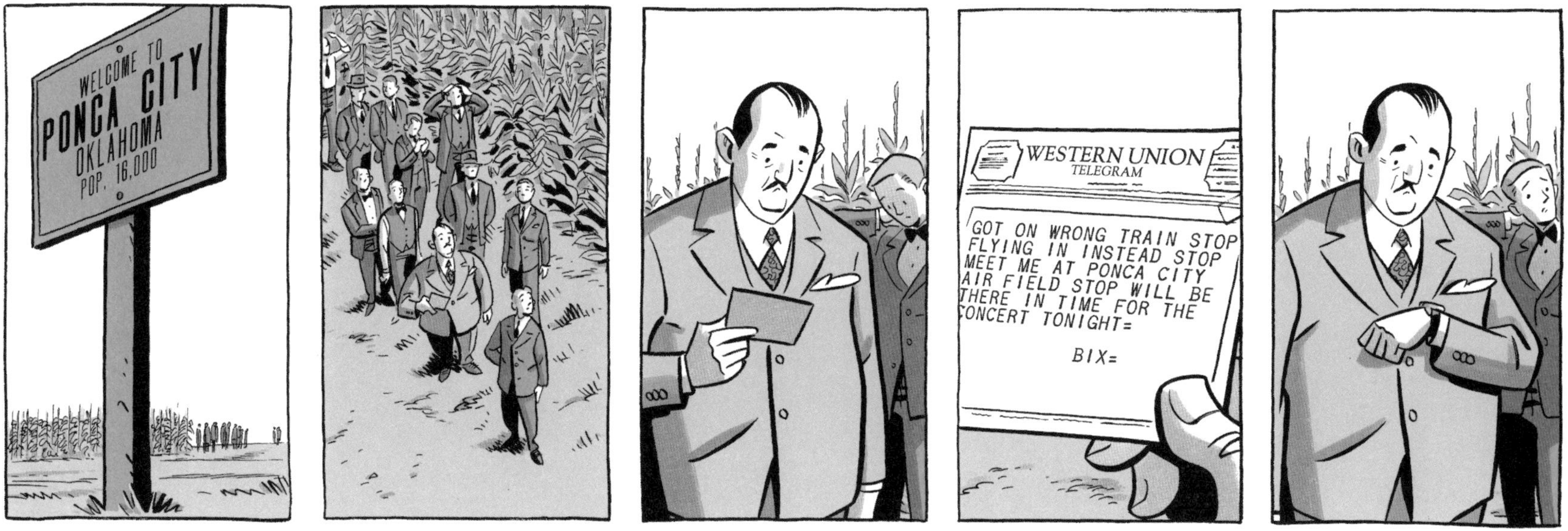
WELCOME TO
PONCA CITY
OKLAHOMA
POP. 16,000
WESTERN UNION
TELEGRAM
GOT ON WRONG TRAIN STOP
FLYING IN INSTEAD STOP
MEET ME AT PONCA CITY
AIR FIELD STOP WILL BE
THERE IN TIME FOR THE
CONCERT TONIGHT=
BIX=

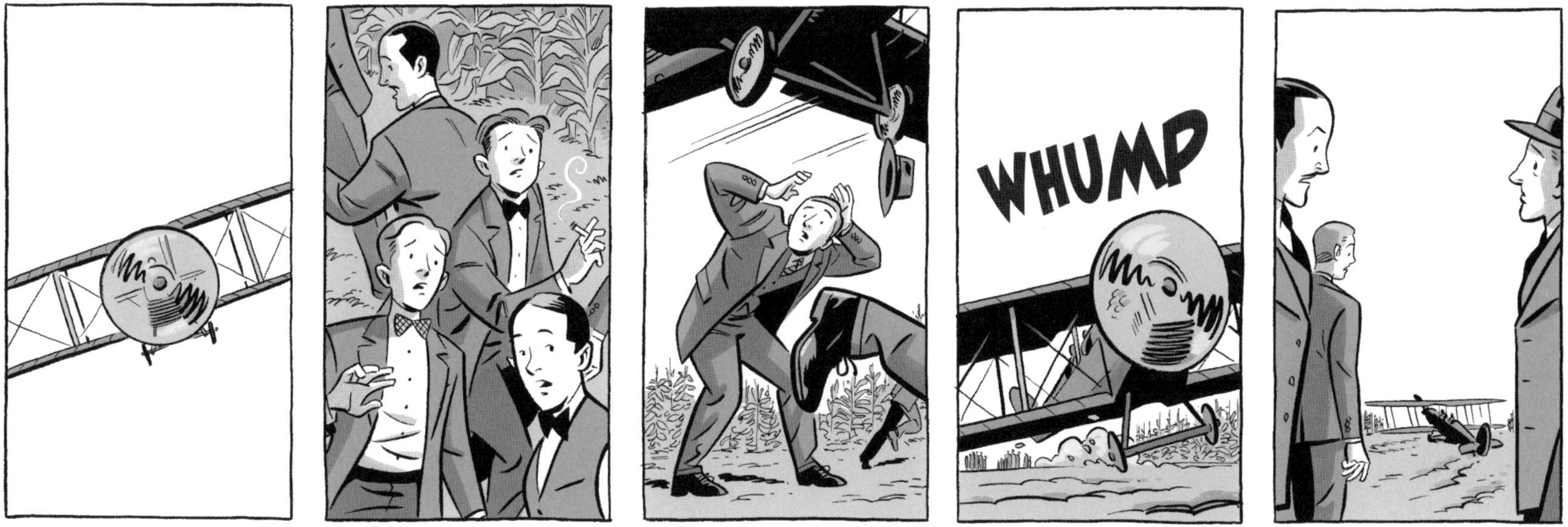
WHUMP

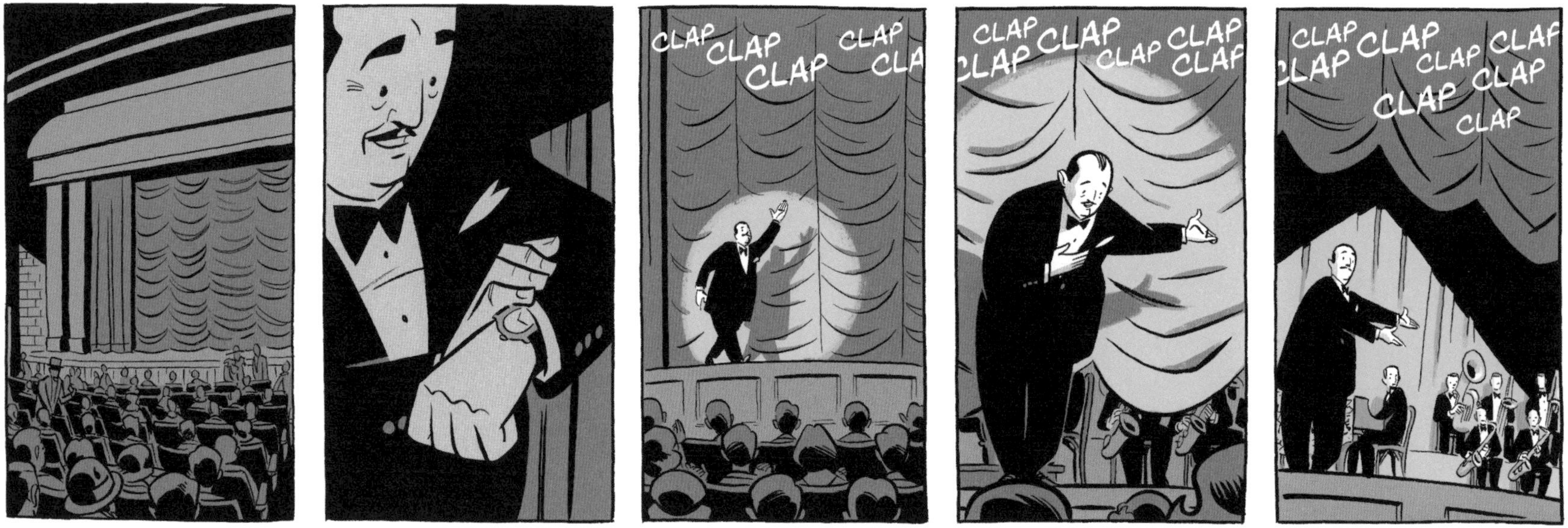
CLAP
CLAP
CLAP
CLAP
CLAP
CLAP
CLAP
CLAP
CLAP
CLAP
CLAP
CLAP
CLAP
CLAP
CLAP

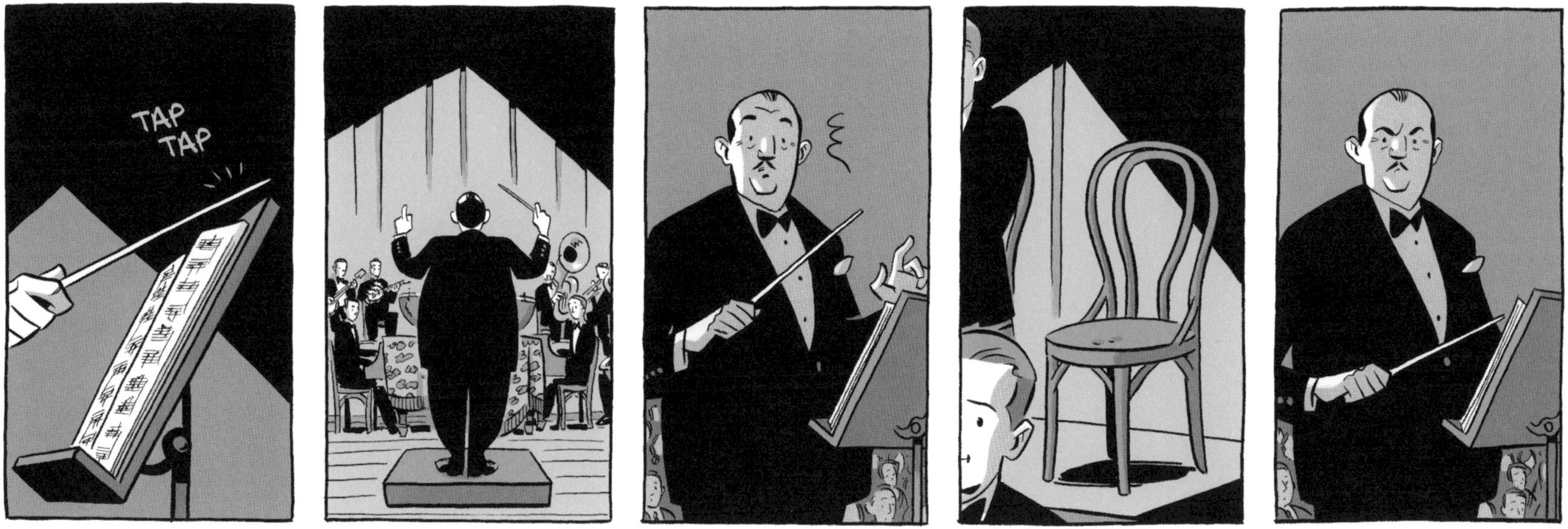
TAP
TAP

TAK

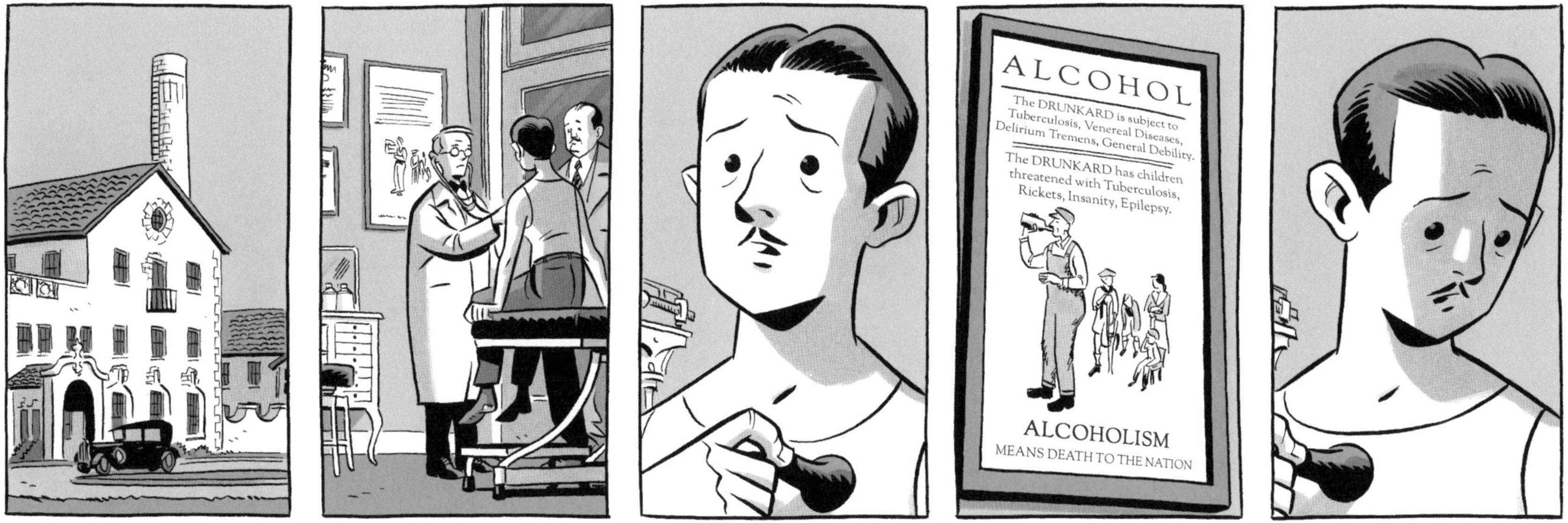
ALCOHOL
The DRUNKARD is subject to Tuberculosis, Venereal Diseases, Delirium Tremens, General Debility.
The DRUNKARD has children threatened with Tuberculosis, Rickets, Insanity, Epilepsy.
ALCOHOLISM
MEANS DEATH TO THE NATION

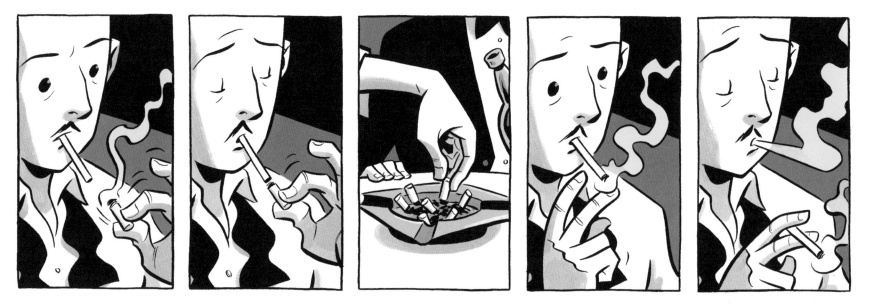

B.F. Keith's
Palace

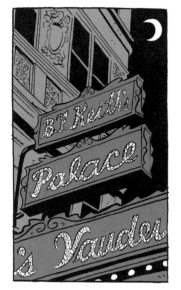

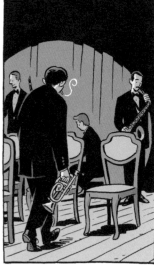

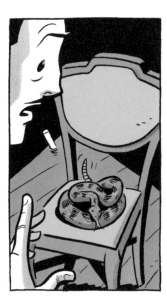

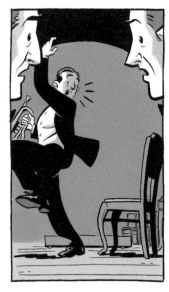

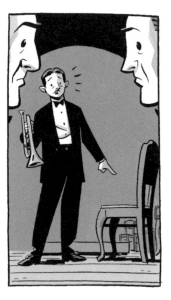

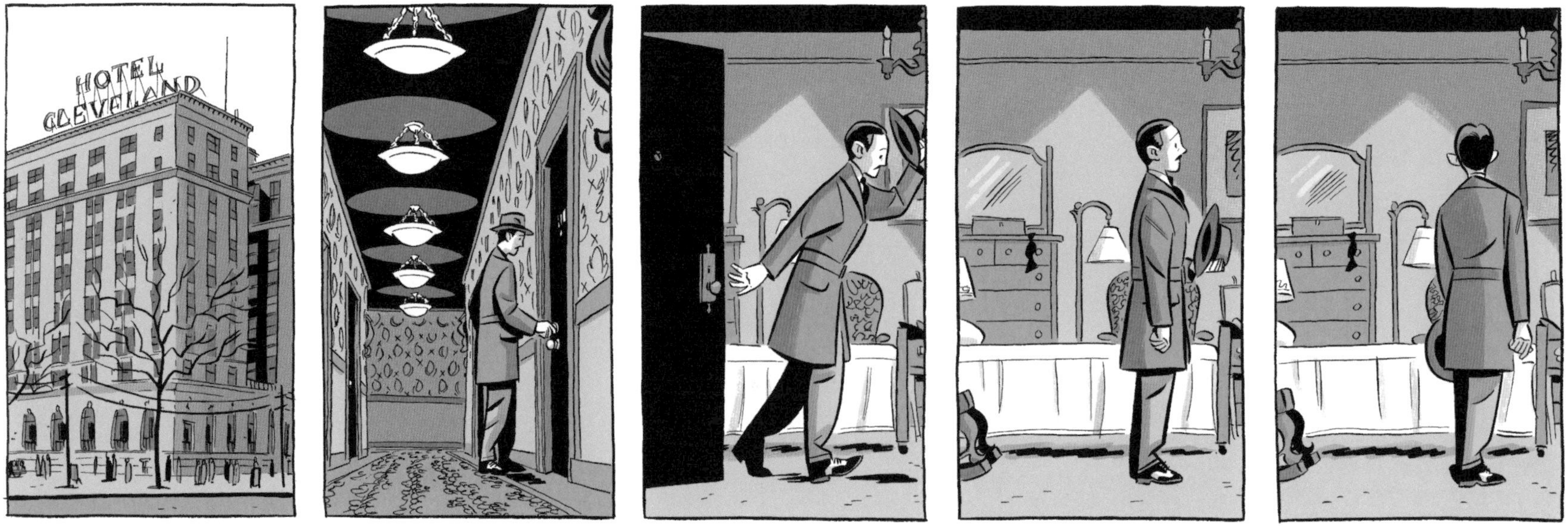
HOTEL
CLEVELAND

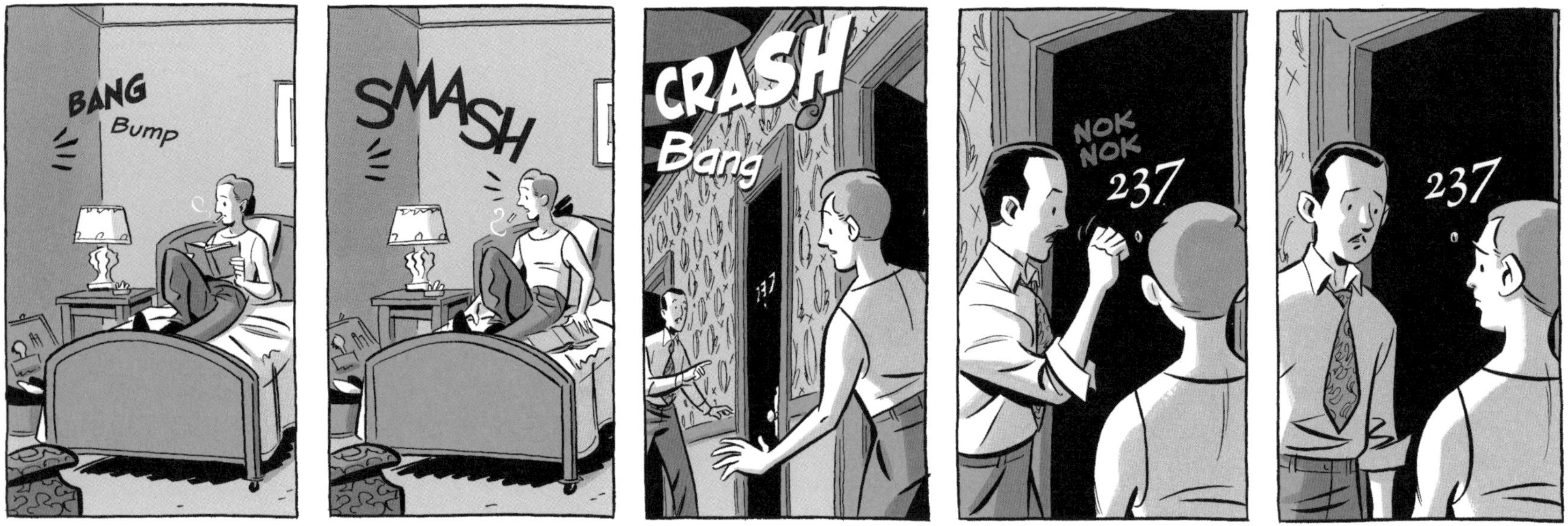
BANG
Bump
SMASH
CRASH
Bang
NOK NOK
237
237

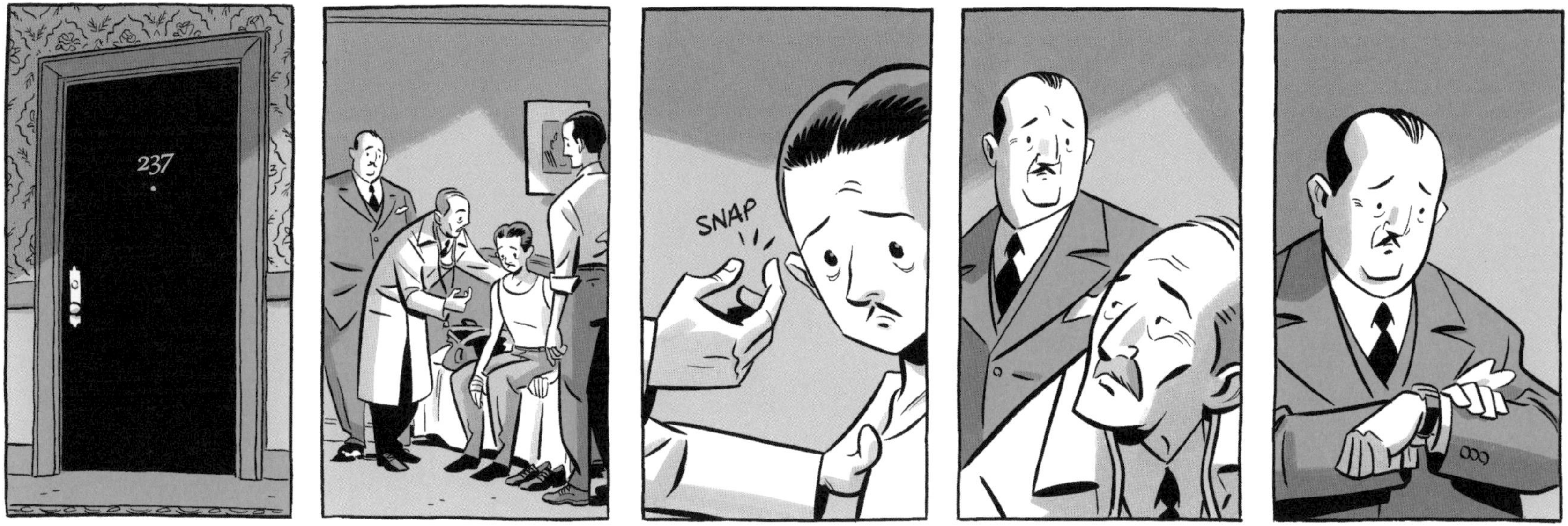
237
SNAP

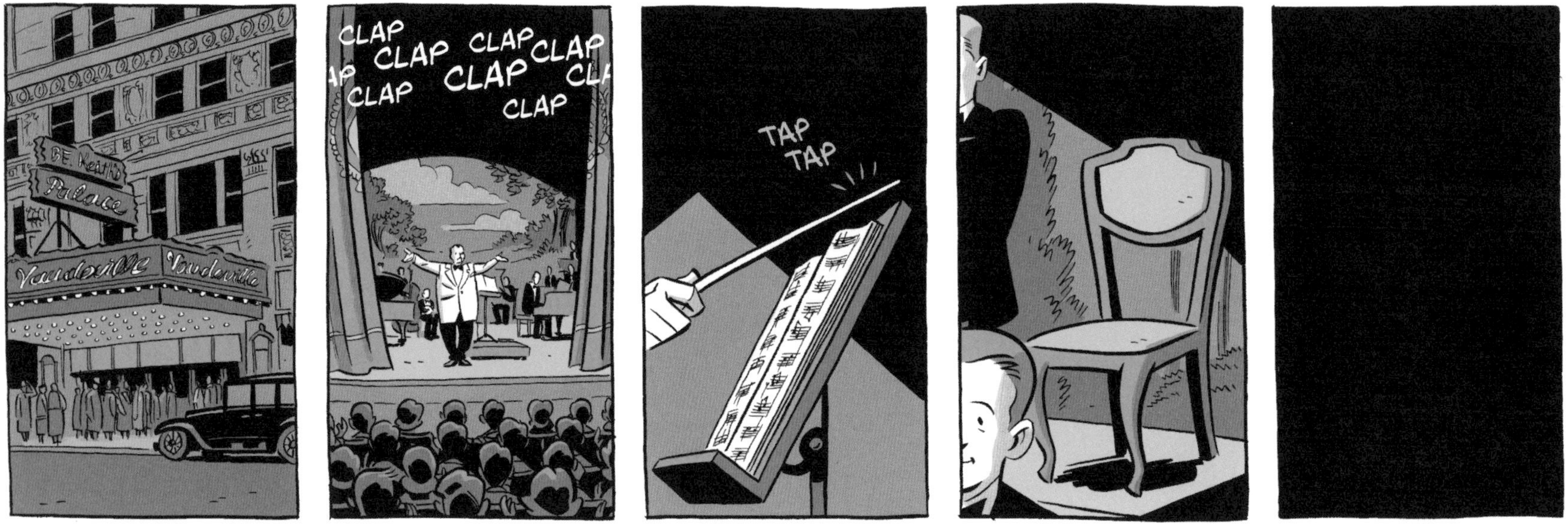
Palace
Vaudeville
Vaudeville
CLAP
CLAP
CLAP
CLAP
CLAP
CLAP
CLAP
TAP
TAP

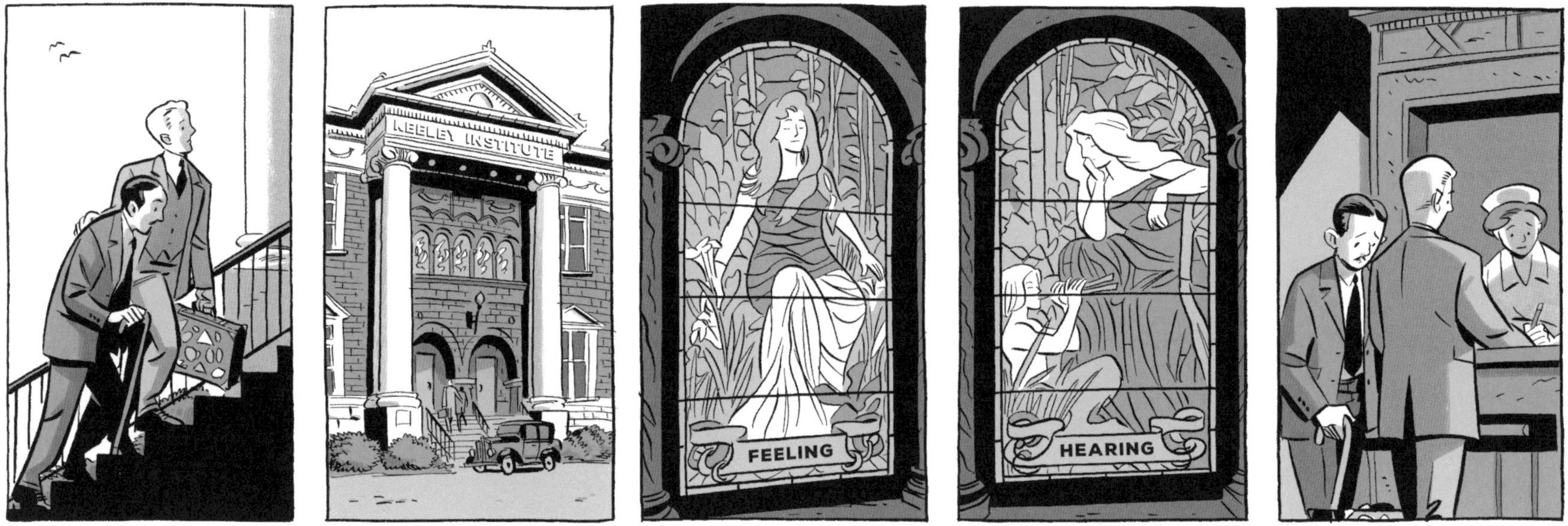
KEELEY INSTITUTE
FEELING
HEARING

KLIK

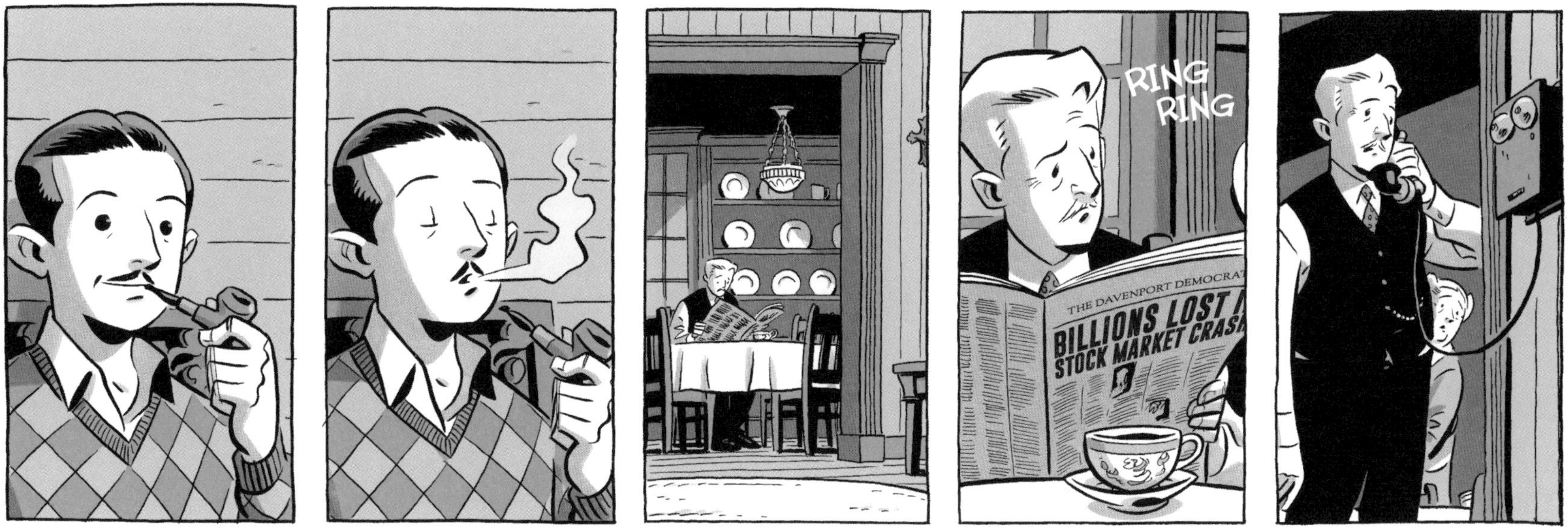
RING
RING
THE DAVENPORT DEMOCRAT
BILLIONS LOST
STOCK MARKET CRAS

KLIK

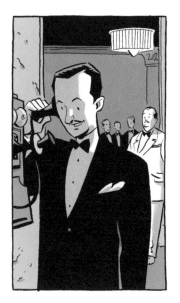

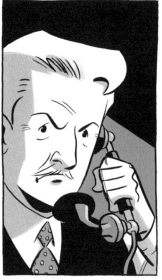

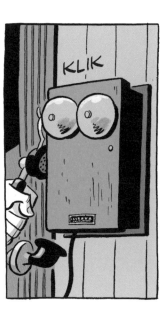

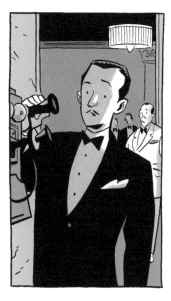

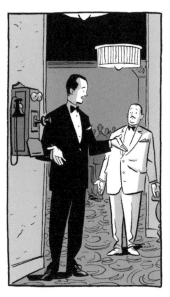

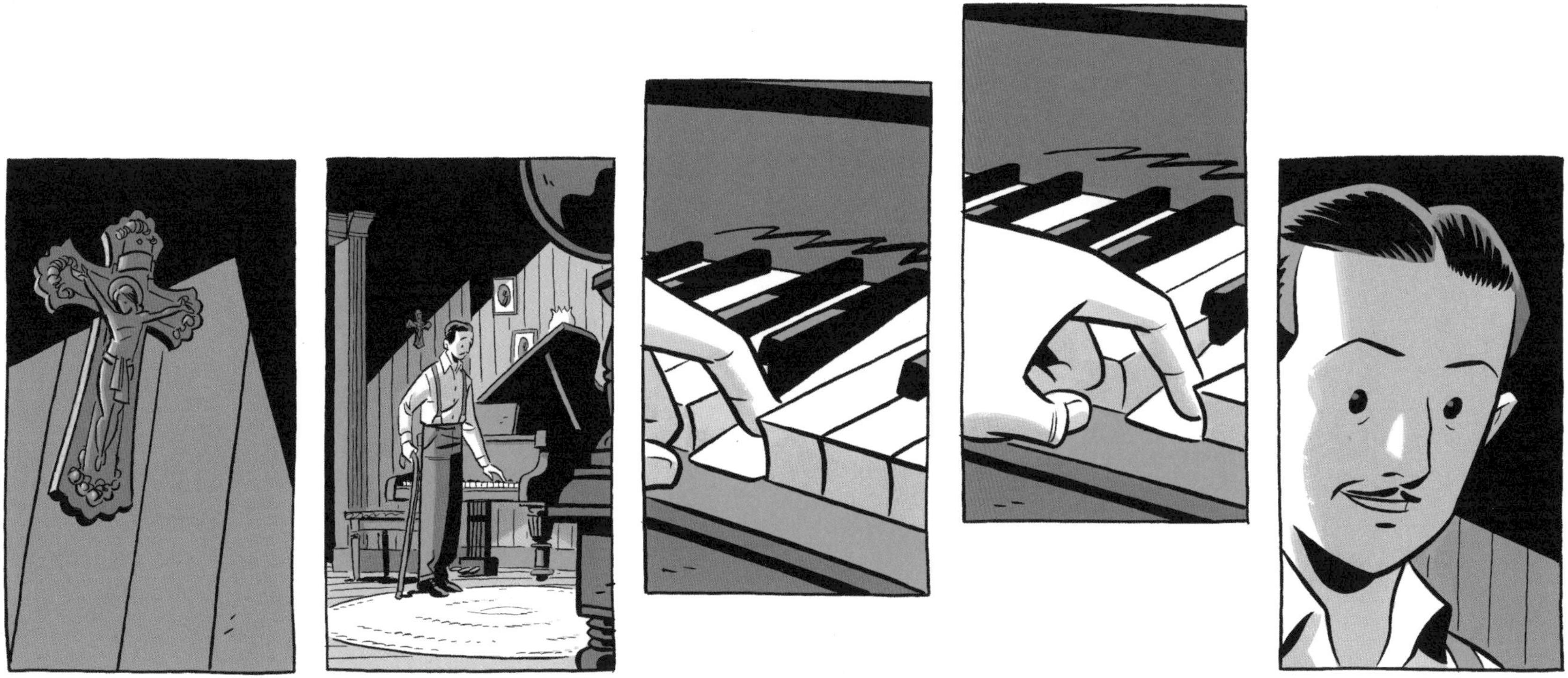

Harmony
JESUS,

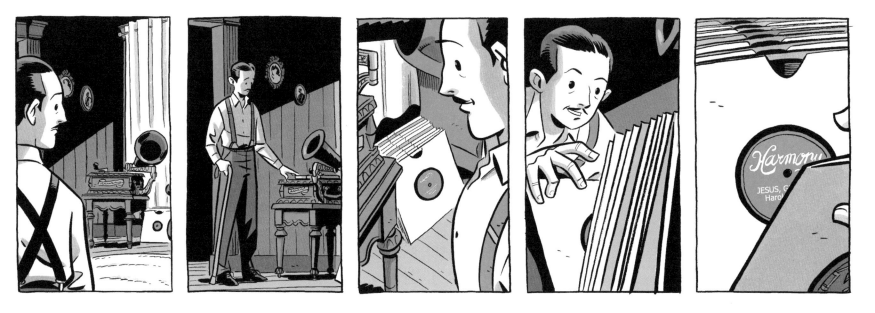

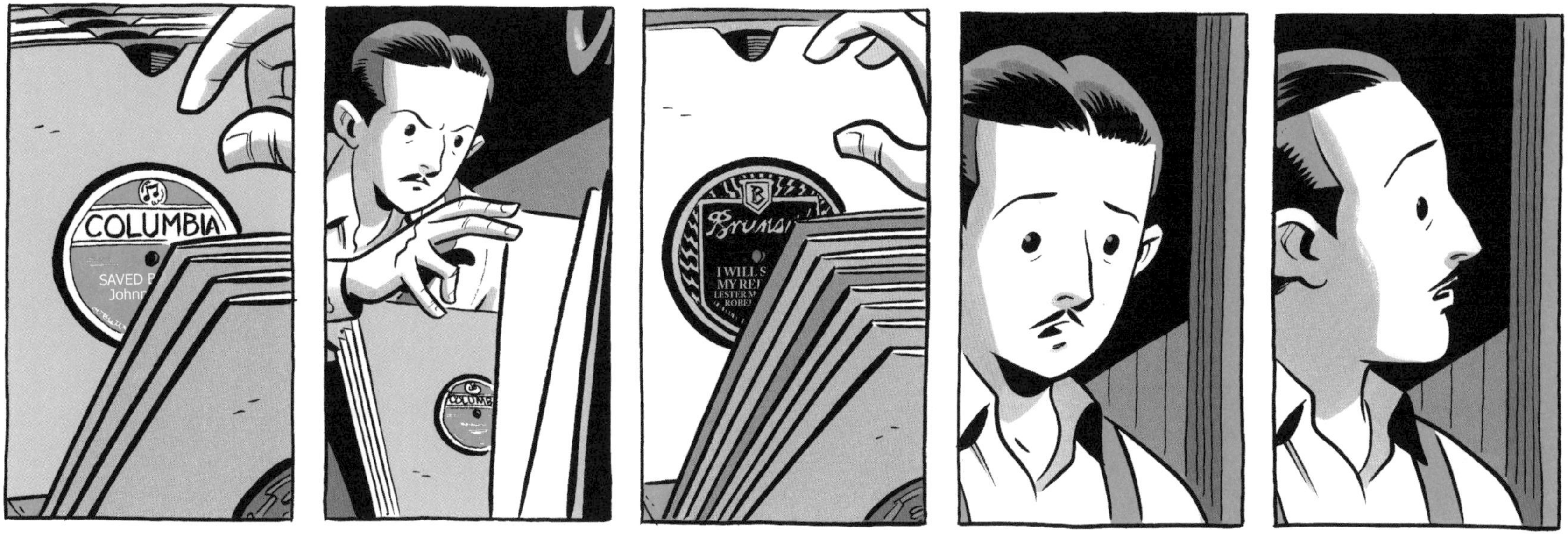
COLUMBIA

203

Part Five
IN THE DARK

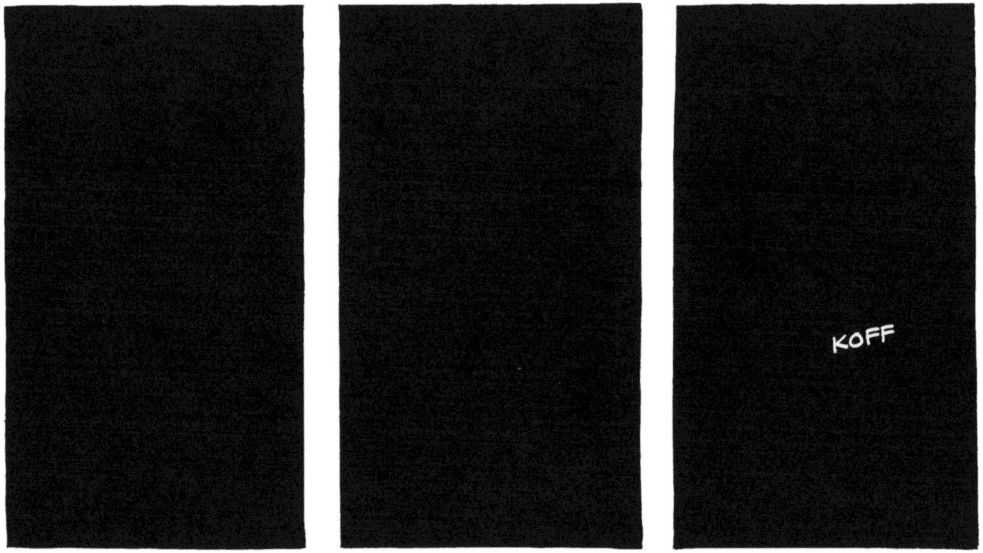

KOFF

KOFF
KOFF
CITY
LIGHTS

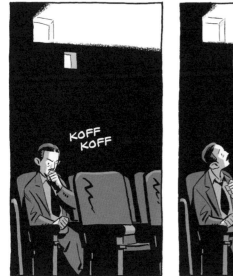

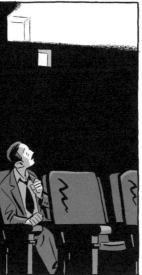

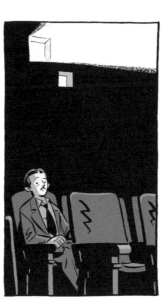

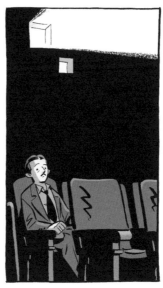

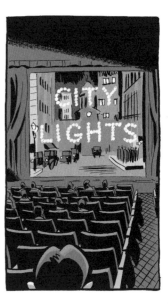

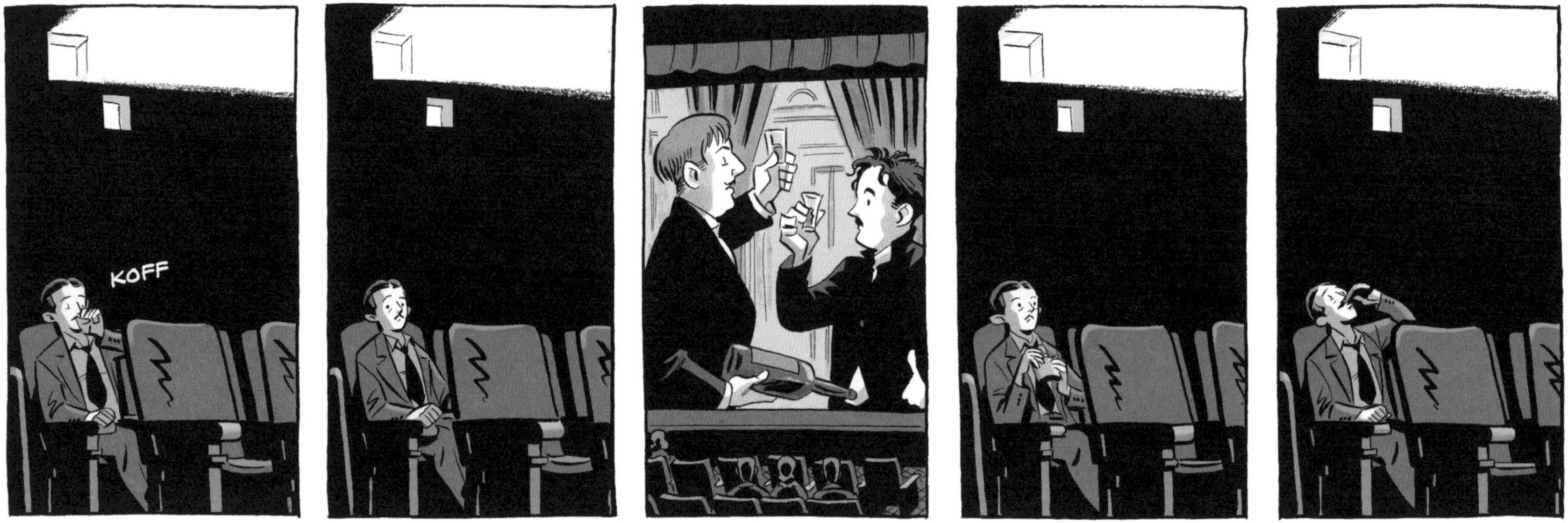
KOFF

Saltzman's
SHOW ROOM
SHOW 7 | DANCE 9
SMITH BALLEW
and His Orchestra
Star of STAGE & SCREEN
NUDGE

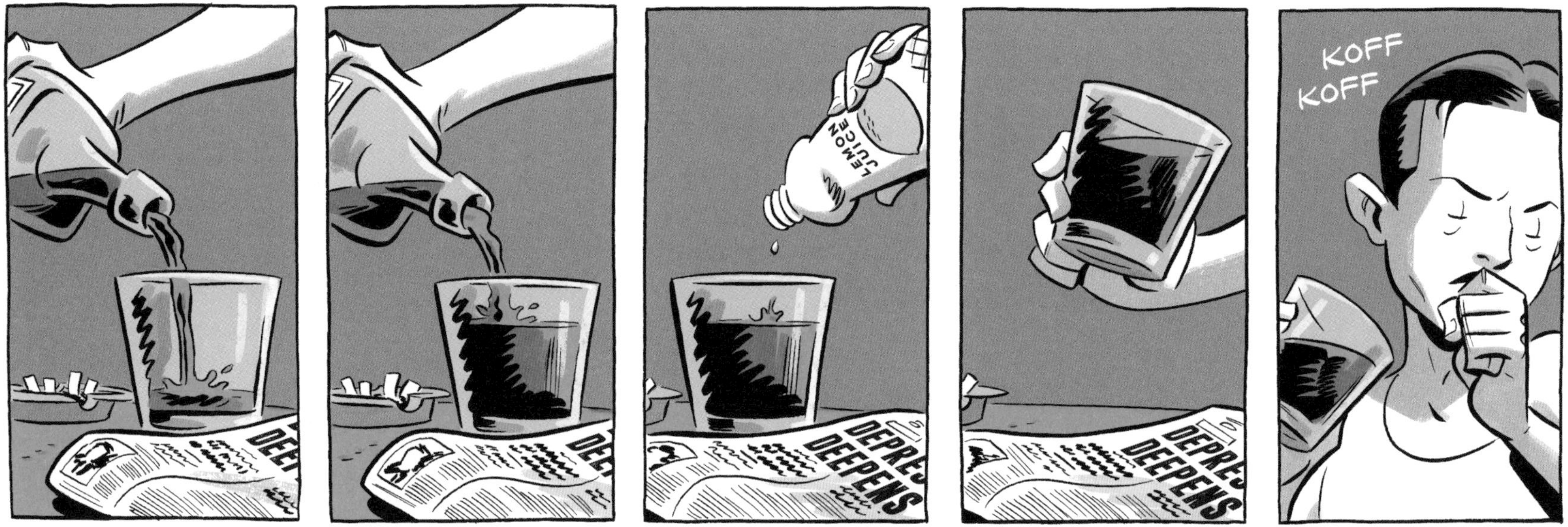
LEMON JUICE
DEPRES
DEEPENS
DEPRES
DEEPENS
KOFF
KOFF

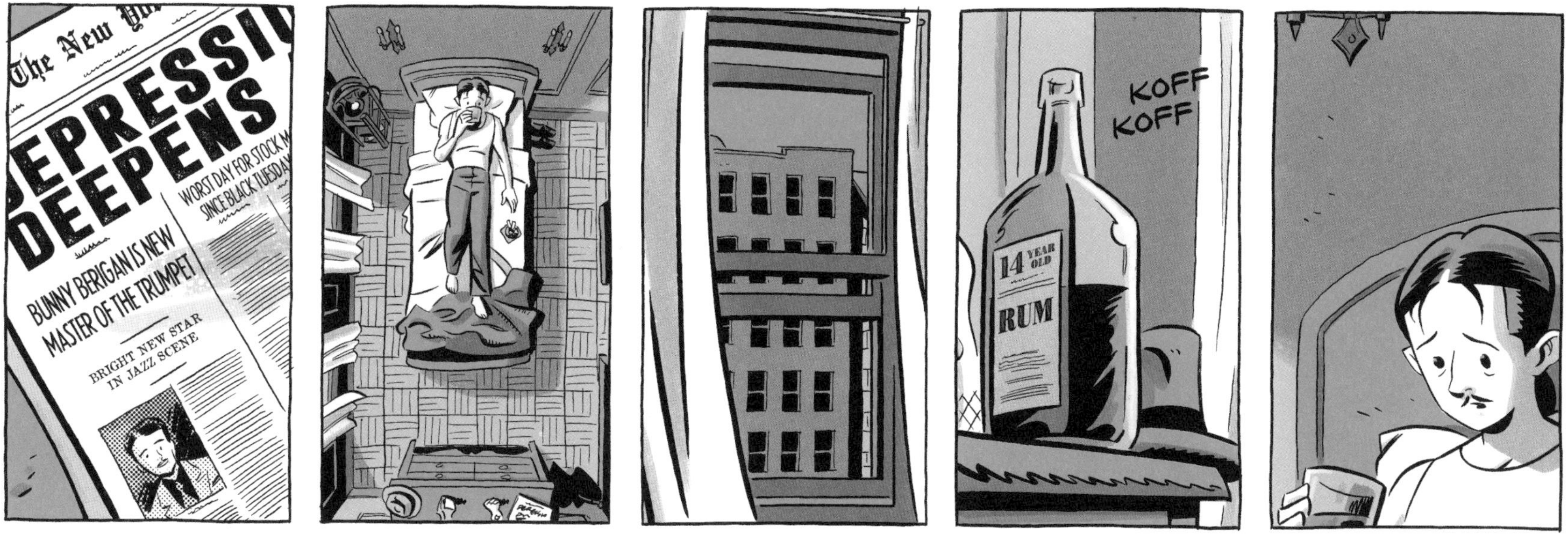
The New
DEEPENS
BUNNY BERIGAN IS NEW MASTER OF THE TRUMPET
BRIGHT NEW STAR IN JAZZ SCENE
14 YEAR OLD
RUM
KOFF KOFF

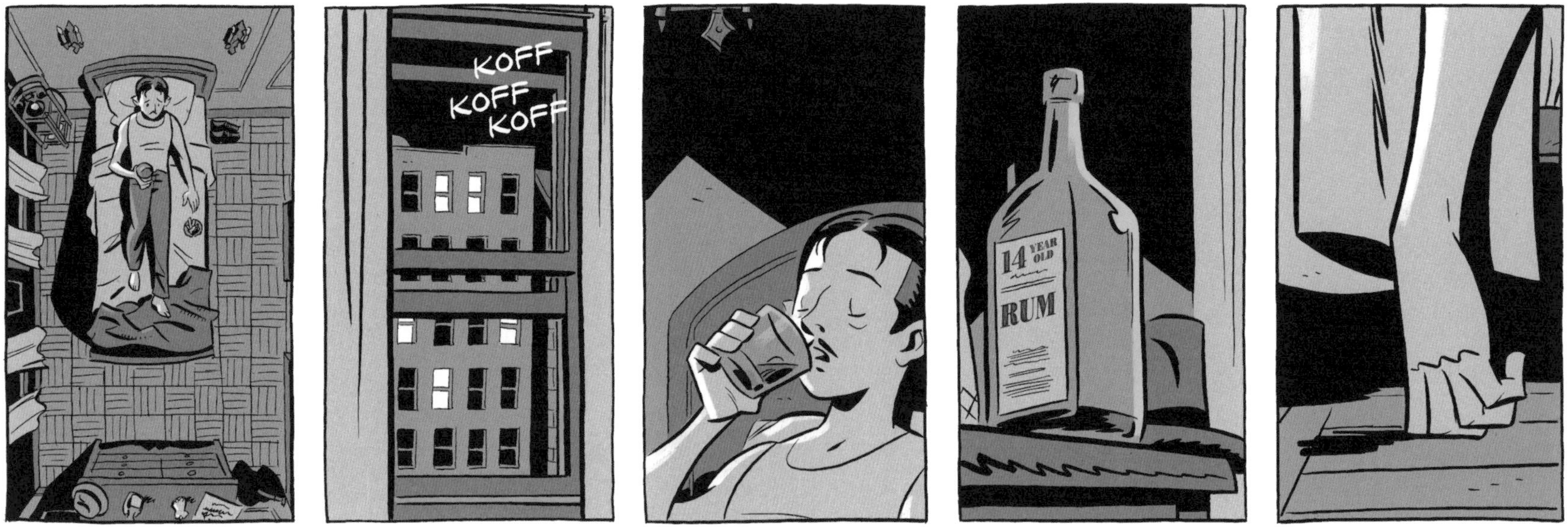
KOFF
KOFF
KOFF
14 YEAR OLD
RUM

KOFF
KOFF

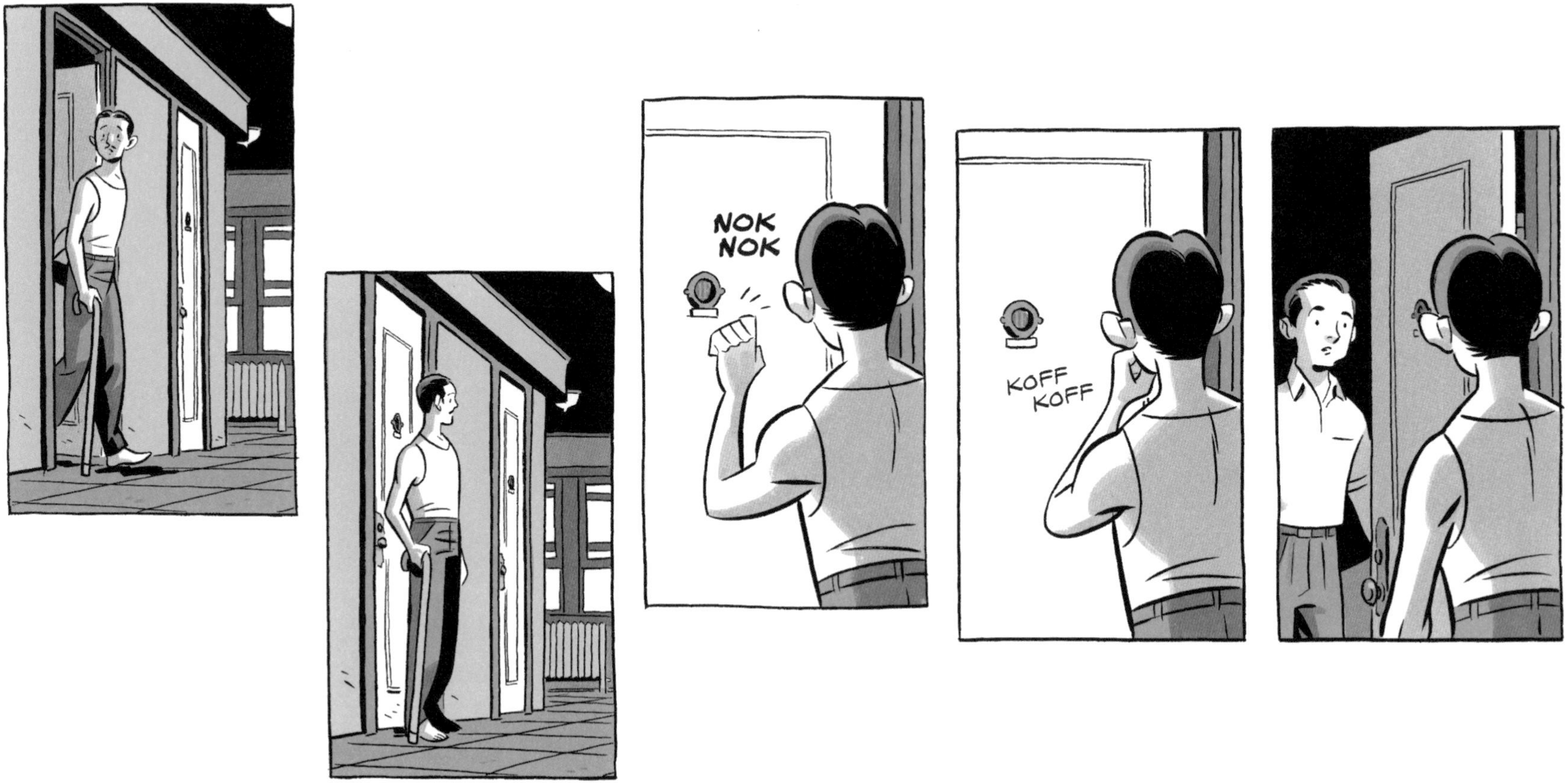
NOK
NOK
KOFF
KOFF

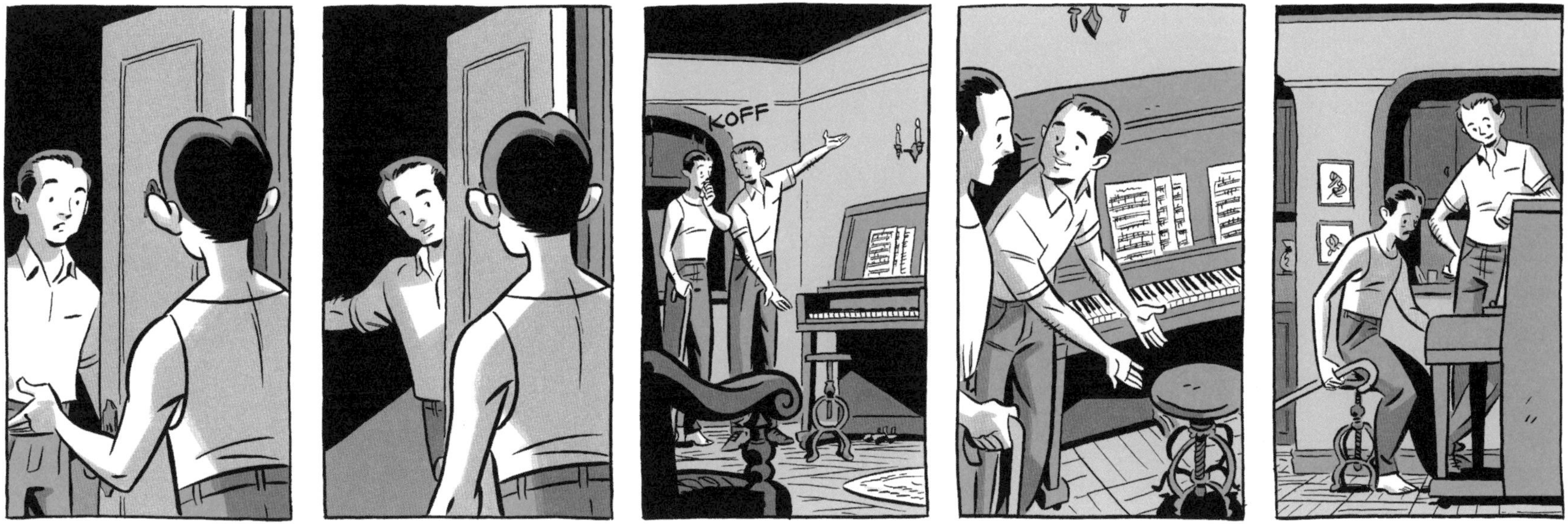
KOFF

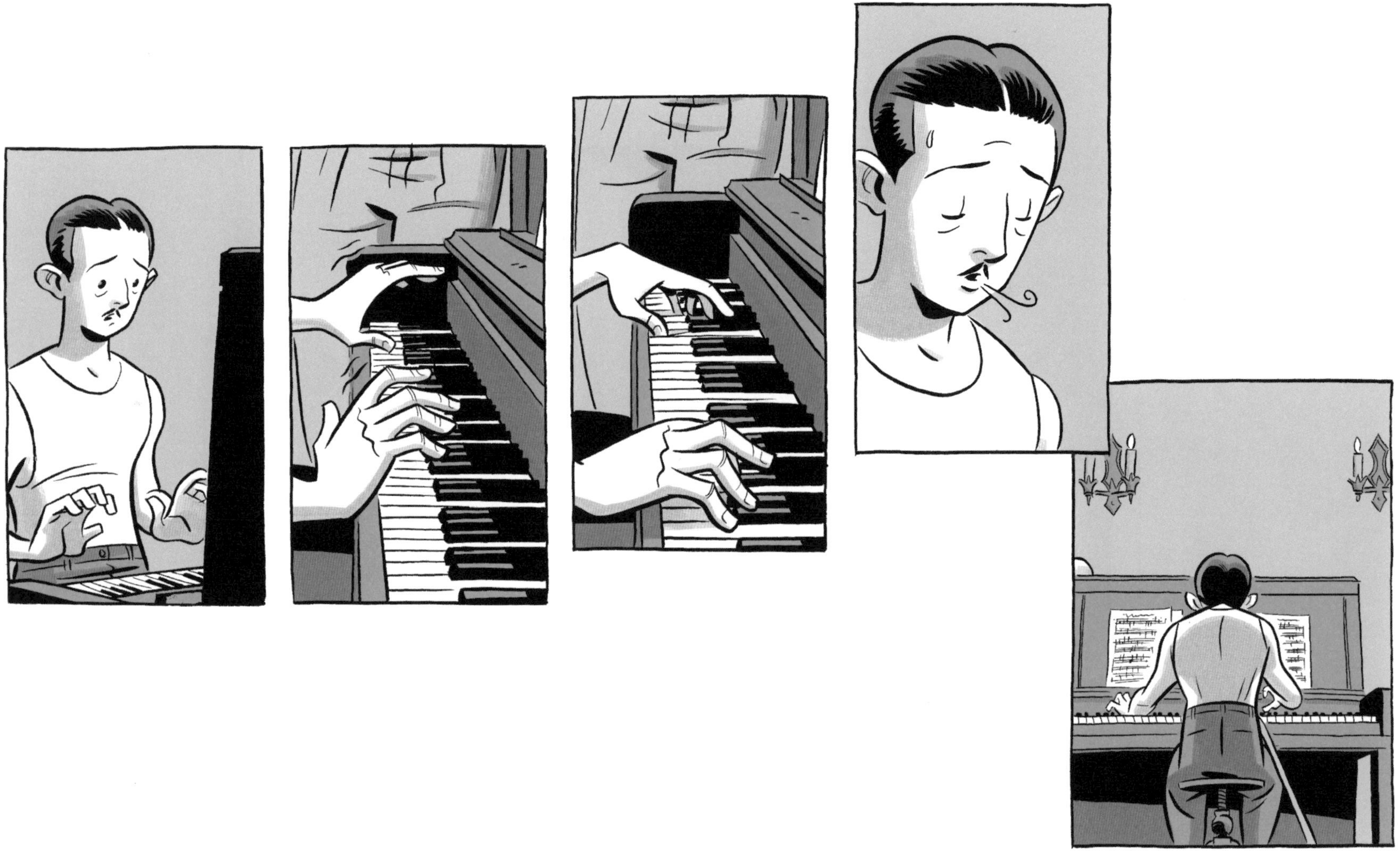

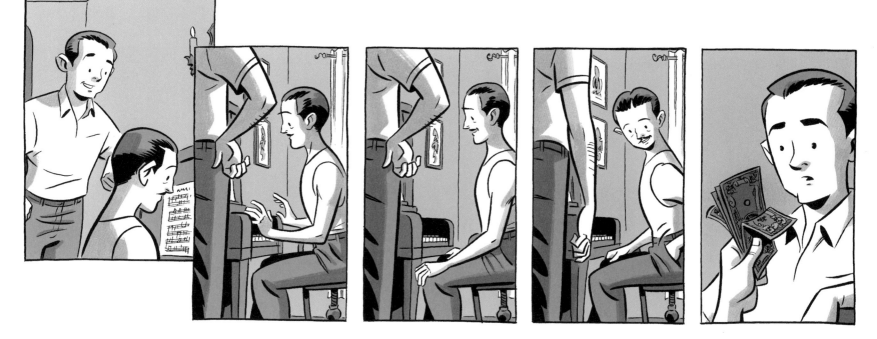

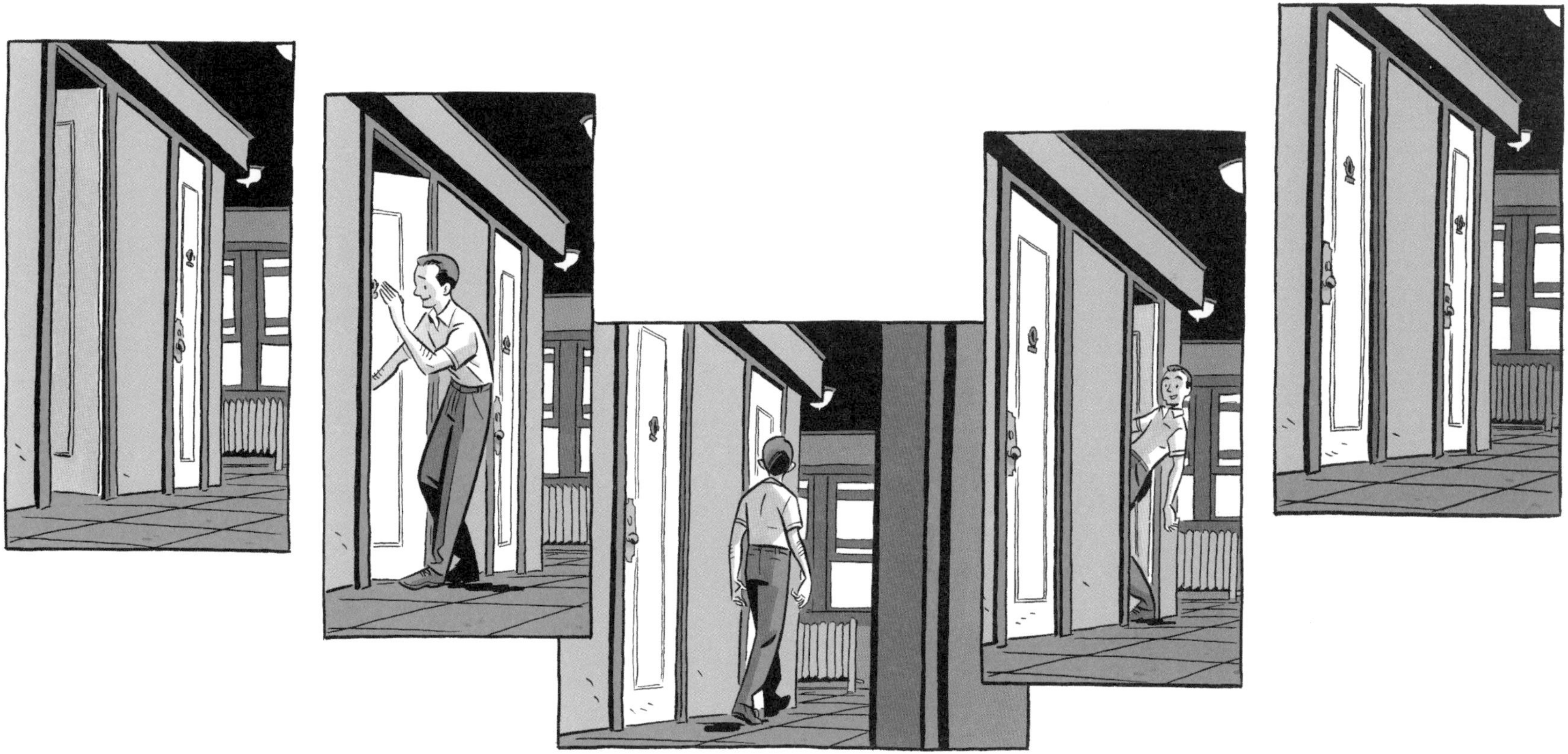

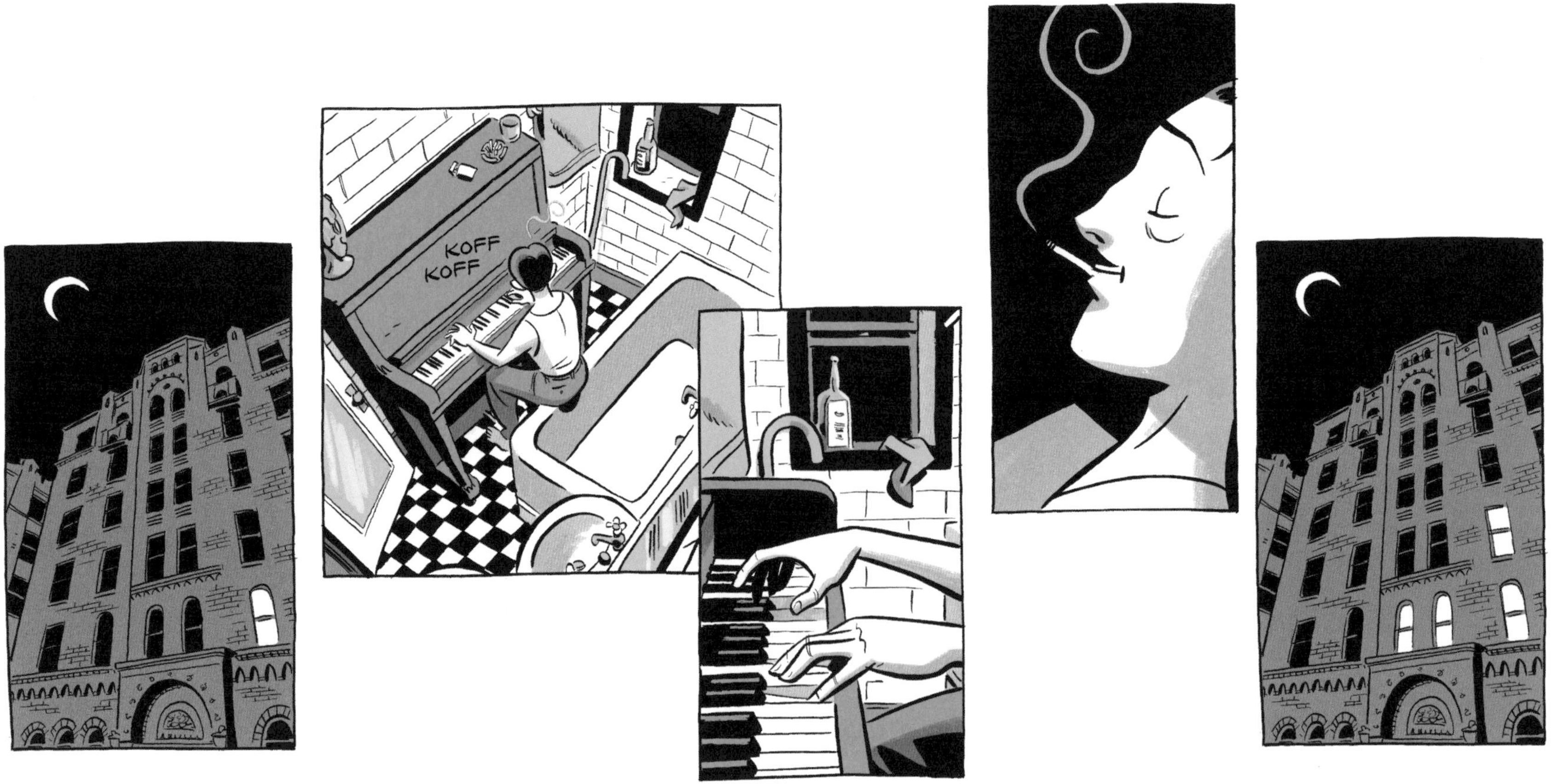
KOFF
KOFF

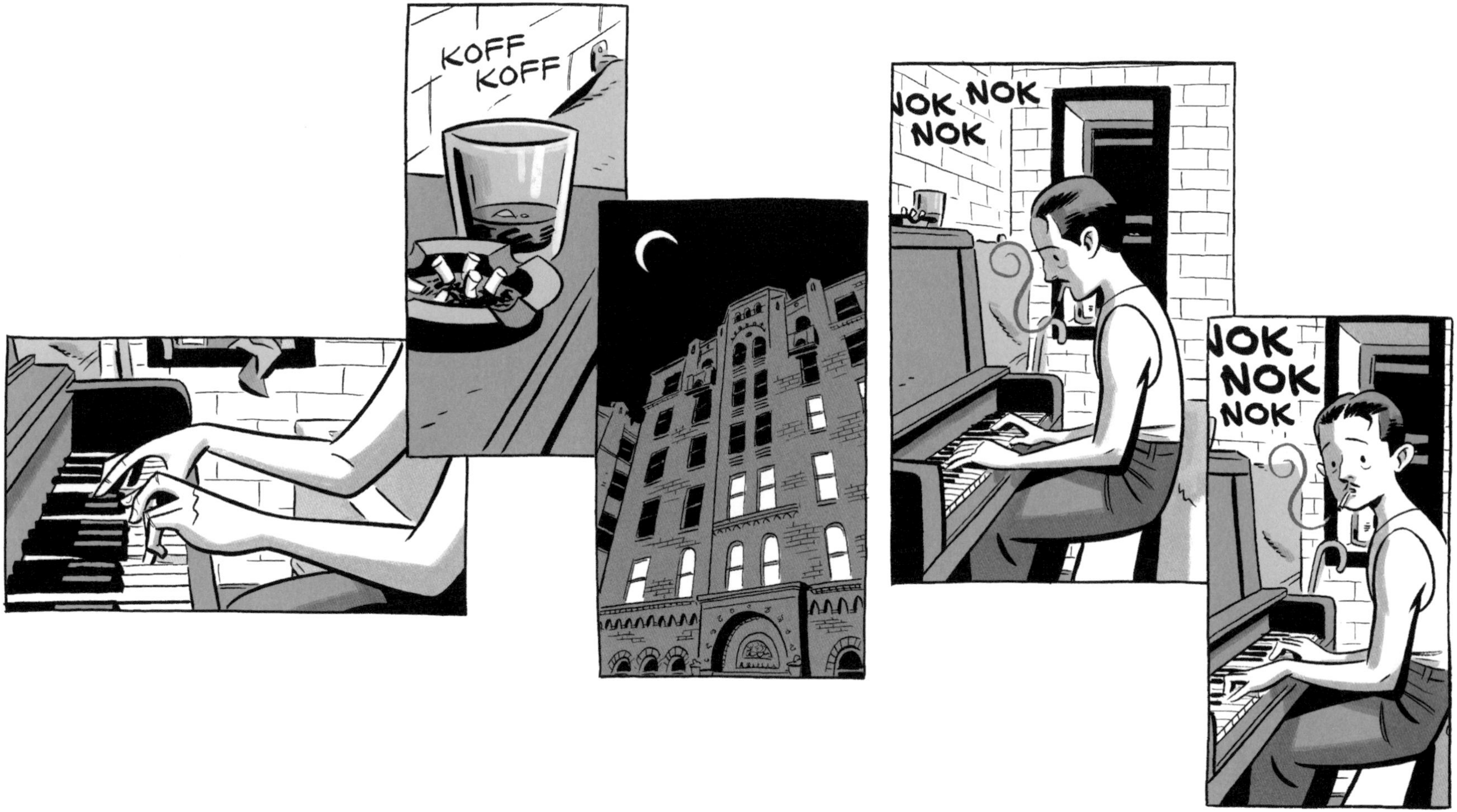
KOFF
KOFF
NOK NOK
NOK
NOK
NOK
NOK

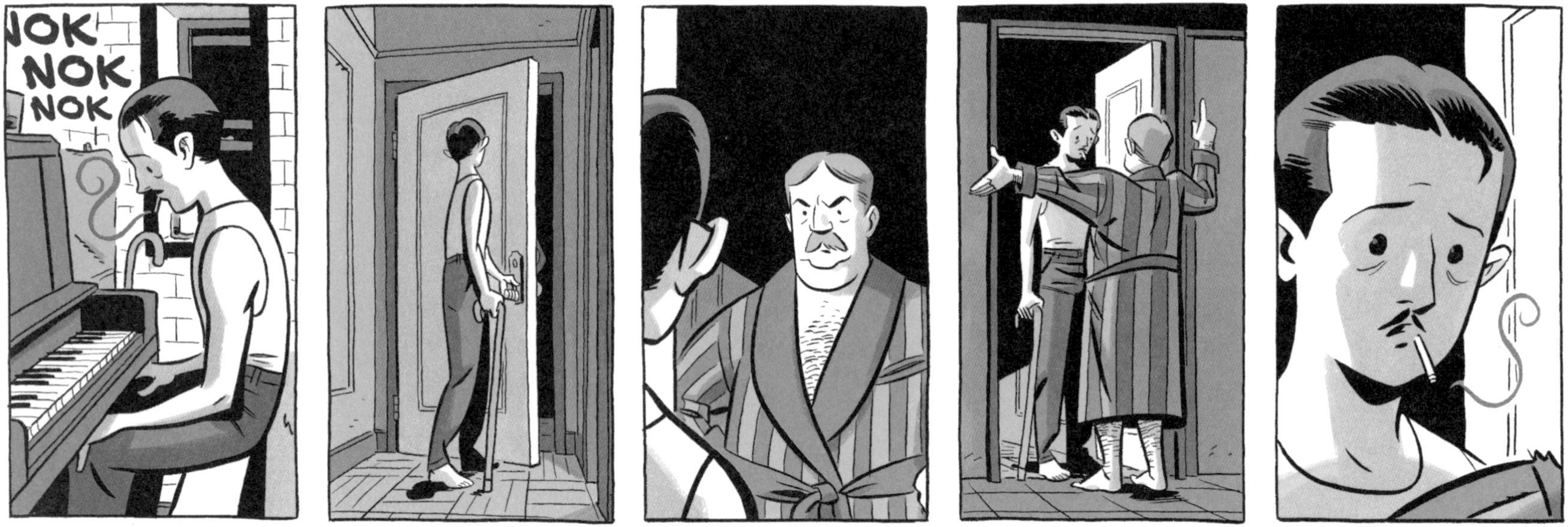
NOK
NOK
NOK

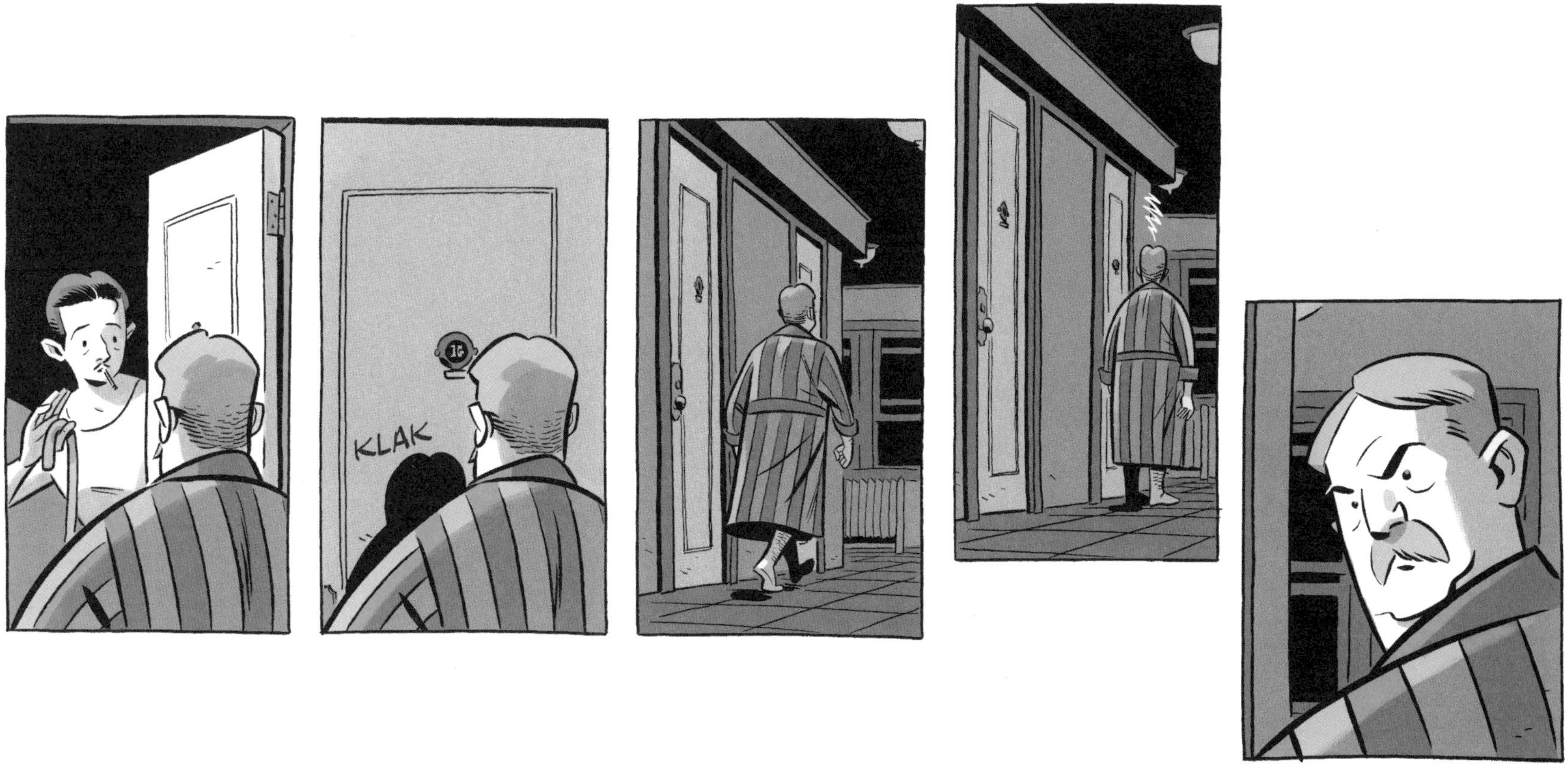
KLAK

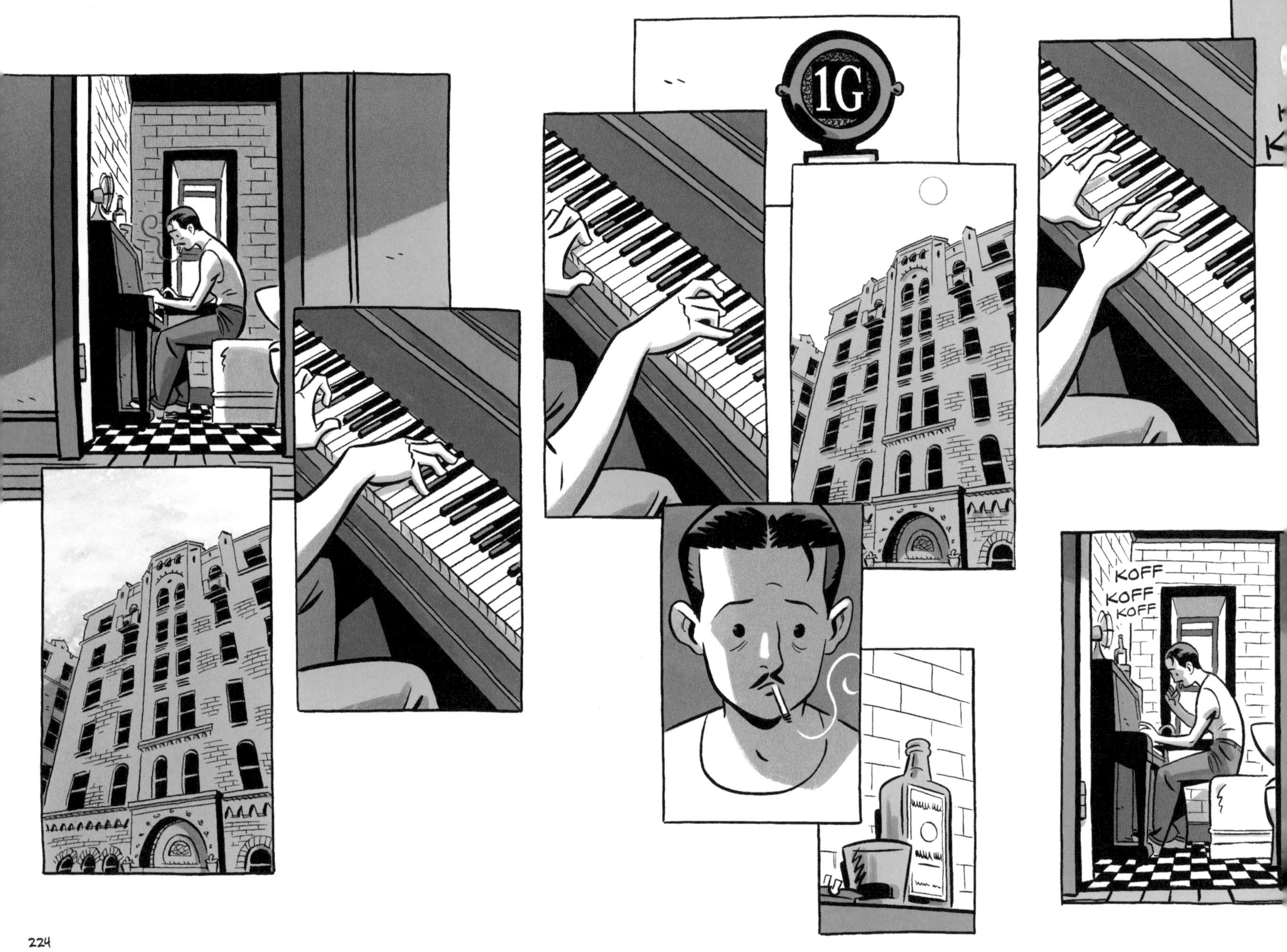
1G
KOFF
KOFF
KOFF

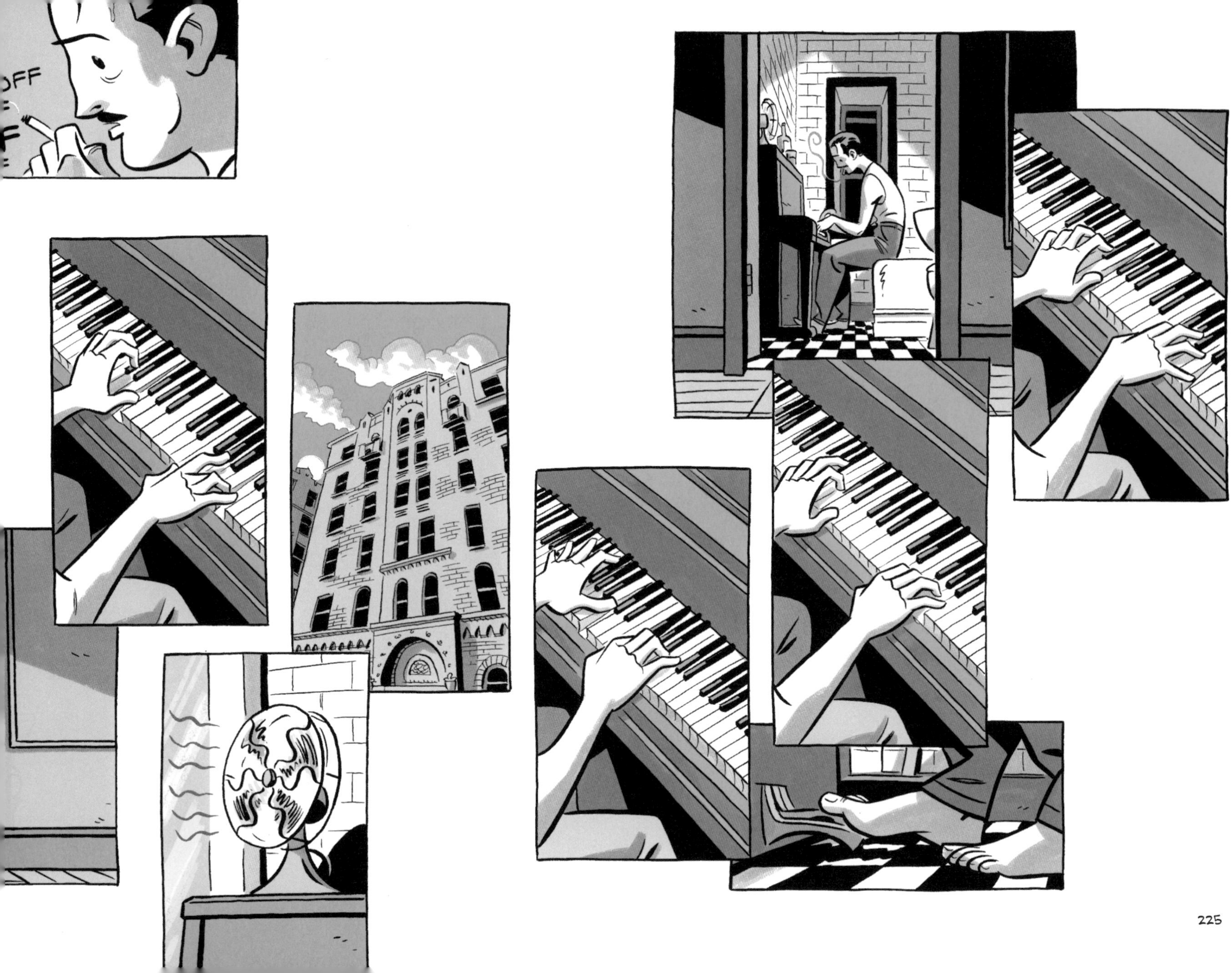

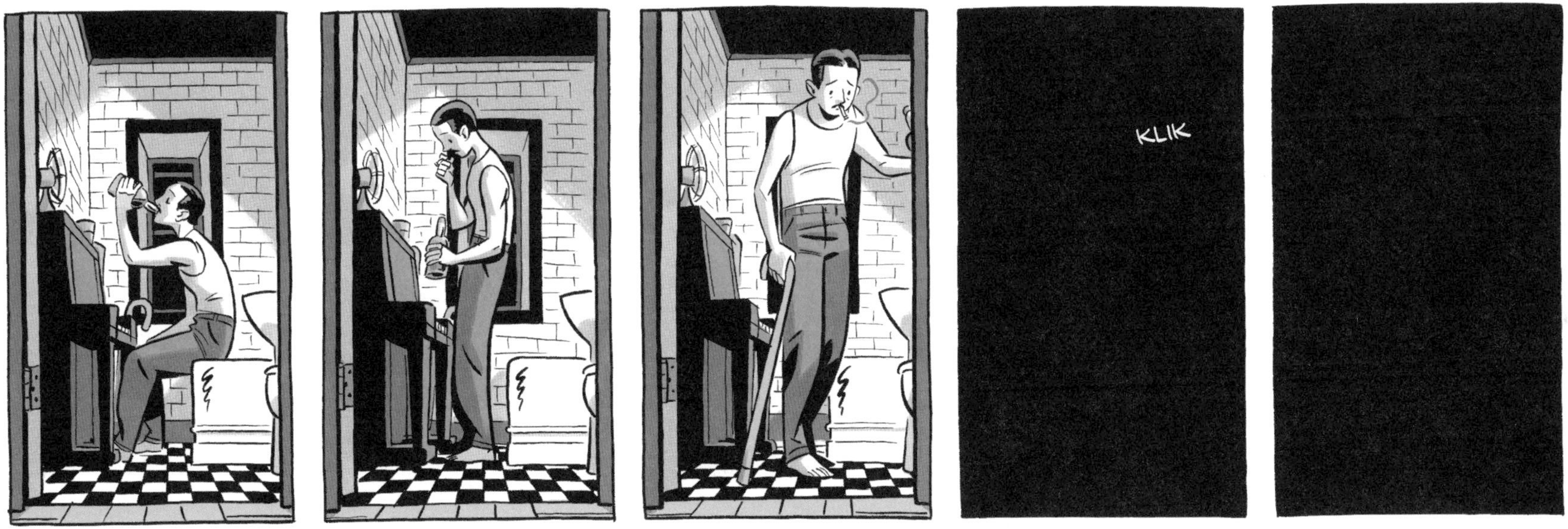
KLIK

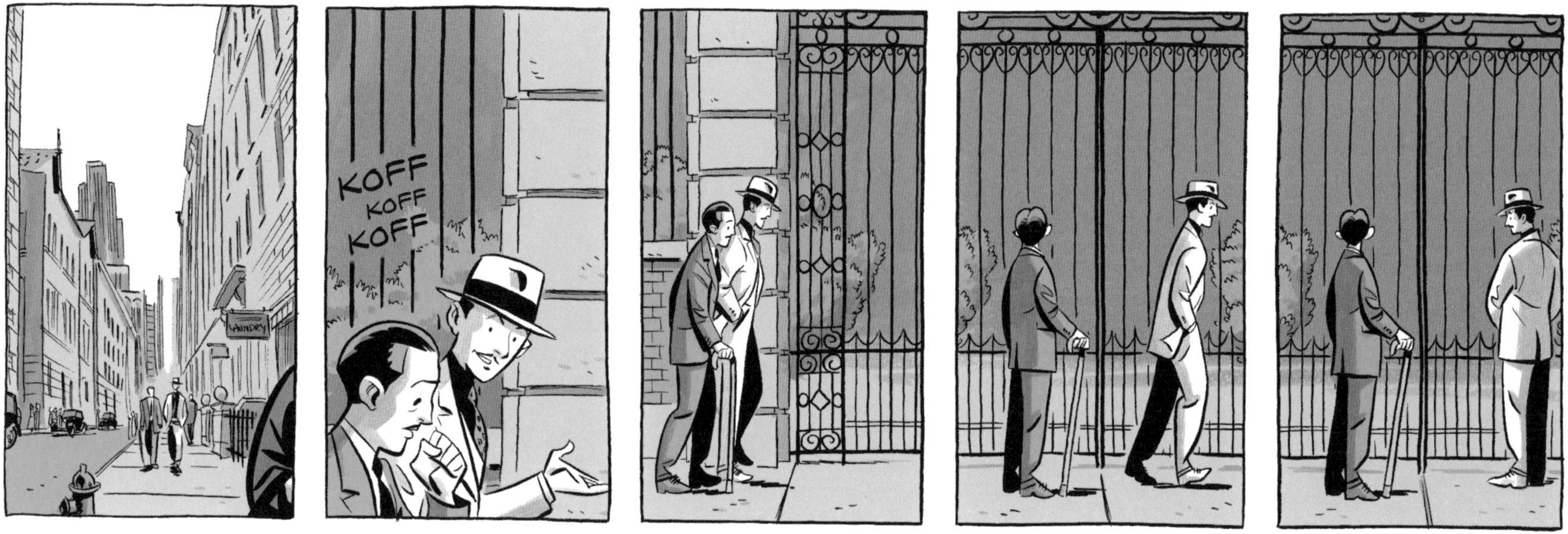
LAUNDRY
KOFF
KOFF
KOFF

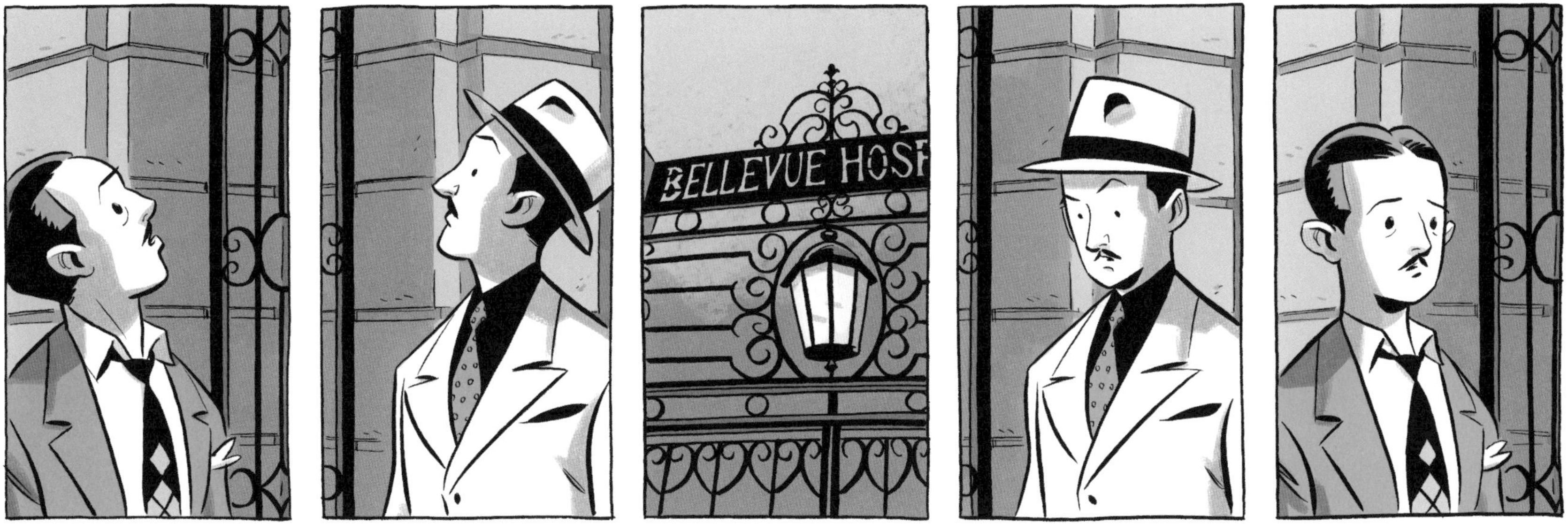
BELLEVUE HOS

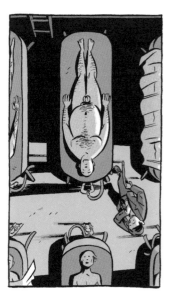

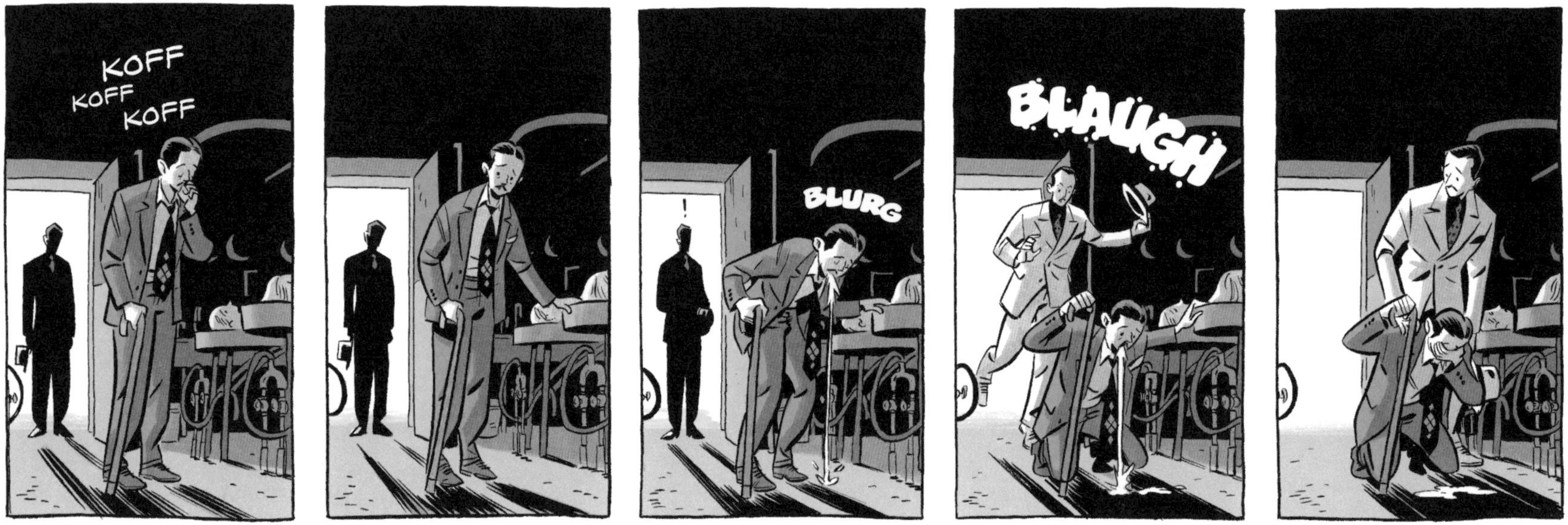
KOFF
KOFF
KOFF
!
BLURG
BLAUGH

KOFF
KOFF
KOFF
KOFF
KOFF
KOFF
KOFF
KOF
KOFF
OFF
KOFF
KOFF
KOFF
KOFF
KOFF
OFF
FF

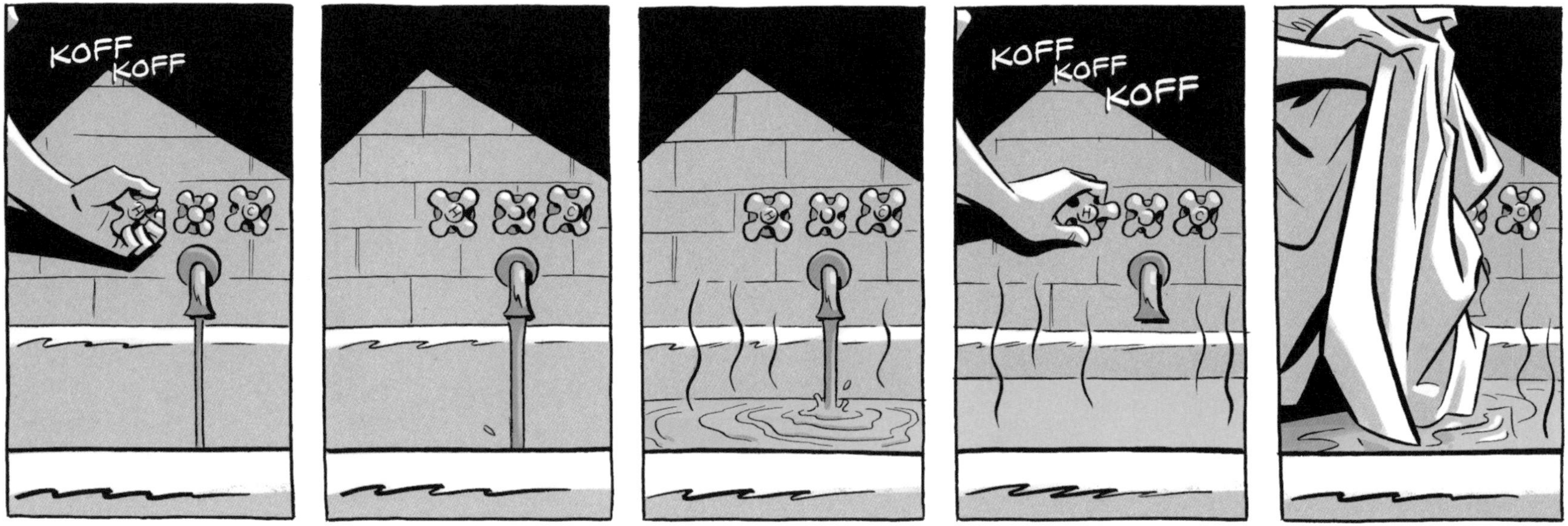
KOFF
KOFF
KOFF
KOFF
KOFF

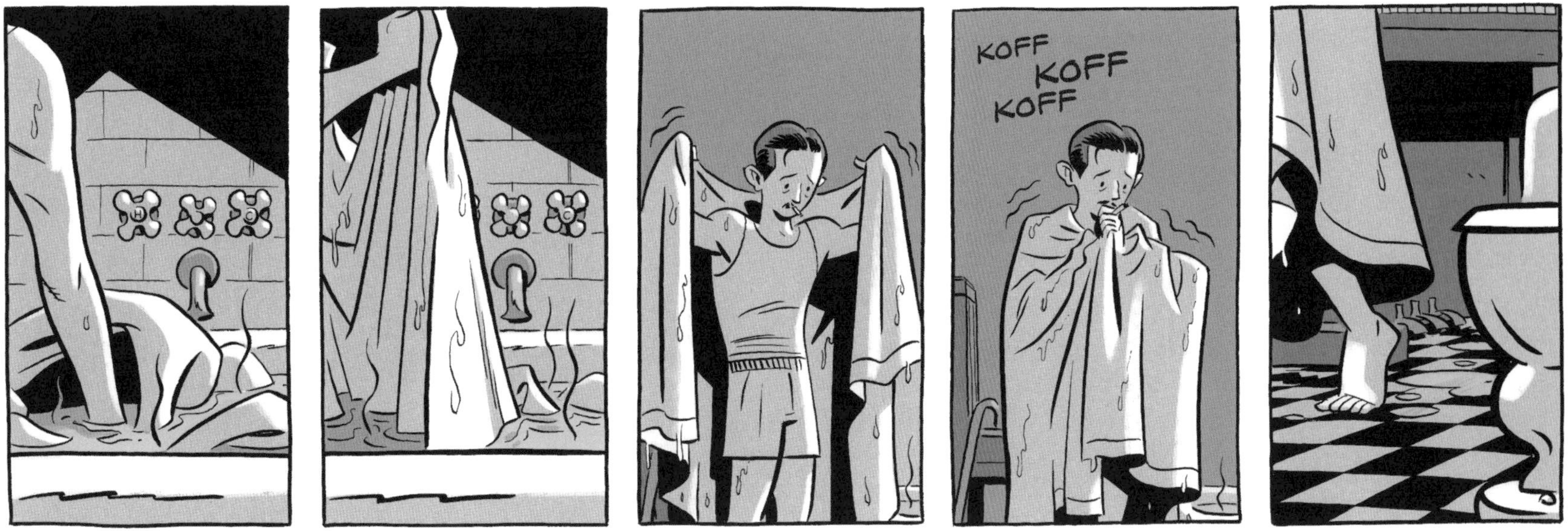
KOFF
KOFF
KOFF

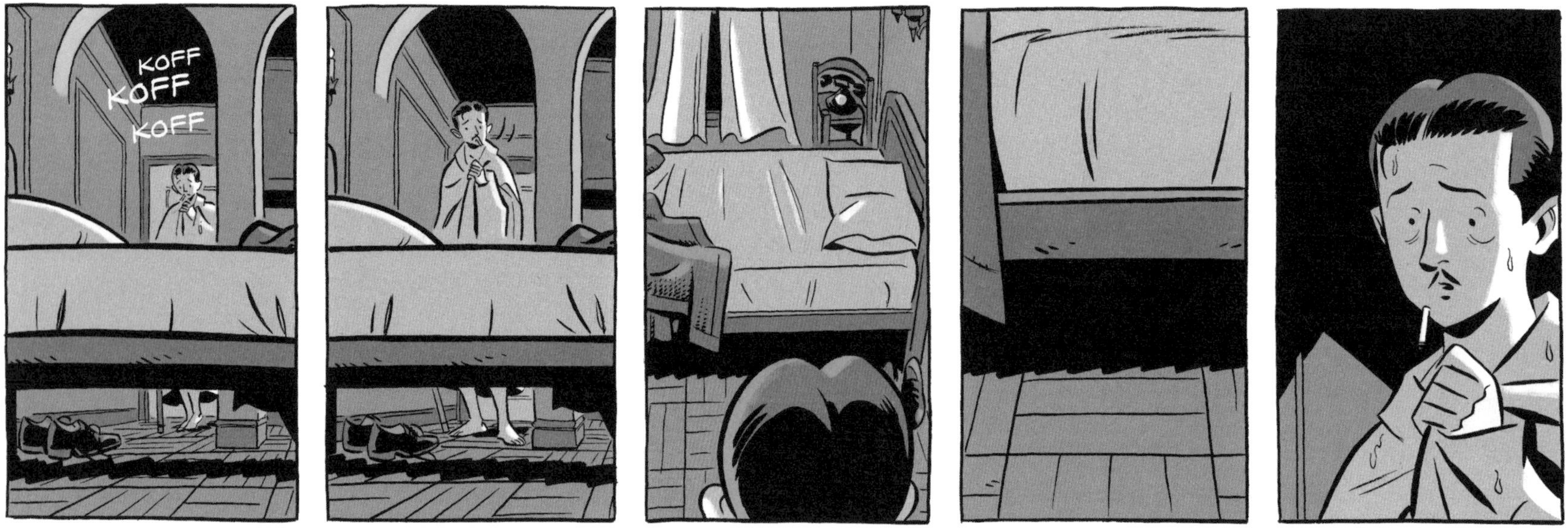
KOFF
KOFF
KOFF

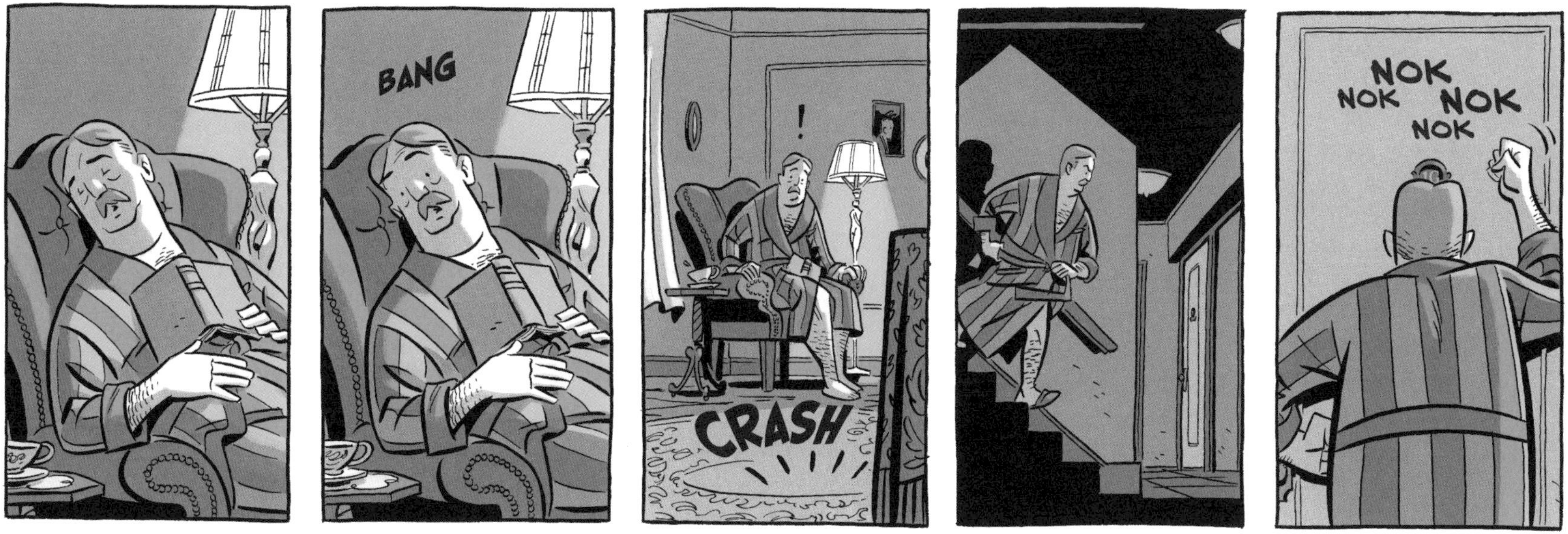
BANG
!
CRASH
NOK
NOK
NOK
NOK

ACKNOWLEDGMENTS

This book saved my life.

Within a span of just over a year in 2016–2017, during which I began researching and writing *Bix*, I lost a friend and mentor to cancer, ended my twenty-one-year marriage, and lost my mother to mental illness and then suicide. Just over a year later, my father suffered a debilitating stroke. None of these things were expected. Each was devastating in turn, and the combined weight of them was nearly overwhelming.

It's a stereotype for traumatized people to bury themselves in work. I fully embraced that stereotype. I don't know if this long-planned dream project of mine will mean nearly as much to other people as it did to me. But whatever else it may be, *Bix* functioned as a life raft for my battered sense of self at a time when it was definitely in danger of drowning. Letting go of it now is bittersweet. There will, of course, be other projects. But *Bix* will always, for me, remain a record of those turbulent years. It's a work of great pain, and great healing.

I didn't do it alone, of course.

Thanks are due to my amazing agent, Samantha Haywood of Transatlantic Agency, for selling this unconventional book, and to Ed Schlesinger at Gallery 13 for buying it.

To the Canada Council for the Arts for their generous financial support.

Grateful acknowledgments to the essential references used in the creation of this work, and their authors: *Bix: The Definitive History of a Jazz Legend* by Jean Pierre Lion, *Bix: Man & Legend* by Richard M. Sudhalter and Phillip R. Evans, and *Remembering Bix* by Ralph Berton. Bix devotees definitely have their favorites (and least favorites) among them, but for my money I think they each got a piece of it.

To James Beiderbecke, Bix's great-great-nephew, for early support of the book.

To the Bix Beiderbecke Museum in Davenport, Iowa, for simply existing. Please visit this great place and support them with your donations.

There's not a lot of lettering in this book, but where there is I've mostly used Blambot fonts by the terrific letterer Nate Piekos. Buy his fonts; they're a comic book artist's best friend.

To Shawn Richison, who pitched in with some badly needed coloring assistance in the home stretch.

To Ray Fawkes, whose haunting graphic novel *One Soul* inspired and challenged me to create a narrative that could only be told in comics form.

To Todd Tope, for holding the ladder.

To my sons, Miles and Mason, for their maturity and resilience. I wish more adults had as much character as my kids.

And most of all, to comics scholar Irene Velentzas, who enthusiastically championed this project when it was just an unlikely pitch. Who assisted with research and eventually became a relied-upon reader and second set of eyes. And who cared for a lost dog.

Scott Chantler
November 2019